# ENHANCING
# THE QUALITY OF LIFE
# IN ADVANCED DEMENTIA

# ENHANCING THE QUALITY OF LIFE IN ADVANCED DEMENTIA

*edited by*

## Ladislav Volicer, MD, PhD
## Lisa Bloom-Charette, PhD

Department of Veterans Affairs
Edith Nourse Rogers Memorial Veterans Hospital
Bedford, Massachusetts and
Boston University School of Medicine
Boston, Massachusetts

BRUNNER/MAZEL
Taylor & Francis Group

| USA | Publishing Office: | BRUNNER/MAZEL<br>*A member of the Taylor & Francis Group*<br>325 Chestnut Street<br>Philadelphia, PA 19106<br>Tel: (215) 625-8900<br>Fax: (215) 625-2940 |
| --- | --- | --- |
| | Distribution Center: | BRUNNER/MAZEL<br>*A member of the Taylor & Francis Group*<br>47 Runway Road, Suite G<br>Levittown, PA 19057<br>Tel: (215) 269-0400<br>Fax: (215) 269-0363 |
| UK | | BRUNNER/MAZEL<br>*A member of the Taylor & Francis Group*<br>1 Gunpowder Square<br>London EC4A 3DE<br>Tel: +44 171 583 0490<br>Fax: +44 171 583 0581 |

**ENHANCING THE QUALITY OF LIFE IN ADVANCED DEMENTIA**

1  2  3  4  5  6  7  8  9  0

Printed by Edward Brothers, Ann Arbor, MI, 1999.
Cover design by Joan Wendt

A CIP catalog record for this book is available from the British Library.
∞ The paper in this publication meets the requirements of the ANSI Standard Z39.48-1984 (Permanence of Paper).

Library of Congress Cataloging-in-Publication Data
Enhancing the quality of life in advanced dementia / Ladislav Volicer,
  Lisa Bloom-Charette.
      p.  cm.
  Includes bibliographical references and index.
  ISBN 0-87630-965-1 (hbk : alk. paper)
  1. Dementia—Patients—Care.  2. Quality of Life.  I. Volicer,
Ladislav.  II. Bloom-Charette, Lisa.
  [DNLM:  1. Dementia—rehabilitation—Aged.  2. Quality of Life.
WT 155 E58 1999]
RC521.E53  1999
616.8´3—dc21
DNLM/DLC
for Library of Congress                                    99-12881
                                                           CIP

ISBN 0-87630-965-1 (cloth)

# CONTENTS

# PART II
# SPECIALIZED APPROACHES

# CONTRIBUTORS

**Barbaranne J. Benjamin, PhD,** is a professor in the Department of Public Health and Rehabilitation Services at the University of Toledo. She serves as program director of the speech-language pathology program and is a certified speech-language pathologist. Her research interests include normal and disordered communication in the geriatric population. Dr. Benjamin's research has been published in refereed journals as well as presented to national and international associations.

**Lisa Bloom-Charette, PhD,** is a staff geropsychologist at the Edith Nourse Rogers Memorial Veterans Hospital in Bedford, Massachusetts. She is also a lecturer at the Boston University School of Medicine. Dr. Bloom-Charette has consulted at numerous public and private nursing homes for the past 10 years. Her clinical and research interests include behavioral management, geropsychological assessment, and caregiver support groups.

**Elizabeth J. Brown, RDH, MS,** is a clinical hygienist at the Edith Nourse Rogers Memorial Veterans Hospital in Bedford, Massachusetts. Her duties and research interests involve geriatric dentistry in long-term care settings. She also coordinates the dental-hygiene program at five nursing homes in southern New Hampshire.

**Theressa Burns, OTR,** is the occupational therapist at the Minneapolis VA Hospital Geriatric Research, Education, and Clinical Center and is the current director of the Adapted Work Program. Ms. Burns developed the Cognitive Performance Test (CPT) that occupational therapists use to assess functional abilities related to cognitive impairment.

**Lois Camberg, PhD,** is a health services researcher for the Department of Veterans Affairs and is on the faculties of the Harvard School of Medicine and the Funeral Institute of the Northeast and has published papers and book chapters in the areas of long-term care and mental health. Dr. Camberg has conducted extensive research on topics related to nursing homes, including staffing, contracting, and evaluation services.

**Suzanne B. Hanser, EdD, MT-BC,** is chair of the Music Therapy Department at Berklee College of Music and a lecturer in the Department of Social Medicine at

Harvard Medical School. Dr. Hanser has served as president of the National Association for Music Therapy, senior postdoctoral fellow in geropsychiatry at Stanford University School of Medicine, and program director of the Alzheimer's Association, San Francisco Bay Area.

**David G. Harper** is a PhD candidate in psychology at Tufts University. Mr. Harper has been actively engaged in the study of biological rhythms since 1987. His interest in Alzheimer's disease, and the role biological rhythms play in the illness, dates from 1990.

**Joan Hyde, PhD,** is the chief executive officer of Hearthstone Alzheimer Care, a leading provider of dementia care in assisted living settings. She also holds an appointment as senior policy analyst at the Gerontology Institute, University of Massachusetts Boston. Recent research includes being principal investigator of an NIA-funded project to develop an assessment tool for assisted living; regulation of assisted living for those with dementia; and home adaptation for dementia. She currently serves as chair of the research group of the International Assisted Living Foundation.

**Melitta K. Maddox, MS, RNCS** is a Clinical Nurse Specialist for the Minneapolis VA Hospital Geriatric Research, Education, and Clinical Center (GRECC) and adjunct faculty in the School of Nursing at the University of Minnesota. Ms. Maddox is a Principle Investigator for a VA Health Service Research and Development (HSR&D) grant to teach caregivers strategies for dementia care.

**Barbara C. Manning, MEd,** received her master's degree from Cambridge College and did postgraduate work at Brasenose College in Oxford. Inspired by Dr. Snowdon's nun study, she made a shift from education to medical research. Ms. Manning is currently at the McLean Hospital in Belmont, Massachusetts, and is investigating with Ladislav Volicer the effects of Alzheimer's disease on circadian rhythms.

**Kevin McIntyre, MD,** is a physician specializing in cardiovascular medicine. His activities include patient care in medicine and cardiology, research, and teaching at the Harvard Medical School. The author of over 200 publications, Dr. McIntyre conceptualized simulated-presence therapy for patients with Alzheimer's disease in 1987 and initiated clinical testing with Patricia Woods at that time.

**Paul Raia, PhD,** is the director of patient care and family support at the Alzheimer's Association of Eastern Massachusetts and a consultant to several nursing homes, assisted-living facilities, and day programs, training staffs on the application of habilitation therapy. Dr. Raia has special interests in the management of problem behaviors, the environmental design of Alzheimer's units, and the special needs of those dually diagnosed with Down syndrome and Alzheimer's disease.

**Yvette Rheaume, BSN, RN,** is a nurse manager in the dementia study unit of the Geriatric Research, Education, and Clinical Center at the Edith Nourse Rogers

Memorial Veterans Hospital in Bedford, Massachusetts. Certified in Gerontological Nursing by the American Nursing Association, Ms. Rheaume has published a number of articles on the care of patients with Alzheimer's disease.

**Linda Shi** has held several research positions including research coordinator for Hearthstone Alzheimer Care, research associate for Brigham and Women's Hospital in Boston, and independent researcher for Wesleyan University, Middleton, Connecticut. She was responsible for data collection and preliminary data analysis for the project on specialized care unit design that formed the basis of the chapter in this book, "Environmental Design as a Treatment for Alzheimer's Disease."

**Joyce Simard, MSW,** is the vice president of Alzheimer's programs for CareMatrix Corporation. Ms. Simard has over 20 years of healthcare experience and has written many articles on Alzheimer's disease. She also has traveled throughout the United States speaking to caregivers.

**Scott A. Trudeau, MA, OTR/L,** is an occupational therapist at the Geriatric Research, Education, and Clinical Center of the Edith Rogers Memorial Veterans Hospital. A lecturer at the Boston School of Occupational Therapy, Tufts University, Mr. Trudeau's primary research interests center around the lived experience for the person with dementia, and the exploration of interventions that may contribute positively to that experience.

**Ladislav Volicer, MD, PhD,** is the clinical director of the Geriatric Research, Education, and Clinical Center at the Edith Nourse Rogers Memorial Veterans Hospital, and professor of pharmacology and psychiatry at the Boston University School of Medicine. Dr. Volicer investigates various aspects of dementia care, including behavioral symptoms, medical complications, and eating difficulties. He also has published over 200 articles and chapters and two books on the clinical management of dementia.

**Patricia Woods, RN, MSN,** is a clinical nurse specialist in the Department of Health Services Research and Development at the West Roxbury VA Medical Center. Ms. Woods has been involved in the development and implementation of the simulated presence intervention. She has worked extensively with family members and long-term care staff to provide simulated presence to individuals with Alzheimer's disease.

**John Zeisel, PhD,** is the president of Hearthstone Alzheimer Care, a company with its headquarters in Lexington, Massachusetts. He has served as a senior housing and healthcare consultant and has written numerous articles and books including *Inquiry by Design*, a standard reference in many social-science courses. Dr. Zeisel is also a founding member of the National Association for Senior Living in North American and has won numerous awards for his work in senior housing and healthcare including Progressive Architecture, the First Honor Award from the American Institute of Architects in 1982; and the First Massachusetts Governor's Design Award in 1986.

# PREFACE

Quality-of-life issues, important for all, are particularly important for those who have the least control over their environments, individuals with advanced dementia. Because quality of life consists of both affective and cognitive components, individuals with significant cognitive deficits experience decreased levels of well-being. Because these individuals are unable to verbalize their psychological discomfort, their frustrations often are displayed as agitation and other problem behaviors (Weiner et al., 1996). The 1985 National Nursing Home Survey (U.S. Department of Health and Human Services, 1989) found that approximately 62% of all nursing-home residents were so cognitively impaired that this impairment affected their everyday level of adaptive functioning, with many displaying disruptive and aggressive behaviors. Historically, the treatment approaches of chemical and physical restraints to counter problem behaviors have proved unsuccessful and at times countertherapeutic and even dangerous to the patients (Beers et al., 1988). Federal guidelines such as the Omnibus Reconciliation Act of 1987 have addressed these issues and mandated that alternative methods of care be considered. Instead of focusing on eliminating the problem behaviors, this book focuses on alternative methods of facilitating positive behaviors.

Alternative methods of care have been the topics of a number of recent publications; however, many of these approaches are not individualized or patient-focused. It is important to remember that individuals with dementia are a diverse group of all religions, races, and socioeconomic levels, so that one approach would not work with all.

The 11 approaches described in this book are divided into two groups: general strategies and specific approaches. In the first section, generalized approaches such as habilitation, the lifestyle approach, sheltered workshops, and functional techniques are described. The chapters on specialized approaches focus on various activities specifically designed for this population, such as validation therapy, simulated-presence therapy, the Bright Eyes group protocol, music therapy, SNOEZELEN®, light therapy, and environmental approaches.

The book is also unique in that it is directed primarily towards patients with advanced dementia, an underserved and difficult population. Where traditional approaches may fail, this book provides new and proven techniques to enhance the lives of those individuals afflicted with advanced dementia. Although each technique may not work with each and every individual, these innovative approaches are successful in a great number of cases. Each chapter provides guidelines for the appropriateness of each technique with individuals with different manifestations of the illness. For example, SNOEZELEN (a multisensory stimulation), although effective for withdrawn individuals, may be too stimulating for some agitated persons. In fact, many of these techniques may be useful with milder forms of dementias, as well as with other populations.

Another unique aspect of this book is that many of the techniques can be group-oriented. In this era of managed care, there is an increased emphasis on cost-effective approaches such as group therapies. Group interventions are often difficult to do with individuals with advanced dementia because of poor concentration and associated behavioral problems. All of the techniques described in this book such as Bright Eyes, music therapy, SNOEZELEN, validation, and light therapy can be set up individually or in groups. Many of these approaches even can be done by paraprofessionals under the direction of licensed staff.

Written by a multidisciplinary team of experts in the fields of psychiatry, psychology, public health, social work, occupational therapy, nursing, music therapy, and speech pathology, this patient-focused book provides cutting-edge and cost-effective techniques to deal with this challenging population. This book is organized around the most basic principle of all: to enhance the quality of life for those who have the most difficulty with life.

# ☐ References

Beers, M., Avorn, J., Soumerai, S., Everitt, D., Sherman, D., & Salem, S. (1988). Psychoactive medication use in intermediate-care facility residents. *Journal of the American Medical Association, 260,* 3016–3020.

U.S. Department of Health and Human Services, Public Health Service, Centers for Disease Control, & National Center for Health Statistics. (1989). *The National Nursing Home Survey, 1985: Summary for the United States.* (DHHS Publication No. PHS)89-1758. Hyattsville, MD: Author.

Weiner, M. F., Koss, E., Wild, K. V., Folks, D. G., Tariot, P., Luszczynska, H., & Whitehouse, P. (1996). Measures of psychiatric symptoms in Alzheimer patients: A review. *Alzheimer Disease and Associated Disorders, 10,* 20–30.

PART

I

# GENERAL STRATEGIES

1 CHAPTER

Ladislav Volicer
Lisa Bloom-Charette

# Assessment of Quality of Life in Advanced Dementia

The evaluation of psychological well-being in individuals suffering from progressive dementia is important for measuring the quality of care in long-term care settings and for determining the effectiveness of therapeutic programs. Traditionally, the assessment of quality of life has been a difficult task because of inconsistencies in the definition of terms. One difficulty is the subjective experience that each individual embodies in his or her definition of what constitutes the quality of life. The assessment of quality of life becomes progressively harder as the individual ages, the biological systems become more diverse, and environmental resources may become increasingly limited. As one enters a system such as long-term care, issues around quality of life become even more complex because of constraints of the setting. The most difficult population in which to assess quality of life is those individuals with advanced dementia. This chapter explores quality of life for older individuals, focusing on the definition and assessment and a model of quality of life in individuals with advanced dementia.

## ☐ Characteristics of Quality of Life in Normal Elderly Persons

The quality of life in older individuals has been the subject of considerable literature and debate because of confusion in terms. In general, *quality*

3

*of life* suggests a subjective evaluation of either life in general or individual components such as social, occupational, or financial functioning (Campbell, Converse, & Rodgers, 1976). What makes the definition of quality of life so challenging is the assessment of these subjective states. Another challenge in defining the quality of life is deciding what areas or domains to include in the definition.

Arnold (1991) identifies a number of overlapping factors that may influence the quality of life in normal elders. These factors include physical, emotional, intellectual, and social functioning, life satisfaction, health perceptions, economic status, leisure activities, sexual functioning, and vitality and energy. Although there appears to be agreement on the general domains within quality of life, there may be variations in the definitions of these domains. Stewart and King (1994) suggest that each domain needs a content or subject area as well as a response dimension consisting of both behavioral states and subjective evaluations.

In terms of assessment of these domains, there are a number of quality-of-life instruments for the normal elderly population. These instruments include measures of both single and multiple domains. Some single-domain instruments include the Instrumental Activities of Daily Living Scale (Lawton & Brody, 1969), the Katz Activities of Daily Living Index (Katz, 1983), the Pleasant Events Schedule (MacPhillamy & Lewinsohn, 1982; Teri & Lewinsohn, 1982), the Unpleasant Events Schedule (Lewinsohn, Mermeistein, Alexander, & MacPhillamy, 1985; Teri & Lewinsohn, 1982), the Satisfaction with Life Scale (Diener, Emmons, Larson, & Griffin, 1985) and the Geriatric Depression Scale (Yesavage et al., 1983).

Multidimensional instruments for a normal elderly population include the Life Satisfaction Index A and B (Neugarten, Havighurst, & Tobin, 1961), the Life Satisfaction in the Elderly Scale (Salamon, 1988), Life Satisfaction Instrument–Z (Wood, Wylie, & Sheafur, 1969), the Philadelphia Geriatric Center Morale Scale (Lawton, 1975), the Quality of Well-Being Scale (Kaplan, Bush, & Berry, 1976), the Medical Outcomes Study Functioning and Well-Being Profile (Stewart et al., 1992), the Functional Status Questionnaire (Jette et al., 1986), the Older Americans Resources and Services Multidimensional Functional Assessment Questionnaire (George & Fillenbaum, 1985), and the Multidimensional Functional Multilevel Assessment Instrument (Lawton, Moss, Fulcomer, & Kleban, 1992). With the plethora of available instruments, the choice of an appropriate instrument may seem daunting at first to the investigator. The choice of instruments is dependent upon the population, the definition of quality of life, and the purpose of the study.

In terms of assessment, the quality of life may be conceptualized differently in older individuals than in their younger counterparts. Older individuals may face a number of losses, such as social, role, physical, or financial losses. Despite these losses, many older individuals are able to maintain a positive self-image and quality of life. Brandstadter and Greve (1994) suggest that it is the process and not context that is most influential in quality of life in older adults in the face of potential losses. These authors detail three strategies: assimilation, accommodation, and immunization. Assimilation is the maintenance of current activities, interests, and goals. Accommodation is the replacement of previous activities with new adaptive ones in the face of change. Immunization is the adaptation to these changes by filtering out incongruous information.

Lawton (1983) presented one of the first well-defined conceptualizations for quality-of-life issues for normal elderly persons and later for individuals with Alzheimer's disease (Lawton, 1994). Lawton (1983) suggests that quality of life involves four dimensions: psychological well-being, behavioral competence, the environment, and perceived quality of life. Psychological well-being describes an individual's emotional state, such as lack of anxiety or depression. Behavioral competence consists of physical health, cognition, and functional competence. The objective environment comprises the physical attributes of the environment. The perceived quality of life is one's subjective life satisfaction.

## ☐ Characteristics of Quality of Life in Long-Term Care Settings

Defining the quality of life for residents in long-term care facilities may be even more difficult than for elders in the community. One reason for this difficulty may be the notion of limited choice and control within these diverse settings. Coon, Mace, and Weaverdyck (1996) attempted to outline factors that may enhance the quality of life in long-term facilities. These include freedom of choice and control, individuality, privacy, continuity with past, age-appropriate activities, pleasant ambiance of home, and opportunities for enjoyment.

Freedom of choice and control over one's environment are salient points in most people's lives. The very setting of a long-term care unit may be paradoxical to an individual's choice and control for a number of reasons. One reason is that the nursing-home industry is one of the most regulated industries, because of a number of building, federal, and state codes and mandates. Cost-cutting measures that may affect staffing and other resources also may affect a resident's sense of freedom and control over his or her environment. Fostering a sense of individuality is another important aspect of quality of life in long-term care settings. Recognizing an individual's tastes, likes, dislikes, ethnicity, and accomplishments, to name a few things, is very important in creating a therapeutic environment.

# ☐ Characteristics of Quality of Life in Late-Stage Dementia

The most difficult population in which to delineate quality-of-life issues is individuals with advanced dementia, because cognitive changes affect one's subjective experience and subsequent verbalization of quality-of-life issues. Several diseases cause development of progressive dementia, characterized by memory deficits and other cognitive dysfunctions. The most common of these diseases are Alzheimer's disease, vascular dementia, frontotemporal dementia (including Pick's disease), and dementia with Lewy bodies (Klein & Kowall, 1998). An individual suffering from dementia may have had more than one of the types of pathological changes characterizing these diseases, confirmed if his or her brain is examined after death. Unfortunately, we do not have an effective treatment to prevent or reverse any of these diseases. Therefore, caregiving efforts are directed towards improvement or maintenance of quality of life for the individual with advanced dementia.

## Measurement of Quality-of-Life Issues in Advanced Dementia

The evaluation of psychological well-being among persons with an advanced dementia is primarily dependent on verbal and nonverbal cues and behaviors that are observed and interpreted by others, as these individuals are no longer able to express their feelings about their lives and changes in their quality of life. The way to interpret these behaviors is open to debate. Ronch ( 1996) suggests that in order to understand the quality of life in persons with Alzheimer's disease, it is important to experience it from the patient's perspective. This approach, however, does not delineate how to assess behaviors from the patient's point of view.

There are, however, two instruments designed to assess the subjective experience of quality of life of the individual with dementia. The Pleasant Events Schedule–Alzheimer's Disease (Teri & Logsdon, 1991) is a 53-item self-report questionnaire of potentially reinforcing events assessed on a two- or three-point Likert scale. Designed for individuals with cognitive deficits, it may not be appropriate for individuals with advanced dementia. The instrument is also limited in that it only addresses the single domain of meaningful activities. Most recently, Brod, Stewart, Sands, and Walton (1999) developed the Dementia Quality of Life Instrument, a 29-item multidimensional self-report instrument designed to assess the quality of life in individuals with mild to moderate dementia (Mini-mental Examination [Folstein, Folstein, & McHugh, 1975] score greater than 12). The domains of this quality-of-life assessment instrument are self-esteem, positive affect and humor, negative affect, feelings of belonging, and sense of esthetics.

Much about the quality of life of an individual with advanced dementia needs to be gleaned from interviews with family members and staff. There are a couple of observer instruments designed to assess the quality of life of individuals with advanced dementia.

## Discomfort Scale

The Discomfort Scale (Hurley, Volicer, Hanrahan, Houde, & Volicer, 1992) measures physical discomfort in noncommunicative patients with advanced Alzheimer's disease. This nine-item rating scale notes the frequency, intensity, and duration of behavioral characteristics during a 5-minute observation, with ratings from 0 (no observed discomfort) to 27 (high level of discomfort). One limitation of the instrument in terms of quality of life is that it focuses on only a specific aspect of one of the domains and on negative rather than on positive emotion.

## Philadelphia Geriatric Center Affect Rating Scale

The Philadelphia Geriatric Center Affect Rating Scale (Lawton, 1994) is an affect-rating scale that focuses on both positive and negative emotions such as pleasure, interest, contentment, anger, anxiety, and depression. Like the Discomfort Scale, this scale only focuses on the affective component.

## Cornell Scale for Depression in Dementia

The Cornell Scale for Depression in Dementia (Alexopoulos, Abrams, Young, & Shamoian, 1988) is a well-known scale for measuring depression in patients with advanced dementia. It is a 19-item four-choice response set assessing five areas of emotional functioning: behavioral disturbance, mood, physical symptoms, lability, and ideational disturbances. This instrument is administered by both family and staff, and congruency of the two reports is compared. Like previously mentioned scales, the Cornell Scale for Depression in Dementia measures only one domain of quality of life, affect.

## Progressive Deterioration Scale

The Progressive Deterioration Scale (DeJong, Osterlund, & Roy, 1989) is a 27-item scale measuring activities of daily living, instrumental activities of daily living, social behaviors, and cognitive functioning. The scale, which gives an overall score for quality of life, does not measure the affective component.

### Resident Behavior/Life Quality Inventory

The Resident Behavior/Life Quality Inventory (Coon et al., 1996) is one of the few multidimensional instruments designed for individuals with dementia. This observation instrument assesses 12 behavioral categories for behaviors: functional and nonfunctional behaviors, null behaviors (disengagement), aggressive behaviors, sickness behaviors, emotional behaviors, purposeful motor behaviors, parasocial behaviors, task-oriented behaviors, leisure behaviors, social behaviors, and self-initiated behaviors. The limitation of this multidimensional instrument is that it is intended for individuals with mild to moderate stages of dementia. Thus far there exist no multidimensional quality-of-life instruments for individuals with advanced dementia.

## A Model of Quality of Life in Advanced Dementia

In moderate and severe dementia, there are three main areas that determine quality of life: meaningful activities, medical issues, and psychiatric symptoms (see Figure 1.1). Only if we consider all of these areas may we be able to achieve optimal quality of life for an individual with advanced dementia.

### Meaningful Activities

Provision of meaningful activities is the most important factor but the hardest to achieve in maintaining quality of life of demented individuals. Because the individual with advanced dementia cannot initiate such an activity alone, caregiver involvement is required. The main problem regarding meaningful activities is how to provide them with limited resources: limited caregiver time and energy for an individual living at home, and limited staffing available in a long-term care setting. Various strategies detailed in this book are designed to help address this problem.

Activities have to be tailored continuously to the remaining strengths and abilities of the individual, taking into consideration his or her life history and likes and dislikes. It is up to the caregiver to pick and choose appropriate activities for the individual and his or her current medical and emotional status. Engagement of the individual should not be restricted to short periods of special programs. Instead, the individual should get involved in all housekeeping and daily-living chores such as folding laundry, even if such an involvement requires more time and effort on the part of the caregiver (see Chapter 3).

There are two important interfaces between engagement in meaning-

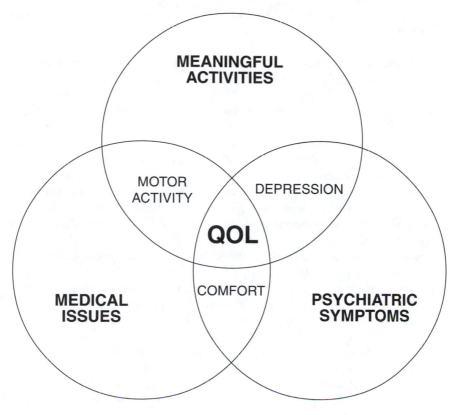

**FIGURE 1.1.** Factors involved in quality of life (QOL) in dementia.

ful activities and the two other quality-of-life domains, medical issues and psychiatric symptoms. The interaction between meaningful activities and psychiatric symptoms involves the effect of activities on mood. The interaction between activities and medical issues involves the impact of dementia-induced impairment of mobility.

**Depression.**    Demented individuals commonly show signs of depressed mood. In a study of 175 community-living demented individuals, 97% of them showed sad mood or loss of interest, and 87% had vegetative symptoms of depression (Merriam, Aronson, Gaston, Wey, & Katz, 1988). Eighty-six percent of these individuals had both sad mood and vegetative symptoms and therefore fulfilled criteria for diagnosis of depression. However, distraction by a meaningful activity improved mood in 90% of these individuals who were depressed. These results show the importance of meaningful activities for management of symptoms of depression in demented individuals.

**Maintenance of Mobility.**    As dementia progresses, patients lose their ability to walk independently. This loss of independent ambulation may be caused either by a lack of visual recognition of obstacles or by neuromotor changes. The neuromotor changes lead to unsteady gait and gait abnormalities including extremely narrow gait (scissoring). Both lack of visual recognition of obstacles and neuromotor changes lead to an increased risk for falls. Management of this risk by restraining the patient leads to deconditioning and development of contractures, which further impair the ability of the patient to ambulate. As a result of these impairments, one half of patients suffering from Alzheimer's disease lose the ability to walk independently by 7.8 years after the onset of dementia (Volicer et al., 1987).

Inability to walk independently restricts the involvement of a patient in activities. It precludes pacing, which is a desirable activity in a safe environment, because it provides an outlet for physical energy and alleviates agitated behavior. Patients who are not able to walk independently also may have fewer opportunities for activities outside the home or long-term care setting.

Loss of independent ambulation is a significant risk factor for development of infections. It was reported that such loss makes the risk for development of a urinary tract infection 3.4 times higher and the risk for development of lower respiratory infections 6.6 times higher than the risks for development of infections in ambulatory individuals (Magaziner et al., 1991). Each day of bed confinement increased the risk of development of pneumonia by 10% (Sahn, 1991), and the inability to ambulate is a risk factor for the development of deep vein thrombosis and pressure ulcers (Volicer, Brandeis, & Hurley, 1998). Therefore, it is very important for both psychological and physical reasons to maintain patient's mobility as long as possible.

## Medical Issues

The second area determining quality of life in moderate and severe dementia includes medical issues such as management of eating difficulties, intercurrent infections, chronic medical conditions, and comfort.

**Eating Difficulties.**    Eating difficulties include chewing difficulties, food refusal, and swallowing difficulties (Frisoni, Franzoni, Bellelli, Morris, & Warden, 1998). As dementia progresses, individuals may forget how to chew and start choking on food or liquids. Chewing difficulties can be managed by changing the texture of the diet. Swallowing difficulties are caused by the loss of coordination of oral muscles involved in the swallowing process. Individuals may start to choke on thin liquids, which require the best coordination. Adjusting the diet and switching to thick liquids may decrease the danger of aspiration. In patients who have forgotten how to swallow, changes of the diet texture and composition, and cueing during the feeding process, can assure adequate nutrition even in advanced dementia (Frisoni et al., 1998).

Food refusal could be related to the patient's food preferences but also may be a symptom of depression. Antidepressant treatment is quite effective in improving not only mood but also food intake in patients who are refusing food (Volicer, Rheaume, & Cyr, 1994). Another medication that is effective in improving nutritional status of patients with advanced dementia who refuse food is dronabinol (Volicer, Stelly, Morris, McLaughlin, & Volicer, 1997).

Initiation of long-term tube feeding is not indicated in patients with progressive degenerative dementia because there is a limited evidence to support long-term benefits and it is not clear that long-term tube feeding improves quality of life (Sheiman, 1996). One study actually reported that tube feeding increases the risk of aspiration pneumonia (Pick et al., 1996). This increased risk of aspiration is present not only with nasogastric tubes but even with gastrostomy tube feeding. A review of 1386 nursing-home residents showed that tube feeding does not provide any survival benefit if similar groups of cognitively impaired residents with and without tube feeding are compared (Mitchell, Kielly, & Lipsitz, 1997).

**Intercurrent Infections.**   Aspiration pneumonia and other intercurrent infections are more common in individuals with dementia than in cognitively intact individuals, because advanced dementia affects immunological defenses and causes incontinence and swallowing difficulties. Management of intercurrent infections in advanced dementia should take into consideration decreased effectiveness of antibiotic therapy in this patient population. Because of the recurrent nature of infections, antibiotic therapy does not extend survival in individuals who are unable to ambulate and are mute (Fabiszewski, Volicer, & Volicer, 1990). Aggressive treatment of infections also leads to increased discomfort of demented individuals, who are not able to understand the need for medical procedures. Treatment in a hospital, commonly using intravenous therapy, often requires restraining demented individuals to prevent removal of intravenous catheters and precipitates behavioral problems such as agitation and restiveness to care. Because antibiotic treatment is not always effective, a palliative approach to management of intercurrent infections, which assures maximal comfort without striving for maximal survival, may be appropriate.

**Chronic Medical Conditions.**    Treatment of chronic medical conditions in demented individuals needs to take into consideration three factors: inability to report symptoms, reduced life expectancy, and induction of discomfort by therapeutic interventions. Severe aphasia prevents reporting of symptoms by patients, but even patients with mild dementia are less likely to report symptoms, such as cough, rash, gastrointestinal symptoms, or joint pain, than cognitively intact individuals (McCormick et al., 1994). Therefore, the patients are also unable or less likely to report side effects of treatments. This inability to report side effects of treatments is especially important in treatment of hypertension, in which unreported dizziness can lead to falls and serious injuries. Similarly, patients treated with hypoglycemic agents or insulin can experience hypoglycemia, which they cannot report.

Reduced life expectancy is the second important consideration. Both Alzheimer's disease and vascular dementia shorten survival of affected individuals (Katzman et al., 1994). Survival of institutionalized demented patients is also significantly shorter than survival of patients institutionalized for other invalidating conditions (Hébert et al., 1995). Therefore, in demented individuals there is less need for preventive interventions that do not have an immediate impact. Thus, diet restrictions such as of cholesterol, fat, or salt may not be appropriate, especially because these restrictions may decrease palatability of food. Similarly, treatment of chronic conditions, such as hypertension and diabetes, should be less aggressive and should keep prevention of side effects as the main emphasis.

Significant discomfort may be induced in demented individuals by even the most routine diagnostic or therapeutic procedure. This discomfort may lead to significant abnormal behaviors, such as agitation, repetitive vocalization, and combativeness. In addition, patients do not understand the need for procedures and appliances and often have to be restrained to allow the procedure or to prevent removal of an appliance. Restraints also increase discomfort and the incidence of behavioral problems. Therefore, maintenance of comfort is an important interface between medical issues and psychiatric symptoms.

**Comfort.**    A risk-benefit analysis always should be made before a management decision. This analysis has to take into consideration the latest information not only about effectiveness of therapeutic interventions but also about the burden these interventions pose to the patient. Thus, long-term tube feeding may be rejected because of induction of significant discomfort and limited effectiveness. Rankings of discomfort resulting from 16 common procedures, which were obtained from hospitalized, nondemented adults, showed that nasogastric tube feeding was considered more uncomfortable than mechanical ventilation, and mechanical restraints were only slightly less uncomfortable than mechanical ventilation (Morrison et al., 1998).

Considerations regarding risks and benefits also should be made if considering initiation of an antibiotic therapy. Antibiotic therapy has limited effectiveness in patients with severe dementia (as noted previously) and may inflict significant burden on the patient. Rational selection of an antibiotic requires drawing of blood, suctioning of sputum, and sometimes intravenous therapy, and all of these procedures induce discomfort. At the same time, it is possible to maintain comfort of a patient suffering from an infection by analgesics and antipyretics without the use of antibiotics.

In patients with advanced dementia, it is not possible to determine discomfort from their reports. However, it is possible to determine their levels of discomfort by observation. Patients were found to be equally comfortable if treated with antibiotics as if treated with analgesics and antipyretics (Hurley, Volicer, Mahoney, & Volicer, 1993). Thus, antibiotics have limited effectiveness not only on patients' survival but also on patients' comfort.

## Psychiatric Symptoms

The third main area determining quality of life of individuals with advanced dementia includes psychiatric symptoms. Psychiatric symptoms can be classified into three categories: primary, secondary, and peripheral (Volicer, Hurley, & Mahoney, 1998c) There are three primary symptoms or consequences of dementia: functional impairment, depression, and delusions or hallucinations. One or more of these three main consequences can cause secondary symptoms: inability to initiate meaningful activities, dependence in activities of daily living, spatial disorientation, and anxiety. Functional impairment leads to inability to initiate meaningful activities and to dependence in activities of daily living. Because of this impairment, patients also may lose spatial orientation and become anxious if they are aware of their limitations. Depression can lead to decreased interest in social activities and decreased willingness to perform activities of daily living. In addition, anxiety is a common symptom of depression. Delusions and hallucinations may prevent a patient from participating in activities and make a patient unaware of need for bathing and grooming. Delusions also may cause spatial disorientation, and paranoid delusions may cause anxiety.

Combination of one or more primary and secondary symptoms leads to peripheral behavioral symptoms, such as apathy, agitation, repetitive vocalization, resistiveness, food refusal, elopement, and interference with other residents. It is important to analyze the behavior of each individual to establish the primary cause of these peripheral symptoms, because treatment of a primary cause, such as depression, may improve many peripheral symptoms. Such an approach is preferable to treatment of the individual peripheral symptoms by sedatives or hypnotics.

There is a lack of uniformity in classification of behavioral symptoms. Some authors call all problem behaviors "agitation" and separate agitation into physical and verbal, aggressive and nonaggressive behaviors (Cohen-Mansfield & Werner, 1995). Other investigators use the terms *aggressive behavior* (Ryden, Boseenmaier, & McLachlan, 1991), *catastrophic reaction* (Tiberti et al., 1998), and *obstreperous behavior* (Drachman, Swearer, O'Donnell, Mitchell, & Maloon, 1992). Behavioral symptoms often are evaluated more for negative impact on caregivers and other residents than for their impact on patients themselves. We believe that it is important to distinguish between two main problem behaviors, agitation and resistiveness, because they have different causes, and interventions for their management also may be different.

**Agitation.**    We reserve the term *agitation* for an uninvoked state of negative excitement that is characterized by restlessness and either physical or vocal repetitive behaviors, unrelated to known physical need of the patient that can be remedied, and without known motivational intent (Hurley et al., in press). Agitation often is caused by a patient's boredom and can be improved by providing a meaningful activity (see Chapter 8). Agitation may be also a symptom of depression or a consequence of delusions and hallucinations. Therefore, either antidepressant or antipsychotic medications are effective in decreasing agitation, according to the underlying cause. Some patients oscillate between agitation and apathy, and sedative medications used to treat agitation increase their apathetic behavior.

Agitation and apathy are important determinants of psychological well-being of demented individuals. An observational study showed that it is possible to distinguish three components of psychological well-being in individuals with moderate to severe dementia: agitation versus calm, engagement versus apathy, and happiness versus sadness (Volicer, Camberg, et al., 1998). These components are to some extent independent of each other and influenced by different interventions. The base of a cone in Figure 1.2 consists of the complex of emotions present in a normal individual (Russell, 1997). As dementia progresses, the ability to express complex emotions is impaired, but it is still possible to observe and measure agitation, engagement, and mood. In severe and terminal dementia, a patient may not be able to express any emotions, although he or she is not in a persistent vegetative state (Volicer, Berman, Cipolloni, & Mandell, 1997). Our interventions attempt to increase psychological well-being of

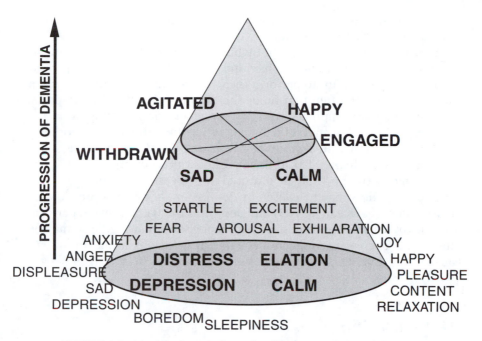

**FIGURE 1.2.** Model of psychological well-being in advanced dementia.

demented individuals by providing an optimal level of engagement, preventing agitation, and maintaining a happy mood.

**Resistiveness.**    We define *resistiveness* as the repertoire of behaviors with which persons with dementia withstand or oppose the efforts of a caregiver (Mahoney et al., 1997). Resistiveness is one of the most common problem behaviors (Patel & Hope, 1992), occurring during bathing in over 40% of nursing-home residents (Sloane et al., 1995). Nursing staff have identified resistive behaviors as the most difficult aspect of providing care to nursing-home residents with dementia (Herz, Volicer, Ross, & Rheaume, 1992).

Resistiveness is caused by the patient's lack of understanding of why an activity of daily living needs to be performed. This lack of understanding may be secondary to comprehension difficulties or may be caused by delusions regarding the patient's condition and identity of caregivers. Patients also may try to assert their independence without understanding their situations. If a patient's resistance is challenged by insistence of the caregiver that an activity has to be performed, the patient may become combative and even strike out to prevent an activity from happening. However, it is a mistake to label such behavior "aggression," because it is actually the staff person who insists on providing care who is perceived as an aggressor by the patient.

Resistiveness may be managed by both behavioral and pharmacological approaches. The simplest behavioral approach is to leave the patient for a while and attempt to perform the activity after few minutes, when the patient has forgotten that he or she did not want the activity done. Another behavioral approach uses two caregivers for providing care: One caregiver (a "joker") distracts the patient while the other one (a "worker") performs the activity. Relaxation before an activity also may decrease resistiveness (see Chapter 10). If behavioral approaches are not effective, pharmacologic therapy may be required to decrease a patient's resistiveness. Resistiveness may be caused by depression, because depression increases anger (Fava et al., 1993) and decreases the willingness to perform activities of daily living. Therefore, antidepressant treatment also may be effective in decreasing resistive behavior. If delusions are a prominent cause of resistiveness, neuroleptic therapy is often effective (Herz et al., 1992).

## ☐ Conclusion

Quality-of-life issues, complex for any population, are particularly difficult to define for individuals with advanced dementia. Thus far, there are no multidimensional quality-of-life instruments for individuals with advanced dementia. Informal evaluation, however, that considers the three main areas that determine quality of life in advanced dementia—meaningful activities, medical issues, and psychiatric symptoms—can be used by all caregivers for patients with dementia.

Meaningful activities are the most important factor in the quality of life of dementia patients. If proper activities are available, the patient can be engaged with either the physical or social environment. Activities may prevent states of apathy and agitation, which are indicators of impaired quality of life. We hope that information contained in this book will be used by professional caregivers to promote involvement in meaningful activities for individuals suffering from dementia.

Medical issues are important for prevention of the suffering caused by inappropriate aggressive medical interventions. The staff always should weigh the benefits of an intervention against the burden the intervention poses for the patient. Because advanced dementia is a terminal disease for which no curative therapy exists, comfort of the patient instead of maximal survival may be the appropriate goal of care. Aggressive interventions that produce discomfort and require patient restrants should be avoided as much as possible.

Psychiatric symptoms are most commonly expressed by disturbed behaviors. However, not all symptoms impair quality of life. Some patients may have hallucinations that are not bothersome and do not interfere with their involvement in other activities. In those patients, treatment of hallucinations may lead to drug side effects that decrease quality of life. However, caregivers have to be very sensitive to any signs and symptoms suggesting that a patient may be depressed. These symptoms include labile mood with episodes of sadness and crying spells, impaired appetite or food refusal, sleep disturbances, isolative behavior with a lack of interest in activities, and angry behavior during interaction with other residents or staff. Treatment with antidepressants may lead to improvement of some of these symptoms and increase quality of life.

Only if all three areas are considered can we be sure that we did everything possible to enhance or at least maintain the quality of life of a demented individual.

## ☐ References

Alexopoulos, G. S., Abrams, R. C., Young, R. C., & Shamoian, C. A. (1988) Cornell Scale for Depression in Dementia. *Biological Psychiatry, 23,* 271–284.

Arnold, S. (1991). Measurement of quality of life in the frail elderly. In J. Birren, J. Lubben, J. Cichowlas, J. Rowe, & E. Deutchman (Eds.), *The concept and measurement of quality of life in the frail elderly.* San Diego: Academic Press.

Brandstadter, J., & Greve, W. (1994). The aging self: Stabilizing and protective processes. *Developmental Review, 14,* 52–80.

Brod, M., Stewart, A. L., Sands, L., & Walton, P. (1999). Conceptualization and measurement of quality of life in dementia: The Dementia Quality of Life Instrument (DQoL). *The Gerontologist, 38,* 25–35.

Campbell, A., Converse, P. & Rodgers, W. (1976) *The quality of American life.* New York: Russell Sage Foundation.

Cohen-Mansfield, J., & Werner, P. (1995). Environmental influences on agitation: An integrative summary of an observational study. *American Journal of Alzheimer's Care, 10*(1), 32–39.

Coon, D., Mace, N., & Weaverdyck, S. E. (1996). Resident Behavior/Life Quality Inventory. In D. Coon & N. Mace (Eds.), *Quality of life in long-term care.* New York: Haworth Press.

Diener, E., Emmons, R. A., Larson, R.J., & Griffin, S. (1985). The Satisfaction with Life Scale. *Journal of Personality Assessment, 4,* 92–101.

DeJong, R, Osterlund, O. W., & Roy, G. W. (1989) Measurement of quality-of-changes in patients with Alzheimers disease. *Clinical Therapy, 11,* 545–554.

Drachman, D. A., Swearer, J. M., O'Donnell, B. F., Mitchell, A. L., & Maloon, A. (1992). The caretaker obstreperous-behavior rating assessment (COBRA) scale. *Journal of the American Geriatric Society, 40,* 463–470.

Fabiszewski, K. J., Volicer, B., & Volicer, L. (1990). Effect of antibiotic treatment on outcome of fevers in institutionalized Alzheimer patients. *Journal of the American Medical Association, 263 ,* 3168–3172.

Fava, M., Rosenbaum, J. F., Pava, J. A., McCarthy, M. K., Steingard, R. J., & Bouffides, E. (1993). Anger attacks in unipolar depression, part 1: Clinical correlates and response to fluoxetine treatment. *American Journal of Psychiatry, 150,* 1158–1163.

Folstein, M., Folstein, S., & McHugh, P. J. (1975). "Mini-mental State," a practical method for grading the cognitive state of patients for clinicians. *Journal of Psychiatric Research, 12,* 189–198.

Frisoni, G. B., Franzoni, S., Bellelli, G., Morris, J., & Warden, V. (1998). Overcoming eating difficulties in the severely demented. In L. Volicer & A. Hurley (Eds.), *Hospice care for patients with advanced progressive dementia* (pp. 48–67). New York: Springer Publishing Company.

George, L. K., & Fillenbaum, G. G. (1985). OARS methodology: A decade of experience in geriatric assessment. *Journal of the American Geriatrics Society, 33,* 607–-615.

Hébert, M., Parlato, V., Lese, G. B., Dabaj, A., Forette, F., & Boller, F. (1995). Survival in institutionalized patients: Influence of dementia and loss of functional capacities. *Archives of Neurology, 52,* 469–476.

Herz, L. R., Volicer, L., Ross, V., & Rheaume, Y. (1992). Single case study method for treatment of resistiveness in Alzheimer patients. *Hospital and Community Psychiatry, 43,* 720–724.

Hurley, A. C., Volicer, L., Camberg, L., Ashley, J., Woods, P., Odenheimer, G., Ooi, W. L., McIntyre, K., & Mahoney, E. (in press). Measurement of observed agitation in patients with Alzheimer's disease. *Journal of Mental Health and Aging.*

Hurley, A. C., Volicer, B. J., Hanrahan, P., Houde, S., & Volicer, L. (1992). Assessment of discomfort in advanced Alzheimer patients. *Research in Nursing & Health, 15,* 369–377.

Hurley, A. C., Volicer, B., Mahoney, M. A., & Volicer, L. (1993). Palliative fever management in Alzheimer patients: Quality plus fiscal responsibility. *Advances in Nursing Science, 16,* 21–32.

Jette, A. M., Davies, A. R., Cleary, P. D., Callans, D. R., Rubenstein, L. V., Fink, A., Kosecoff, J., Young, R. T., Brook, R. H., & Delbanco, T. L. (1986). The Functional Status Questionnaire. *Journal of General Internal Medicine, 1,* 143–149.

Kaplan, R. M., Bush, J. W., & Berry, C. C. (1976) Health status: Types of validity and index of well-being. *Health Services Research, 11,* 478–507.

Katz, S. (1983). Assessing self-maintenance: Activities of daily living, mobility, and instrumental activities of daily living. *Journal of the American Geriatrics Society, 31,* 721–727.

Katzman, R., Hill, L. R., Yu, E. S. H., Wang, Z.-Y., Booth, A., Salmon, D. P., Liu, W. T., Qu, G. Y., & Zhang, M. (1994). The malignancy of dementia: Predictors of mortality in clinically diagnosed dementia in a population survey of Shanghai, China. *Archives of Neurology, 51,* 1220–1225.

Klein, A., & Kowall, N. (1998). Alzheimer's disease and other progressive dementias. In L. Volicer & A. Hurley (Eds.), *Hospice care for patients with advanced progressive dementia* (pp. 3–28). New York: Springer Publishing Company.

Lawton, M. P. (1975). The Philadelphia Geriatric Center Morale Scale: A revision. *Journal of Gerontology, 30,* 85-89.

Lawton, M. P. ( 1983) Environment and other determinants of well-being in older people. *Gerontologist, 23,* 349–57.

Lawton, M.P. (1994). Quality of life in Alzheimer disease. *Alzheimer Disease and Associated Disorders, 8*(Suppl. 3), 138–150.

Lawton, M. P., & Brody, E. M. (1969) Assessment of older people: Self-maintaining and instrumental activities of daily living. *The Gerontologist, 9,* 179–186.

Lawton, M. P. , Moss, M., Fulcomer, M. & Kleban, M. H. (1982) A research and service oriented Multilevel Assessment Instrument. *Journal of Gerontology, 37,* 91–99.

Lewinsohn, P. M., Mermeistein, R. M., Alexander, C., & MacPhillamy, D. J. (1985). The Unpleasant Events Schedule: A scale for the measurement of aversive events. *Journal of Clinical Psychology, 41,* 483–489.

MacPhillamy, D. J., & Lewinsohn, P. M. (1982) The Pleasant Events Schedule (#1): Studies on reliability, validity and scale intercorrelation. *Journal of Consulting and Clinical Psychology, 50,* 363–380.

Magaziner, J., Tenney, J. H., DeForge, B., Hebel, R., Munice, H. L., & Warren, J. W. (1991). Prevalence and characteristics of nursing home-acquired infections in the aged. *Journal of the American Geriatrics Society, 39,* 1071–1078.

Mahoney, E. K., Hurley, A. C., Volicer, L., Bell, M., Lane, P., Hartshorn, M., Rheaume, Y., Gianotis, P., Lesperance, R., Novakoff, L., Sullivan, J., Timms, R., Warden, V., & McDonald, S. (1999). Development and testing of the resistiveness to care scale. *Research in Nursing and Health, 22,* 27–38.

McCormick, W. C., Kukull, W. A., Van Belle, G., Bowen, J. D., Teri, L., & Larson, E. B. (1994). Symptom patterns and comorbidity in the early stages of Alzheimer's disease. *Journal of the American Geriatric Society, 42,* 517–521.

Merriam, A. E., Aronson, M. K., Gaston, P., Wey, S.-L., & Katz, I. (1988). The psychiatric symptoms of Alzheimer's disease. *Journal of the American Geriatric Society, 36,* 7–12.

Mitchell, S. L., Kiely, D. K., & Lipsitz, L. A. (1997). The risk factors and impact on survival of feeding tube placement in nursing home residents with severe cognitive impairment. *Archives of Internal Medicine, 157,* 327–332.

Morrison, R. S., Ahronheim, J. C., Morrison, G. R., Darling, E., Baskin, S. A., Morris, J., Choi, C., & Meier, D. E. (1998). Pain and discomfort associated with common hospital procedures and experiences. *Journal of Pain & Symptom Management, 15*(2), 91–101.

Neugarten, B. L., Havighurst, R. J., & Tobin, S. S. (1961) The measurement of life satisfaction. *Journal of Gerontology, 16,* 134–143

Patel, V., & Hope, R. A. (1992). A rating scale for aggressive behavior in the elderly: The RAGE. *Psychological Medicine, 22,* 211–221.

Pick, N., McDonald, A., Bennett, N., Litsche, M., Dietsche, L., Legerwood, R., Spurgas, R., & LaForce, F. M. (1996). Pulmonary aspiration in a long-term care setting: Clinical and laboratory observations and an analysis of risk factors. *Journal of the American Geriatrics Society, 44,* 763–768.

Ronch, J. (1996). Assessment of quality of life: Preservation of the self. *Psychogeriatrics, 8,* 267–275.

Russell, J. A. (1997). How shall an emotion be called? In R. Plutchik & H. R. Conte (Eds.), *Circumplex models of personality and emotions* (pp. 205–220). Washington, DC: American Psychological Association.

Ryden, M. B., Bossenmaier, M., & McLachlan, C. (1991). Aggressive behavior in cognitively impaired nursing home residents. *Research in Nursing & Health, 14,* 87–95.

Sahn, S. A. (1991). Continuous lateral rotational therapy and nosocomial pneumonia. *Chest, 99,* 1263–1267.

Salamon, M. J. (1988) Clinical use of the life satisfaction in the elderly scale. *Clinical Gerontologist , 8*(1), 45–54.

Sheiman, S. L. (1996). Tube feeding the demented nursing home resident. *Journal of the American Geriatric Society, 44,* 1268–1270.

Sloane, P. D., Honn, V. J., Dwyer, S. A. R., Wieselquist, J., Cain, C., & Meyers, S. (1995). Bathing the Alzheimer's patient in long term care. Results and recommendations from three studies. *American Journal of Alzheimer's Disease, 10*(4), 3–11.

Stewart, A., & King, A. (1994). Conceptualizing and measuring quality of life in older populations. In R. Abeles, H. Gift, & M. Ory (Eds.), *Aging and quality of life.* New York: Springer Publishing Company.

Stewart, A. L., Sherbourne, C. D., Hays, R. D., Wells, K. B., Nelson, E. C., Kamberg, C. J., Rogers, W. H., Berry, S. D., & Ware, J. E., Jr. (1992). Summary and discussion of MOS measures. In A. L. Stewart and J. E. Ware, Jr. (Eds.), *Measuring functioning and well-being: The medical outcomes study approach.* Durham, NC: Duke University Press.

Teri, L., & Lewinsohn, P. M. (1982). Modification of the Pleasant and Unpleasant Events Schedule for the use with the elderly. *Journal of Consulting and Clinical Psychology, 50,* 444–445.

Teri, L., & Logsdon, R. G. (1991). Identifying pleasant activities for Alzheimer's disease patients: The Pleasant Event Schedule–AD. *Gerontologist, 31*(1), 124–127.

Tiberti, C., Sabe, L., Kuzis, G., Cuerva, A. G., Leiguarda, R., & Starkstein, S. E. (1998). Prevalence and correlates of the catastrophic reaction in Alzheimer's disease. *Neurology, 50,* 546–548.

Volicer, L., Berman, S. A., Cipolloni, P. B., & Mandell, A. (1997). Persistent vegetative state in Alzheimer disease: Does it exist? *Archives of Neurology, 54,* 1382–1384.

Volicer, L., Brandeis, G., & Hurley, A. C. (1998). Infections in advanced dementia. In L. Volicer & A. Hurley (Eds.), *Hospice care for patients with advanced progressive dementia* (pp. 29–47). New York: Springer Publishing Company.

Volicer, L., Camberg, L., Hurley, A. C., Ashley, J., Woods, P., Ooi, W. L., & McIntyre, K. (in press). Components of decreased psychological well-being in advanced dementia. *Journal of the American Geriatrics Society.*

Volicer, L., Hurley, A. C., & Mahoney, E. (1998). Behavioral symptoms of dementia. In L. Volicer & A. Hurley (Eds.), *Hospice care for patients with advanced progressive dementia* (pp. 68–87). New York: Springer Publishing Company.

Volicer, L., Rheaume, Y., & Cyr, D. (1994). Treatment of depression in advanced Alzheimer's disease using sertraline. *Journal of Geriatric Psychiatry and Neurology, 7,* 227–229.

Volicer, L., Seltzer, B., Rheaume, Y., Fabiszewski, K., Herz, L., Shapiro, R., & Innis, P. (1987). Progression of Alzheimer-type dementia in institutionalized patients: A cross-sectional study. *Journal of Applied Gerontology, 6,* 83–94.

Volicer, L., Stelly, M., Morris, J., McLaughlin, J., & Volicer, B. J. (1997). Effects of dronabinol on anorexia and disturbed behavior in patients with Alzheimer's disease. *International Journal of Geriatric Psychiatry, 12,* 913–919

Wood, V., Wylie, M. L., & Sheafur, B. (1969). An analysis of a short self-report measure of life satisfaction. *Journal of Gerontology, 24,* 465–474.

Yesavage, J. A., Brink, T. L., Rose, T.L., Lum, O., Huang, V., Adey, M., & Leirer, V. O. (1983) Development and validation of a geriatric depression screening scale: Preliminary report. *Journal of Psychiatric Research, 39,* 37–49.

CHAPTER **2**

Paul Raia

# Habilitation Therapy: A New Starscape

Knowledge often depends on how we define what we want to know. Before Galileo, Western astronomers claimed the sun revolved around the Earth, which conveniently defined Earth, and man, as the center of the cosmos.

## ☐ Galileo Redux

Until recently, it could be said that the life of the person with Alzheimer's disease was defined as revolving entirely around inevitable loss—sun around Earth.

This shortsightedness permeates several common, broad "definitions" of Alzheimer's disease. It has led not only to different responses to the disease, but to dramatically different approaches to care.

The first view is essentially no definition at all. Memory loss, confusion, and disorientation occurring later in life are considered just facets of normal aging. And because these symptoms are "normal," no specific approach to care is needed. Few state or federal programs, for example, recognize the need or provide funds for specialized dementia-care programs in either community or long-term care settings.

A second, and equally disturbing, definition tends to see Alzheimer care as a backwater, a low-technology area of medicine and professional caregiving with minimal challenges and scant rewards. The emphasis here is on palliative care—that is, providing basic comfort as patients wait to die.

The third definition emphasizes that Alzheimer's disease is a disease for which there is no cure and no treatment. Hence, our only hope to alleviate the pain and suffering associated with the disease process is to devote all of our resources to biomedical research. The inviolable quest for the "magic pill" obscures the need for new ways to better manage symptoms of the disease in those who are presently afflicted. Although a cure is nowhere in sight, this paradigm holds enormous power among professionals and the public at large.

## ☐ A New Starscape

In contrast, another view of Alzheimer's disease and related disorders has emerged, in which these diseases are defined more as disabilities, albeit caused by progressive and fatal neurological illness. In this view, individuals respond to their disease according to how supportive their environments are. Here, the emphasis is on active treatment of the symptoms of the dementia through a careful focus on the utilization of those capacities that remain, particularly the person's psychological capacity. Developing a better understanding of the psychology of dementia—how a person thinks, feels, communicates, compensates, and responds to change, to emotion, to love—may bring some of the biggest breakthroughs in treatment.

This new paradigm has led to a radically different orientation to dementia care—a model called *habilitation*, first discussed by Raia and Koenig-Coste in 1996. Drawn for the most part from the common experiences of professional and family caregivers, habilitation is more a disposition, or a way of thinking, than a complete therapeutic model. It reflects the humanistic perspective of psychologist Abraham Maslow (1968), meaning that habilitation starts with the premise that there is an innate drive in all people to maximize their potential, even, as we would apply it, if the person is afflicted with a dementing illness.

The aim of habilitation therapy is not to restore people with a dementia such as Alzheimer's disease to what they once were (i.e., *re*habilitation), but to maximize their functional independence and morale. This approach also allows minimization or elimination of many difficult symptoms of the dementia in spite of the person's progressive physical, cognitive, and emotional limitations.

For caregivers, the primary learning task becomes how to value what is still there and not dwell on functions the person has lost. To borrow from the philosopher Erich Fromm (1976), family and professional caregivers need to emphasize "being" rather than "having." This model is no cure. But it is a system of treating symptoms that can benefit both the person with Alzheimer's disease and the caregiver.

## ☐ Realigning the Planets

The goal of habilitation is deceptively simple—to bring about a positive emotion and to maintain that emotional state over the course of the day. Clinically, however, it presents a challenge. If cognitive capacities involving memory, logic, reason, decision making, judgment, language, attention, perception, and motor control all are being gradually lost to the disease, what remains? What cognitive capacity can we then use as a channel to the brain?

The collective experience of caregivers tells us that the capacity to feel and exhibit emotions persists among people with Alzheimer's disease far into the disease process. What is lost is the insight into what may have triggered a particular emotion, or how to control it. The ability to feel emotions, then, may be our best inroad to the mind of the person with Alzheimer's disease.

That said, habilitation can be defined as a proactive environmental therapy characterized by what we refer to as "domains," six critical areas in which positive emotions can be created and maintained (see Table 2.1). This therapeutic intervention supports the person's remaining cognitive capacities, respects his or her adult needs, and emphasizes meaningful activity. It can be established in the home, day center, assisted-living, or long-term care setting.

The challenge, of course, is for family and professional caregivers to recognize, within the six-domain construct, what will evoke—and what will inhibit—positive emotions, and then to address those positive emotions over the course of the day.

## ☐ The Domains

### The Physical Domain

Even a once-familiar environment can become frightening and confusing to someone with Alzheimer's disease. Within the physical domain, the habilitation model attempts to reduce the potential for fear and disorientation by "directing" cognition, often without the person's awareness. In this way, the manipulated environment becomes a prosthetic for the brain.

**TABLE 2.1. The six domains of habilitation**

| | Goal | Outcome |
| --- | --- | --- |
| Physical environment | To create a physical environment that directs cognition without the patient's awareness | Positive emotions because of greater mastery of environment |
| Communication | To enhance the patient's capacity to understand language as well as to make him- or herself better understood | Positive emotions because of less frustration |
| Functional assistance | To reduce excess disability | Positive emotions because of greater perception of independence |
| Social | To help the patient hold on to cognitive and social skills longer via practice | Positive emotions because of meaningful activity and sense of purpose |
| Perceptual | To make sensory cues more easily perceived | Positive emotions because of less confusion |
| Behavioral | To reduce unsafe as well as annoying behavior | Positive emotions because of fewer negative interactions with staff and other patients |

A well-designed prosthetic environment, like all the other domains in this model, has as a goal to bring about a positive emotion and to maintain that emotion.

To illustrate, I was asked to consult on a case in which a 73-year-old woman with Alzheimer's disease, living at home with her husband, was having difficulty dressing herself in the morning. When I arrived at the home I asked the husband to show me how he assisted her in the morning. He took me to the bedroom, where there was an enormous walk-in closet. He indicated that he simply would say to his wife that it was time to get dressed and he would leave. When he would return 20 minutes later he would find his wife still standing in the closet in her nightgown.

Because it is well known that Alzheimer patients have problems making decisions, the environment had to be altered in such a way as to reduce the number of choices. I instructed the husband to remove all but two or three outfits from the closet and begin the morning by taking two outfits from the closet. I suggested that he say something like: "We have two very pretty outfits here, a blue one and a red one. I like the blue one because it matches your eyes. Which one would you like to wear today?" Once we limited the number of choices, she was able to get dressed on her own. With her environment structured so that she can use her remaining skills, chances are that she will hold on to these skills longer. It also serves to bring about a positive emotion because she feels more independent.

Perhaps the single most important adaptation to an environment is enhanced lighting. Experience indicates that by increasing artificial light from approximately 45-foot-candle power (typical lighting in a home) to 80-foot-candle power and controlling the glare and shadows from outside, ambient light we can improve independence, reduce late afternoon and early evening agitation, and stabilize mood.

Another principle of habilitative design is that we use color and textural contrast to draw attention to important features of the environment, and we camouflage or hide dangerous or distracting elements of the environment. Again, to illustrate, I was called to a caregiver's apartment because her husband, a midstage Alzheimer's patient, was urinating in a closet. The problem as I saw it was that the couple had recently moved to a new apartment and he more often than not chose the wrong door when he felt he needed to use the bathroom. In fact, the bathroom and closet doors were adjacent to one another. By painting the bathroom door red, the color automatically drew the gentleman's attention and he reliably chose the correct door. However, once in the bathroom he was confronted by white walls and floor, a white sink, toilet, and bathtub. He often would urinate in the bathtub. I instructed the caregiver to purchase a red toilet seat, and the problem was solved.

These are just some of the physical enhancements that can reduce the environmental demands on the person's already challenged perception. They, in combination with the other domains of this model, can increase dramatically levels of functioning. More importantly, they lessen the frustration, which often results in behavioral outbursts, and promote feelings of accomplishment, security, and belonging.

## The Social Domain

Structured activities are the engine that drives the social domain. Understandably, people with Alzheimer's disease who spend significant amounts of time doing nothing experience more psychiatric symptoms, such as depression, anxiety, paranoia, delusions, and hallucinations, than people who are occupied by a meaningful activity; however, the increased amounts of leisure time with which these people find themselves can be addressed successfully through enriching activities that promote feelings of purpose and accomplishment.

By developing a failure-free activities plan, we can avoid cognitive skill areas that have been lost. This plan may require that the person's cognitive strengths and weaknesses be assessed through a battery of neuropsychological tests. A cautionary note should be mentioned here: For some patients, these tests can cause frustration and bring about negative emotions. In these instances our knowledge of the patient and observation of his or her skill level are better indicators of how to design failure-free activities. Practice with remaining skills with these failure-free activities can help slow the rate of decline of those skills.

In the social domain, time is filled with opportunities for reminiscence (e.g., cooking classes, word games, and holiday reflections), for fun (dancing, sing-a-longs), and for creativity (herb gardening, jigsaw puzzles, and art projects). However, these activities are not "time fillers"; rather, they are carefully and individually selected cognitive enhancers that maintain healthy neural connections and promote branching or arborization of neurons. Branching of neuronal axons allows an electrical impulse in the brain to bypass damaged areas of the brain and make connections with healthy cells. So, failure-free activities help individuals hold on to capacities longer and maintain positive emotions. Another benefit of activities, especially musical activities, is that they very quickly change emotions. Thus, activities can be used prophylactically to avoid anticipated swings in mood or increased confusion. An activity cannot be introduced once the person is already agitated. At the same time, therapeutic activities facilitate orientation, maintain interests and strengths, and minimize isolation.

Again, activities should be commensurate with the person's cognitive level. They should offer opportunities for success and interaction and be based on previous interests expressed throughout the person's lifetime. If the person is especially uncooperative in a particular activity, one can try it again later on or forget it for that day. One should avoid jeopardizing a positive emotion in order to adhere to a schedule.

Activities also should have an adult focus and not be childish. In this way they can provide a medium for caregivers to interact with the person in new ways, or to connect with aspects of that person's character, personality, and experience that appear to have been lost to the disease. One caregiver, for example, to address his wife's "sundowning" behavior (late-day confusion), began ballroom dancing with her late every afternoon. She enjoys it, she does not experience sundowning, and they are able to relive some previously inaccessible intimate emotions of their youth.

There is an unfortunate but persistent myth that people with Alzheimer's disease, because they may not remember friends or be able to contribute to a relationship, no longer have a need for social experience and interaction. In fact, they have an increasing need for all of the social benefits that derive from relationships. Victims of Alzheimer's disease may lose the ability to initiate social interaction, but not their need for it.

In the social domain, the caregiver's aim should be to build the person's social competence by fostering opportunities for mutual support. One way to do that is to create social groupings in which the person's feelings of alienation and isolation can be countered by feelings of belonging, mutual respect, and purpose. Groups can be formed for people in the early through the middle stages of the disease and may focus on general activities or on very specific therapeutic goals.

## The Functional Domain

All too frequently in Alzheimer's care we note an inability to perform routine tasks even before the person has reached the point in the downward trajectory of the disease process at which that degree of dysfunction would be expected. Dysfunction caused by the person's emotional reaction to the disease (e.g., depression) or to physical or care factors in the environment is said to be an "excess disability." But depression, like many other psychiatric symptoms seen in Alzheimer's disease, usually can be treated by the judicious use of medication.

Excess disabilities with environmental causes can be avoided by creating supports that encourage independence in the person's activities of daily living, such as eating, walking, toileting, dressing, grooming, and bathing. As in the activity domain, previous routines become the cornerstones here, as caregivers struggle to keep one step ahead of dependence.

The key is to continue for as long as possible with the person's normal, customary routines. From which side of the bed does she get up in the morning? This information becomes significant, for example, if she were to move to a new setting in which the side of the bed she arose from for the past 50 years now abuts a wall. When he dresses, in what order does he like to put on the articles of clothing? They should be laid out for him accordingly. Did she usually shower, or bathe in a tub? Use a face cloth or sponge?

Is the fact that he has so much difficulty removing his pants the real cause of his apparent incontinence? If she fails at more complicated chores, can she instead help by shredding lettuce or setting the table? No matter how simple the task, we must sustain the person at an appropriate functional level for as long as possible.

Caregivers also can change the task to fit the person and prioritize which activities for daily living (or parts of an activity) are important and which are not. Bathing, for example, may be the most difficult activity asked of the person. One should begin by spending at least 5 minutes just talking and building rapport. This is called the "spend 5 to save 20" rule. Proposing an activity as a question ("Would you like to take a bath?") too often leads to a resounding "no." Assist the person with verbal cues, using a technique called "chunking," which involves a series of short, simple, calmly stated commands, such as "come with me," "unbutton your shirt," "take out your arm," "unbuckle your belt," and so on. Schedule bathing when the person is in the best frame of mind, most alert and cooperative. If necessary, provide hands-on assistance, mindful not to let water pour over the person's face and eyes, which can be frightening. Wash the hair and the face at a different time. Showering for a patient with Alzheimer's disease is best done from the feet, stopping at the neck, rather than the standard practice of working from the head down.

Remember, the goal of habilitation is to bring about a positive emotion and to maintain that emotion over the course of the day. If we start the day, say, with a negative emotion caused by a bad experience with bathing or showering, the person will forget the context for that negative emotion but be left with the emotion without any idea about how it was established. The patient will carry that negative emotion to his or her next interaction, causing it to result in a more intense negative emotion. By the end of the day the person is agitated, confused, and disruptive. So it is important not to start the day on a slippery slope of escalating negative emotion. As illustration of this point, Tom, a 53-year-old patient with Alzheimer's disease had great difficulty with his morning shower. Not only was he combative during the ordeal of the shower, but his behaviors dramatically worsened in the afternoon. Under habilitation therapy it is imperative to intervene and prevent the development of the negative emotion. The first step is triage. If showering is so difficult for him, how many times per week are we willing to risk starting off the day with a negative emotion? In this case we said four times per week. We then determined after talking with this man's family that there were four things that calmed him—backrubs, blue sports cars, women in short skirts, and the music of the Beach Boys. So, we developed an intervention that employed these calming agents. To begin with, only one nursing assistant was involved with assisting with this man's shower rather than three aides, as was used before. The aide would come into the man's room and just chat with him for a few minutes—the spend 5 to save 20 rule. She then gave the man a backrub to create a relaxed mood. Once he was relaxed she simply said, "Come with me," and led him down the hall to the shower. On the walls between the "young" patient's room and the shower we had taped pictures of blue sports cars and tasteful pictures of women in short skirts to distract him and avoid any anticipatory anxiety. Once in the shower room the music of the Beach Boys was playing; the room was warm and well illuminated. While singing with the young man the aide undressed him. We had determined that it might be important to put a bathrobe on the man to reduce any modesty problems. Using a handheld shower nozzle, the aide started washing at the man's feet and quickly moved up the body, stopping at the neck. The actual washing took less than 3 minutes. He was not at all resistant or combative during this procedure, and he actually participated in the washing. It also was noted that his behavior did not worsen in the late afternoon as it had under the previous method of showering. Thus, great lengths are taken not to start off the day with a negative emotion, and to make the experience one that brings about a positive emotion.

Habilitation is only successful if we are willing to capitalize on—and discover—remaining skills, to break tasks into simple, easily sequenced steps, to go slowly, and to always to provide only the level of support that the person with Alzheimer's disease needs. Then the person derives meaning and purpose as he or she participates in the task as much as he or she is able. Perhaps the best illustration of these principles involves assisting patients with eating. Many factors can contribute to a patient not eating, and it is entirely too easy for caregivers to take over the task to ensure proper nutritional intake. Some patients can be overwhelmed by too many decisions involved in eating. Consider the typical tray of food in a nursing home. We might have a white tray with a white covered plate, a packet of utensils wrapped in a napkin, a small teapot, a teacup, a salad bowl wrapped in plastic, a dessert, and condiments. The patient, because of problems with executive functioning—planning and implementing a task—does not know where to begin. Some patients may be able to feed themselves if we just get them started; others may need to have only one dish and one utensil presented to them in order to simplify the task. Still other patients may require finger foods to continue feeding themselves. It may take only 10 minutes to feed a patient and an hour if he or she feeds himself or herself, but if caregivers prematurely take over the task, the patient will lose the ability and thus feel more dependent.

## The Communication Domain

Nowhere in the habilitation model is the process of eliciting positive emotions more critical than in the communication domain. As surely as our language system sets us apart from other animals, our loss of communication skills profoundly dismays and unnerves us. In our highly verbal world, expressive and receptive language deficits are catastrophic losses for someone with Alzheimer's disease.

In the communication domain, habilitation calls for increased use of body language, encouraging the use of gestures, demonstrations, signs, and pictures. A drawing of a cup and saucer may better communicate what is in the kitchen cabinet than anything verbal or written.

Habilitation underscores listening techniques related to emotions, directing us to listen not so much to the often misused words and muddled sentences, but to the driving emotion behind them.

For example, if the person is experiencing symptoms of suspiciousness and accuses the caregiver of taking her pocketbook, the caregiver can say something like, "I know how you feel. When I lose my pocketbook [or wallet] I feel panicky. Let me help you find it." Once this offer of assistance is communicated, the outcome is likely to be a change in the person's emotional state.

Within the communication domain there are the rules of communication, straightforward techniques, and the strategies of communication that are more abstract principles of interaction. The following are some of the basic rules of communication.

- Always approach the patient from the front.
- Always indicate your name and say the patient's name every time you have an exchange, even if it is several times in the course of a day.
- Be aware of body language, making sure you are smiling and using a positive tone of voice.
- Always say something positive about the person, such as, "I love your hat," or, "That is a beautiful dress," each time you interact with the patient.
- Try to maintain eye contact with the patient even though the patient may be looking at your mouth. As patients lose the ability to understand language they become inadvertent lip readers. Female staff and family members can wear lipstick, which can be easily seen and facilitate lip reading.
- If the patient is seated you should be at the same level. If the patient is standing you should be standing.
- Never position patients so that a light source (a window or lamp) is behind you as you face them. They will not be able to see the details of your face with the light source in their eyes.
- Always "chunk" information into short, explicit communications. For example, avoid saying, "please set the table," because this may be too abstract. Try a series of short commands such as "come with me"; "take a dish from the shelf"; "put the dish on the table"; and so on.
- Be careful about using metaphors or abstract phrases.
- If the patient loses her or his train of thought, reorient her or him. If she or he is struggling to find a lost word, offer it. If the patient cannot remember something she or he wanted to say, often a reassuring pat on the hand and the comment, "It's OK, it will come back to you later," are helpful.

The less people with Alzheimer's disease are frustrated by their verbal errors, the longer they will continue to interact with others, and the longer they will maintain feelings of personal value.

The more abstract strategies of communication suggest how different habilitation therapy is from everyday methods of communicating with cognitively intact elders. The first strategy of habilitative communication is that one can never change behavior with words, only by changing what one does, the approach to the patient, or the environment. The rationale for this strategy is obvious. Because the patient has no short-term memory and limited capacity to learn, we cannot tell the patient to do something or not to do something and expect him or her to do it the next time.

This point can be illustrated in the following true story. The daughter of a patient with Alzheimer's disease had the custom of taking her mother to a restaurant every Thursday evening. This particular Thursday the daughter arrived at her mother's home to find her mother standing on the porch wearing her mink coat, matching shoes, and pocketbook, ready for an evening out. When they arrived at the restaurant, Mom took off her coat to reveal her slip. She had forgotten to put her dress on. The daughter, realizing that the goal of all habilitative communication is to bring about a positive emotion and that pointing out that her mother forgot to put on her dress only would cause embarrassment, merely said to her mother, "It is a bit chilly. I'm going to put my coat back on." Mom did the same, and they then were able to have a have a wonderful meal together.

The second strategy is to never use the word no. If the patient wakes up at 4 AM and wants to take a walk outside in a rainstorm, one should say, "Sure, let's do it." If one says no, muscles tense up, tone of voice changes, and the patient sees the caregiver as limiting his or her independence. Because of this the situation becomes highly emotional—and emotions are what the patient is good at. Even if the patient is given the most logical, eloquent argument why he or she should not go outside, there is nothing in his or her brain that can appreciate the reasoning. Rather than logic, one should use distraction. Two techniques, refocusing and redirecting, help distract the patient long enough so that his or her faulty memory will work to the caregiver's advantage. For example, one might say, "Sure, let's go, but before we go I need to have a cup of tea and a sandwich. My favorite kind of sandwich is turkey. What's yours?" The caregiver is refocusing the person's attention. He or she then might go on to say, "Help me make the sandwich." Such dialogue redirects behavior. By using these techniques, enough time passes so that the person forgets his or her original intention. Saying no at the outset only makes the person more likely to leave.

A third strategy, perhaps the hardest to learn and apply, is that one never brings a midstage patient back to our sense of reality; rather, the caregiver must go to where she or he is. Reality orientation as a therapeutic technique works just fine for cognitively intact elders, but it is not at all useful for midstage patients with Alzheimer's disease.

Consider this: A 91-year-old lady with Alzheimer's disease becomes increasingly confused in the late afternoon and early evening, a condition referred to as "sundowning." During this period the lady might approach a caregiver and say that she just saw her mother. Using reality orientation, the caregiver would tell the lady that her mother is dead and that she did not really see her. This would propel the patient into mourning because it is the first time she has heard that her mother has died. Two minutes later the patient forgets that her mother is dead, but she is left with the mourning with absolutely no context for it. She carries the negative emotion to her next interaction, and the emotion affects that interaction. And, again because she is feeling anxious and insecure, she says to the caregiver that she saw her mother, thus starting the cycle over.

Within habilitation, rather than tell the patient that her mother is dead, we would say, "Tell me about your mother, I hear that she is a wonderful person." Or, if this happens frequently and predictably, the caregiver could have a picture of the patient and her mother taken many years earlier and use the picture to create a story, which may or may not be true, to bring about a positive emotion.

Still another example emphasizes the creativity required in habilitative communication. An 80-year-old woman in midstage Alzheimer's disease was admitted to a nursing home, and for the first several days there she refused to eat anything. The nursing assistant, having read the patient's social history, learned that she had been a fan of the Boston Pops Orchestra and that she had a crush on Arthur Fiedler, the renowned conductor of the Pops, for many years. Armed with this information, the aide went down into the kitchen and brought up a tray of food. The aide told the patient that while in the lobby she saw Arthur Fiedler and she mentioned to him that the patient was not eating. The aide went on to say that when Mr. Fiedler heard that the patient was not eating, he went into the kitchen and prepared this meal especially for her (keep in mind that this took place many years after Arthur Fiedler had died). The patient then was given the tray of food and she ate every bite, and every meal thereafter Arthur Fiedler prepared.

This sounds as if we are lying to our patients, but these are not lies, these are what I call "therapeutic fiblettes"—inroads into the patient's reality. It is only if we become comfortable and creative in the use of fiblettes that we become effective practitioners of habilitation therapy.

A fourth communication strategy emphasizes our role in reducing fear for the patient and acknowledging underlying emotions. Patients with Alzheimer's disease experience fear throughout their disease course. As they decline and lose capacities, part of what is also lost is the ability to articulate their fears and cope with them. Essentially, what is lost is the person's ability to self-soothe if fears become overwhelming. This is akin to the behavior seen in infants who do not have the neurological and cognitive capacities to overcome their unrealistic fears. The focus of our communications is to make the person feel loved and safe. They need to hear from us what it is that they should be doing, because they live with this nagging feeling that they are supposed to be doing something important but they do not know what it is. Our communications give them purpose and direction. We also need to attend to the underlying feelings behind the inarticulate communications, even if they are difficult emotions.

In a previous example, a patient accused a caregiver of taking her pocketbook. The caregiver's natural reaction was to indicate that she did not take it, and then to offer her assistance in finding the misplaced item. This, however, is only a partial intervention. First, telling the patient that one did not take the item will go nowhere. In fact, it may make things worse. Offering assistance to find the item is appropriate but it still leaves the underlying emotion, in this case panic, ignored and unresolved. It might be better to say, "I know you must be very upset. I get panicky when I lose my pocketbook because all my important stuff is in there. Let's go look for it together." One must look beneath the words to what the patient's basic emotions are and try to address them in a simple, direct way. If these emotions are ignored, they fester and lead to catastrophic behavior.

## The Perceptual Domain

It seems likely that part of the faulty communication system among people with Alzheimer's disease is the result of some sensory deprivation. We have long recognized the link between memory stimulation and odors, sights, and sounds. But how is the person with Alzheimer's disease to communicate if sensory messages to the brain are not fully captured or are no longer recognizable?

Sensory modalities blend together, meaning that senses like sight and sound may not be completely separate experiences. As William James (1890) observed about infants: "Sensory input is a blooming, buzzing confusion." In some cases, the person may lose what is called *proprioceptive memory*; that is, memory related to muscle function. A person in mid-to late-stage Alzheimer's disease, for example, may forget how to open a door, or how to bend the knees in order to sit. If this loss occurs, caregivers can use hand gestures indicating that the person should sit or might even apply some gentle pressure behind the knees to initiate the sitting action.

Caregivers also need to heighten the person's sensory experiences, as well as their own reading of what messages the environment may be giving the person with Alzheimer's disease. Most importantly, we need to be aware of what the person may be connecting to (often in the past) as a result of a current sensate interaction but may be unable to articulate.

The rose's thorny stem, for example, may signal discomfort to the person who is unable to perceive the blooming flower atop it. Or consider the person with Alzheimer's disease whose frustration approaches panic as he rummages for the keys in his pocket because he does not recognize their shape, their feel. When we provide a visual cue by removing the "lost" keys from his pocket and showing them to him, he simply says, "Oh, there they are."

Knowing that the disease process alters perception should prompt caregivers to supply the person with more visual, tactile, and auditory cues. One example of a therapeutic intervention that enhances perception is SNOEZELEN®-based therapy. This form of therapy is detailed in Chapter 10.

## The Behavioral Domain

Although structured activities drive the social domain, properly focused behavior-management techniques are what drive the behavioral domain. To manage problematic (i.e., reactive) behaviors successfully, the habilitation model requires that caregivers adopt a dementia-centered perspective. As stated previously, it accepts that we cannot change the person's behavior directly, but only indirectly by changing either our approach technique or the person's physical environment. Certainly, by the middle stages of the disease we must assume that patients have no short-term memory and only very limited capacity to learn. We cannot say to a patient, "Don't do that," and expect that the command will be remembered and followed in the future. For this reason, traditional forms of behavior modification, that is, new connections between rewards and behaviors, cannot be formed. Likewise, conventional reality-orientation methods have little chance of anchoring the patient to the present or of changing behavior.

So how do family and professional caregivers insinuate themselves into this Alzheimer's reality in order to manage the person's behavior?

Difficult behaviors in people with Alzheimer's disease are most often defensive in nature—a compensation for the confoundedness of an increasingly unfamiliar world. Physical or verbal aggression, for example, is less an arbitrary acting out than a reaction to fear caused by the person's altered perceptions. An important point to stress here is that rarely is behavior a random act; all behavior has a cause or a triggering event. Sometimes these events are obvious because they are external, we can see them, and sometimes triggers are more difficult to see because they are internal, caused by delusions, hallucinations, paranoia, or misunderstood events and motives. Caregivers must assess several possible causes for each challenging behavior. In the habilitation model, these evaluations are ongoing, adjusted, and prophetic.

Assessments should include the physical, medical, and emotional well-being of the person. Is the person hot, cold, hungry, thirsty, ill, in pain, emotionally distressed, in need of toileting? Through a behavioral log that records what happened, when it happened, where it happened, and who was around when it happened, in time patterns begin to emerge. Once a pattern is observed, we can hypothesize about its origin and plan an intervention. Are there too many steps to a given project? Has the person forgotten the sequence of steps? Was this the cause of the outburst that resulted in his or her angrily tossing the project aside?

Try simplifying the task. If setting the table is causing dismay, have the person first put down all of the placemats, then only the plates, then just the glasses, allowing time to process each chore. Assess your communication techniques, carefully evaluating the person's comprehension and your own body language.

Most importantly, try to look at the environment through the person's altered lens of perception. Has a shadow on the wall suddenly taken the shape of an intruder in the room? Are pools of light on a glossy floor perceived as spilled water, which might make the person slip? Has the aroma of baking cookies induced hunger pangs?

Screaming is a good behavior with which to illustrate the last several points. There are at least three different types of screaming that we see with patients with Alzheimer's disease, each with different causes and different interventions.

The first type is a rhythmic sound; it often takes the form of "help me, help me." This is most likely caused by minimal brain stimulation. Too little information is coming into the brain from the senses, so the person creates a form of autostimulation. One can identify this form of screaming by the rhythmic nature and also by the fact that if one approaches the patient it generally does not stop. There are several interventions that work to reduce or eliminate this behavior. One intervention is to replace the stimulation and the rhythm with a more acceptable form. For example, for Catholic patients the rosary recorded on an audiotape creates a kind of rhythmic mantra; a rocking chair or a glider chair does the same. I used an electronic drum pad connected to earphones to reduce screaming in several patients. Music therapy is considered in Chapter 9.

Another form of screaming is identified by its low-pitched and constant sound. When one approaches the patient it does not stop. Often this form is caused by pain. The intervention is to assess the patient for pain and address its source.

Still another form is a loud, shrill, continuous sound that stops when one approaches the patient. This form is often a sign of panic in the patient and sometimes a sign of boredom. The interventions are to make the patient feel safe and secure, such as more one-on-one care, backrubs, or more stimulation.

Family and professional caregivers must be aware of the ongoing need to modify things in the environment—lights, mirrors, plants, electronic equipment, and so many other objects we all take for granted. By manipulating the environment, and with education, patience and practice, caregivers can learn to manage reactive behaviors without, in some cases, resorting to psychoactive medications, or at least with lessened amounts of medication.

Take, for example, the patient with Alzheimer's disease living in a nursing home who occasionally would calmly get up from his chair, walk across the room, and hit another resident. By keeping a log, we began to see that he only would hit someone if he was in the activities room, but not every time he was in that room. There did not appear to be any pattern to whom he hit. Later, we saw that he would only hit people on sunny days, but not on every sunny day on which he was in the activities room. Then, we saw that he only hit people on sunny days if he was sitting on one side of the room. With the log we were able to eventually determine that he would hit people if he sat in the activities room and the sun was shining in his eyes. The intervention was simply to make sure that the blinds were closed on sunny days if this particular man was in the activities room. Thus, with patience and careful analysis of the situation we were able to avoid the use of a psychoactive medication. However, it may be dangerous to allow repeated episodes of assaults to occur in order to gather data to determine the cause of the triggering behavior. Judgment should be exercised to ensure a safe environment for all residents.

## ☐ Conclusion

Through its multiple and interconnected domains, habilitation seeks to create a proactive therapeutic milieu for understanding the needs of people with Alzheimer's disease into the 21st century. It is distinguished from rehabilitation, which seeks to restore external function, by its emphasis on the internal: emotion. It is as much a positive attitude about Alzheimer's disease and related disorders as it is a therapeutic method.

Habilitation's most poignant definition may have been the observation of neurologist A. R. Luria, which appears in a letter written some years ago to Dr. Oliver Sacks, which Sacks (1970) quotes in his book *The Man Who Mistook His Wife for a Hat, and Other Clinical Tales*. "Man," Luria wrote, "does not consist of memory alone. He has feeling, will, sensibility, moral being. It is here you may touch him, and see a profound change." If we choose to see symptoms associated with Alzheimer's disease as potentially treatable, rather than part of inevitable decline, a new starscape materializes before us, as it did for the ancient astronomers.

# ☐ References

Fromm, E. (1976). *To have or to be*. New York: Harper and Row.

James, W. (1890) *The principles of psychology* (Vol. 1). New York: Holt.

Maslow, A. H. (1968). *Toward a psychology of being* (2nd ed.). New York: Van Nostrand.

Raia, P., & Koenig-Coste, J. (1996). Habilitation therapy. *Alzheimer's Association of Eastern Massachusetts Newsletter, 14*(2), 1–2, 4–6.

Sacks, O. (1970). *The man who mistook his wife for a hat, and other clinical tales*. New York: Harper and Row.

Joyce Simard

# The Lifestyle Approach

Each year, thousands of people with Alzheimer's disease or a related memory disorder are admitted to a long-term care facility. It is estimated that more than 50% of all nursing-home residents have Alzheimer's disease or a related dementia (Brawley, 1997). In assisted-living communities, a relatively new choice for people with Alzheimer's disease, it is believed that 30% to 40% of residents have some type of dementia (Morton, 1995). Moving a loved one to another living situation is often a heartbreaking and painful decision for families (Cohen & Eisdorfer, 1987; Manning, 1992) Because of memory loss and impaired cognitive abilities, it is even more difficult for newly admitted residents to comprehend what is happening. Everything and everyone is unfamiliar. Sounds such as the overhead paging system and the sight of residents in wheelchairs are frightening. Smells from cleaning solutions are troublesome. They miss the soothing odor of coffee brewing and bacon cooking on the stove, the familiar sight of family and friends, and the warmth of their homes.

Along with the strange sights, sounds, and smells, the disruption of the residents' familiar daily routines makes the adjustment to new activities and routines difficult (Alzheimer's Disease and Related Disorders Association, 1997). Residents with a memory disorder are usually unable to verbally communicate or understand what has happened to them when their routine has been disrupted. Anxious behavior may be the only method they have to communicate (Bell & Bell, 1997).

People with Alzheimer's disease who have moved into a long-term care facility also miss the attention formerly given to them from their caregivers, usually family members. One of the first books to help caregivers of people with Alzheimer's disease was written in 1981 and is titled *The 36-Hour Day* (Mace & Rabins, 1991). This book, which was updated in 1991, gives a description of what a day feels like for caregivers. And a recently published study of caregivers for the Alzheimer's Association found that "on average caregivers spend 69 hours per week caring for their loved ones. Those with loved ones that have Alzheimer's Disease may spend up to 100 hours per week providing care" (Alzheimer's Disease and Related Disorders Association, 1996). Even in the best of circumstances, neither a nursing facility nor an assisted-living community is able to provide the level of care and attention given at home.

For people with memory disorders, moving to a long-term care facility or assisted-living community has been associated with increased behavioral problems. Relocation trauma—the adjustment of newly admitted nursing-home residents—has been found to be associated with functional decline (Dehlin, 1990). As a social worker in a nursing home, I found that many residents became isolated in their rooms, refusing to attend activity programs. Although I am not qualified to diagnose depression, the residents' loss of appetite and episodes of crying that I observed during the first month after admission were indicative of the onset of depression.

To alleviate problems associated with the move and smooth the transition from home the "lifestyle approach," a new method of care, was developed and found to be helpful in decreasing anxiety and depression for both the residents and their families associated with the move. This interdisciplinary approach helps the resident with a memory disorder to reengage in his or her life and establish a daily routine that is comfortable and familiar, and it can be established without the costs of adding activity staff, which is difficult for many long-term care facilities that rely on Medicaid for reimbursement.

The lifestyle approach is useful in nursing facilities with or without a special care unit (SCU) designated for the care of residents with Alzheimer's disease. It can be used successfully with both ambulatory and nonambulatory residents.

The lifestyle approach has five components:

- Assessment
- Implementation
- Programming
- Documentation
- Environment

## ☐ Lifestyle Assessment

The lifestyle approach begins with an assessment that provides staff with information concerning the resident's previous daily routine. The assessment is more detailed than the minimum data set required by federal regulations. Although the minimum data set required for all nursing-home residents supplies some information regarding resident preferences, it does not go into sufficient detail regarding the resident's daily routine and individual preferences prior to admission (Miller, Peckham, & Peckham, 1995).

The majority of residents admitted to long-term care facilities are not admitted directly from home. Many have experienced some medical emergency that required a hospital stay. Their lives have been seriously disrupted, and their confusion and anxiety have been intensified by new treatments that may precipitate a decline in function. Caregivers often feel pressured by the hospital social workers, who need to discharge patients as soon as the patient is able to leave the acute-care setting (Mace & Rabins, 1991). They often receive little advanced notice of the need to find a long-term care facility. A caregiver described the day of admission as "feeling like the day of the funeral" (Dempsey & Baago, 1998). Filling out paperwork is not high on families' lists of "things they would like to do more of."

Although the lifestyle assessment is lengthy, when the social worker or admission counselor explains the reason this information is important prior to admission, families are usually happy to cooperate. It helps the family to know that staff respect the care they have been providing and want to know the details of what is important to their relative and to the caregiver. The assessment can be completed over the phone just by asking the questions in a conversational tone. For example: "Mrs. Houle, could you tell me what time your husband wakes up in the morning and tell me about a typical day for him?" When asked questions in a nonclinical manner, families often enjoy talking about their caregiving routines. The type of information gathered helps staff know how to approach the resident and how to help him or her adjust during the crucial first days in the facility. In an SCU, residents typically come from home. In special care centers (SCCs) located in assisted-living communities, the move is made easier because the resident's furniture can be used and the room made to resemble his or her room at home. It has been my experience, in 20 years of working with families coping with admission to a nursing home and now 4 years in the assisted-living industry, that families have an easier time with a move into an assisted-living community than into a long-term care facility. The decision has usually not been made in haste. They have visited several communities and made the best choice for them. They seem to feel more in control of the process. Families have additional time to complete the assessment form. Many times they have had an opportunity to meet staff during a home assessment visit from the program director, who may have helped them complete the form. The details regarding the life of the prospective resident and family needs become the foundation of the lifestyle approach.

The following information is contained in the lifestyle assessment:

- Date
- Resident's name
- Name of person completing the form
- Name resident is called by spouse, children, grandchildren, friends
- Daily routine, such as a detailed description of the resident's daily habits before admission, and food and beverage choices, including what time they occur; this section is divided into prebreakfast, breakfast, postbreakfast, midday meal, afternoon, late afternoon, evening meal, after evening meal, bedtime, and sleeping habits.
- Spiritual or religious habits
- Routine prior to onset of disease
- Time in life in which the resident believes he or she is, such as a mother with small children
- Situations in which anxiety may occur
- Successful approaches if resident becomes anxious
- Leisure activities such as hobbies, walking, watching certain television programs
- Household or work-related tasks the resident still can do and enjoy: wiping dishes, sorting food coupons, signing checks, and so forth
- What is important to the family, such as hair fixed a certain way, attendance at church services
- Whether the family wishes to continue to provide any type of personal care, such as bathing, dressing, choice of clothing
- Any other information that will help staff care for the resident

The lifestyle assessment is just one tool for gathering information regarding the resident. The face sheet, social history, and other specific forms for nursing, activities, and dietary departments gather additional information to assess the resident. The difference in the lifestyle assessment versus other assessments is that this information is gathered *prior* to admission or move-in and contains more detailed information regarding the resident's daily routine.

Once the information has been gathered, it is of no use unless it has been communicated to staff. Families do not mind completing the form if they believe the information will be used. Far too many times, important caregiving information is hidden in the resident's chart, and the nursing assistants have no access to that information. There are several ways to insure all caregiving staff members have read the lifestyle assessment. They include the following:

- All department managers (nursing, dietary, maintenance, rehabilitation therapy, activities) and the administrator or executive director receive a copy of the assessment by the day the resident is admitted. If the facility holds a morning meeting, a brief description of the resident being admitted also can be given.
- Each department manager is responsible for making the information available to staff. Some managers place the assessment on a clipboard, others in a three-ring notebook. All staff members who may provide care for the resident are responsible for reading the assessment and initialing that it has been read. The department manager is responsible for ensuring that all caregiving staff has read it.

The social worker or person responsible for admissions is assigned the responsibility for making sure the lifestyle assessment is completed prior to admission day. This person also may follow up with a phone call to the family if the form is not completed in a timely fashion. When the assessment has been communicated to all caregiving staff, the implementation phase begins.

# ☐  Implementation

Each staff person has a role or several roles in the implementation process. In a long-term care facility, the charge nurse has the responsibility of making sure each nursing assistant has the information necessary to provide good care to the resident. The nursing assistant has the responsibility of providing morning care and making sure the resident is fed. If the resident has been admitted from the hospital, his or her routine already has been interrupted. It is important for these residents to return to their old routine as soon as possible. The following example shows what happens if a well-intentioned staff person does not know resident preferences.

> Mrs. Smith was admitted to a long-term care facility from the hospital in which she had recuperated from a broken hip she suffered after falling in her home. She had been diagnosed with Alzheimer's disease several years before, and her daughter had been taking care of her. Before she was admitted to the hospital, Mrs. Smith usually slept until 9:00 and then had black coffee and breakfast. The day after she was admitted, Sara was assigned to care for Mrs. Smith. Sara had not worked the previous day and had missed the morning report, at which she would have been given information about Mrs. Smith's routine. She woke Mrs. Smith at 7:00 and dressed and groomed her. Mrs. Smith was upset and resistive to care. Mrs. Smith then was left in her room for an hour before breakfast was served. She was given coffee with cream and sugar to calm her down. Mrs. Smith became

very agitated when she was unable to communicate how she liked her coffee and threw the coffee across the room, upsetting her roommate. The nursing assistant had to stop and clean up the mess left by the coffee and try to soothe the roommate.

This unfortunate incident could have been avoided had the nursing assistant read the lifestyle assessment. It would have taken fewer than 5 minutes, far less time then was spent dressing the agitated resident, cleaning up coffee, and calming the roommate. In Mrs. Smith's case, the aide could have left her as the last person to be dressed. A cup of black coffee given to Mrs. Smith as the aide was caring for her roommate would have been a pleasant start to the day. One can imagine how difficult it was for the rehabilitative therapist to work with this resident whose day started off in such a negative manner.

In an SCC, usually a secured section of the assisted-living community, the program director is responsible for making the sure that lifestyle assessment is completed and that all caregivers and the SCC team read it. The SCC team includes nursing assistants, housekeeping, maintenance, dietary, and food-service and other staff who interact with residents on a regular basis. The lifestyle assessment is placed in the wellness center or a space in which staff gather. The following example points out how important it is for all staff to know the resident routine.

Mr. Thomas had a habit of waking up early in the morning and having his coffee before he got the newspaper. He liked to have breakfast and tidy up his room. Staff were alert to signs of him waking the first morning of his stay in the SCC. They asked him to accompany them to the country kitchen, where he assisted with making coffee. The maintenance person arrived early and asked Mr. Thomas if he would like to go to the front office for the newspaper. After breakfast, the housekeeper asked Mr. Thomas to "help" her by carpet sweeping his room. This task made Mr. Thomas feel at home and gave him something to do.

If all staff members understand and can support each resident's familiar routine, the adjustment to the long-term care facility or SCC is easier for the resident. This approach decreases aggressive behaviors, which in turn makes the care of the resident easier for the staff (Hegland, 1993). Structure is important to the person with Alzheimer's disease, as studies show that providing routine and structure to the day helps lower the residents' levels of anxiety (Alzheimer's Disease and Related Disorders Association, 1995; Dowling, 1995).

The second phase of the implementation is making sure that the resident has something to do when she or he is awake, and that he or she is taken to programming, as most residents with Alzheimer's disease cannot self-initiate activities (Miller et al., 1995). In a long-term care facility in which the majority of residents are nonambulatory, someone must be responsible for transporting residents to and from any activity outside of their rooms (usually the responsibility of the activity staff). In order for the lifestyle approach to be effective, all staff members must accept responsibility for making sure the residents are taken to programming. Activity staffing is not usually sufficient to allow a great deal of time for individual attention.

Federal regulations for nursing facilities require "an ongoing program of activities designed to meet, in accordance with the comprehensive assessment, the interests and the physical, mental, and psychosocial well-being of each resident" (1987 Omnibus Reconciliation Act). Some states have requirements for the number of staff members per resident or minutes of time spent with each resident; the majority of states do not. In 1990, the ratio of activity staff members to residents was 1 to 50 ( Miller et al., 1995) This ratio does not come close to duplicating the individual attention residents received at home from family caregivers.

There are no federal requirements for what is referred to as "assisted living." States differ as to the name of this residential style of living and formulate their own requirements for activity programming, usually minimal (Miller et al., 1995).

After dressing, grooming, and breakfast have been completed, the activity staff is responsible for keeping residents engaged. There are, however, not enough activity staff hours to provide the individual attention needed for a large number of memory-impaired residents. In many facilities, the activity staff members are the primary providers of programming and also responsible for transporting the residents to and from programs. Along with documentation requirements, meetings, and the other numerous responsibilities of the job, the time actually spent programming, engaging the residents in activities, is limited unless other staff members transport or escort the residents to the program. How then does the lifestyle approach address the problem of transporting or escorting residents to programming?

In long-term care facilities asking nursing assistants to take residents to programming has been a "tough sell." Without the support of the administrator and director of nursing it simply does not happen. Prior to the beginning of the program, nursing staff and others should receive an in-service presentation to explain the benefits of the program for the residents and the need for staff to help with the program. It is then up to the director of nursing, charge nurse, and administrator to make sure that it happens. There is no better way to ensure the cooperation of nursing assistants than if they see individuals in a management capacity taking residents into the program room. James Dowling (1995), who has worked in a community dedicated to the care of people with Alzheimer's disease, states that "activities are the responsibility of everyone involved in an individuals care." This statement is supported by the Alzheimer's Disease and Related Disorders Association (1997, p. 47): "It becomes obvious that programming activities need to include everyone who encounters the person during the course of the day." Sharing the responsibility of activity programming is somewhat easier in an SCC.

In a typical SCC, residents are usually ambulatory and are easier to gather. Staff members are expected to help in all aspects of running a program. The "universal worker" concept, under which staff has overlapping responsibilities (i.e., nursing staff cleaning spills and housekeepers encouraging residents to help with cleaning their rooms) has been very successful in dedicated Alzheimer's programs. In-service presentations to staff members on the expectations of the job and incorporating activities as part of their job descriptions reinforce the concept that everything has the potential to be an activity, and that it is all staff members' responsibility to engage residents in activities.

## Environment in an SCU

The next aspect of the lifestyle approach that needs to be decided on is the location or spaces in which programming takes place. The lifestyle approach is a 7-day-a-week program and needs enough room to handle 25 to 30 residents in gerichairs or wheelchairs. Finding space in a long-term care facility without an SCU may be a challenge. The first choice would be the activity room. Supplies and equipment are readily available and a telephone to summon assistance, if needed, is within reach. The activity room's design can be helpful in adding the proper atmosphere to the program. Whenever possible, make this room look as homey and warm as possible. Exchange glossy vinyl flooring for carpeting or tile that resembles a wood floor. Replace lights with nonglare lighting, hang curtains, and install wall coverings that are residential. If the room is large, use a print on the upper part of the wall, a contrasting-color chair rail, and heavier-grade wall covering below. Whenever possible, create a "country kitchen" atmosphere with sink, refrigerator, and stove. Kitchen cabinets should look like wood, rather than the vinyl institutional type. Hang quilts on the wall; use shelves with old items on them. Make this room help set the scene for the program. Residents will be more comfortable in this setting in which everything around them reminds them of home. From the door entrance with a wreath of dried flowers and welcome sign, everyone who enters this room will feel at home (Brawley, 1997).

Staff members might even want to name the room. One facility named their activity room and program "Our Place." It was a pleasant way for staff to refer to the program. "Let's go to Our Place" was the invitation given to residents. A daughter was greeted by, "Your mother is in Our Place." Somehow, the name softened the fact that this was a long-term care facility.

If there is no activity room available, or it is not large enough, staff must be creative. The living room or dining room are options. The decision on where to locate the program should be made with input from all staff members. They must review the plusses and minuses of each space and then decide together how to get the room ready and transport the residents to that space. For instance, if the dining room is used, housekeeping staff must be ready to clean floors as soon as the residents have left after breakfast, so that the program can begin at 9 AM.

A phone or some way to communicate the need for help is necessary. Overhead paging is to be eliminated. Sounds coming from the ceiling are frightening and confusing to the residents and disruptive to the programming.

Nursing, housekeeping, dietary, and other staff members are responsible for making sure that all residents are taken to the room in which the activity is to take place. The activity staff is responsible for staying in the room and greeting each resident and giving them something to do or engaging them in conversation while the others are being gathered. This means that the activity staff must be organized so that everything it needs is at hand.

If the program is to take place in a place other than the activity room, supplies must be assembled and taken to the room. A cart or table with wheels may be used to take supplies to the program area. In an SCC, space is designed into the secured area. Spaces tend to resemble familiar rooms at home such as kitchens, living rooms, or bedrooms. Programming takes place in the area best suited for the program. Cooking takes place in the kitchen; a card game also might be planned around the kitchen table. Exercises and discussions may be held in the living room. In most SCCs, space for programming is not a problem.

Once the majority of residents are gathered, programming begins. The activity staff acts in the capacity of "hosts" or "hostesses" welcoming residents and providing a warm atmosphere in which everyone is welcomed at any time during the program. A staff member bringing a resident into a program "in process" is asked to "jump start" the person by getting them involved in the activity before leaving. This eliminates the need for the activity person to stop the program and integrate the new person into the "action."

## Environment in an SCC

The environment in an assisted-living community is easier to design because there are far fewer regulations regarding the physical plant. Most

SCCs in assisted-living communities offer a country kitchen setting, a living room, laundry areas in which residents can participate in washing clothes, and a secure courtyard or terrace. Because of the "home-like" atmosphere, programming takes place in a variety of normal settings, such as cooking in the country kitchen, or gardening in the courtyard.

## ☐  Programming: Daily Routine

The days of the "three Bs" (bingo, ball toss, and Bible study) are over. The next component of the lifestyle approach is a change in the type of activities offered. Most activity professionals are just that, professionals. They understand the need to normalize the life of a person with memory loss, incorporating skills and interests that residents still can be successful at and enjoy (Dowling, 1995; Hellen, 1992)

The following leisure-activity program schedule was based on what most people do every day. It was adapted, of course, for the residential life of people with memory loss. Jitka Zgola explains, "Residents are happier when their lives inside a long-term care facility parallel their lifestyle prior to admission" (Hegland, 1993). The lifestyle approach to programming in a long-term care facility is as follows.

### 9:00–9:30  Morning Wake-Up

Residents are escorted to the room in which programming will take place by nursing assistants after breakfast and when activities of daily living have been completed. Music is playing as they enter the room. They are engaged in independent activities designed for their individual interests and capabilities such as looking at a newspaper or magazine, sorting objects (e.g., checkers, multicolored poker chips, coupons), or holding something comforting such as a quilt or stuffed animal. Others are placed in a circle in which they can see everyone who arrives and talk to the activity staff. Each resident is greeted by the activity staff members, who welcome them by name and offer a compliment on their clothing or hairstyle or just say how happy they are to have the resident join them.

### 9:30–10:00  Exercise

Residents who can participate in exercises are placed in a circle for the exercise program. Those residents who cannot participate listen to music they enjoy with earphones or may be placed outside the circle to observe the exercises. Exercises may take the form of dancing to various dance tunes; following an exercise video; using scarves, ribbons, or musical instruments; or following a routine that includes movement of each separate part of the body.

## 10:00–10:30 Coffeeklatch

Morning beverages are served in a social setting. Residents are gathered around tables for a beverage and snack. One nursing assistant is assigned to assist the activity staff in serving the residents. Whenever possible, "regular" beverages are served in place of supplements. In this social setting, residents may eat more, so the use of supplements could be decreased or discontinued. Normal conversation about the day, weather, and what's happening that day takes place while beverages and snacks are served.

## 10:30–10:45 News

The news program is brief, as the majority of residents will not understand or be interested in the current news. The date may be written on a wipe-off board and residents asked what day it is. Residents may be able to read even if they do not understand what they are reading. They also may discuss the weather and other news.

## 10:45–11:30 The Morning Special

Each day a special program is scheduled, such as crafts, art, music, gardening, or intergenerational or spiritual programs. Resident's individual interests are engaged through a variety of programs.

Following the "Morning Special," nursing assistants escort residents back to their rooms for grooming. They then are taken to the dining room for lunch.

## 12:00–1:00 Lunch

## 1:00–3:00 Rest/Siesta

Residents are taken to their rooms for grooming. Some residents may need to return to bed for a rest. Soft music may be played to help residents sleep. Music should be in the style the resident enjoys. If a resident chooses not to rest in his or her room, a quiet movie or video is offered in the activity room. The room must be darkened and efforts made to decrease noise to create a quiet setting for this program. While the residents are enjoying the video, activity staff can make individual room visits or catch up on documentation.

## 3:00–3:30 Afternoon Wake-Up

Nursing assistants groom residents and escort them to the room in which afternoon programming is scheduled. As in the morning, each resident is greeted and told how welcome they are at the program. The "Eden Alternative" approach to quality of life is a part of many afternoons (Thomas, 1994). Programs involve children, animals, and plants and gardening.

## 3:30–4:00 Afternoon Tea

Beverages are served in a social setting. One nursing assistant is assigned to help the activity staff. Whenever possible, nursing staff members should ask a resident to help pass napkins or serve as host or hostess.

## 4:00–4:30 Games

An active game is played, with residents seated in a group. Examples include ring toss, bean-bag toss, basketball, and horseshoes. Residents may be able to do math in their heads. Staff members can keep score by asking what 10 and 20 are. Names and scores are written on a wipe-off board. All residents are encouraged to clap and cheer for each other.

## 4:30–5:00  Afternoon Delight

Residents listen to music, a short story, poetry, or music from the past, or they sing. Each day should be planned to offer a new program. Nursing assistants escort residents back to their rooms for grooming prior to dinner.

## 5:00–6:00  Dinner

Residents are escorted to the dining room by nursing assistants for dinner. Nursing assistants should be assigned to sit with residents to encourage conversation.

## 6:30–8:00  After-Dinner Social

Nursing assistants escort residents to the activity area for some conversation and a video or television show such as *Wheel of Fortune, I Love Lucy, Lawrence Welk,* or so forth. A beverage should be served before bedtime. It is very important for nursing assistants to understand the need to provide programming at night. Most residents do not need to go to sleep at 7 PM. They should retire no earlier than 9:30 PM.

## General Guidelines

Residents with Alzheimer's disease are more comfortable with structure and routine (Alzheimer's Disease and Related Disorders Association, 1997; Dowling, 1995). Therefore, although most days follow a predictable routine, the routine may change because a program residents enjoyed the day before does not work on this day or a group or children are visiting and all eyes are on them. "Go with the flow" is the motto of most activity professionals.

Although there is a schedule of when programs begin and end, it is very loose. The flow from one program to another is an important part of the process. The following example points this out.

> Morning exercises take place when residents are in a circle. When they have been completed, residents are moved and the table for the coffeeklatch is wheeled in with the assistance of a resident or family member who is visiting. Residents in wheelchairs then are placed around the table. A tablecloth is placed on the table and colorful napkins passed around with the assistance of residents. The segue from the exercise program to the coffee may take 15 minutes. Conversation is taking place, and movement of residents and the table is enough to keep residents aware and observant. This is all part of the lifestyle approach.

Some residents involved in the programming may be able to participate only passively. These may be residents in the last stage of the disease process. Special equipment and care is taken to involve them to the extent that they are able to be involved. Examples include the following:

> Mrs. Booth is in a gerichair totally dependent on staff for all care. When a staff person takes her to programming, she is placed by the window so that she can feel the sunlight on her face. A birdcage is near the window, and she can hear the soft chirping of bird songs. She seems to be cold most of the time, so a warm quilt is wrapped around her. She listens to her favorite music or recorded messages using earphones and a portable tape player. The activity staff and others make time to talk and touch her at various

times throughout the morning. One resident, Mrs. Manyard, believes Mrs. Booth to be her sister. This resident's "job" is to hold her hand and sit next to her after coffee. This provides sensory stimulation to Mrs. Booth and gives purpose and meaning to Mrs. Manyard's life.

## Lifestyle Approach in an SCC

There are several differences in the design of the daily routine for residents in a SCC:

- Residents are usually ambulatory.
- Residents are in earlier stages of the disease.
- There are more spaces to use for programming.
- Household and work-related tasks become part of the program.

The lifestyle assessment is easier to follow in an SCC, as the setting lends itself to "normalization" of life. The lifestyle approach involves many aspects of a resident's life and involves all staff members. Activities are not only those that are part of the activity program but also include activities of daily living and work-related tasks. "The most valuable dementia activity is work that is tied to the life of the home. The key is making work: thinking in terms of long-cuts [sic] rather than shortcuts that our normal routine demands" (Dowling, 1995, p. 3): for instance, making muffins from scratch rather than using a cake mix. Roles must be created for residents in their new family. For example the maintenance staff might be helpful with male residents in the following way:

> Mr. Hare always had been happy when he had things to do around the house. The assessment with this information had been communicated to the maintenance staff. Whenever possible, they asked for Mr. Hare's assistance, even if it was just to carry light bulbs as they were being changed or accompany them as they worked. Mr. Hare is now the "assistant maintenance man." He even has a nametag he proudly wears.

With the many spaces for activities and all staff members taking responsibility for keeping residents engaged in their lives, a typical day in an SCC may follow the routine in Table 3.1. The daily routine for nursing facilities and for SCCs also includes a variety of leisure programs. Each day has structure and routine plus a variety of programs to meet the leisure interests of all residents and keep staff interested. Monthly magazines published for activity staff provide a wide range of ideas. Figure 3.1 is an example of the variety of programs offered each day in addition to the daily routine.

| TABLE 3.1. Daily routine in a special care center | |
|---|---|
| Rise and shine | 6:30–7:30 AM |
| Breakfast | 7:30–8:30 AM |
| Freshen up | 8:30–9:00 AM |
| Exercise club | 9:00–9:30 AM |
| Today's news | 9:30–10:00 AM |
| Coffee break | 10:00–10:30 AM |
| Potpourri: programs listed on the life enrichment calendar | 10:30–11:30 AM |
| Freshen up | 11:30AM–12:00 PM |
| Lunch | 12:00–1:00 PM |
| Old-time movies | 1:00–2:00 PM |
| Bits and pieces: individual activities | |
| Afternoon delight: programs listed on the life-enrichment calendar | 2:00–3:00 PM |
| Tea at three | 3:00–3:30 PM |
| Word games | 3:30–4:00 PM |
| Sing-a-long | 4:30–5:00 PM |
| Dinner | 5:00–6:00 PM |
| Table time | 6:00–7:00 PM |
| Walk and talk | 7:00–8:00 PM |
| Television classics | 8:00 PM–bedtime |

## ☐ Documentation

The last component of the lifestyle approach is documentation. Nursing facilities are required to document far more than assisted-living communities. The daily routine and resident preferences must be included in the resident's care plan and must match information recorded on the minimum data set. Nursing assistants also may use a flow sheet that provides them with the normal flow of the day. Activity progress notes should reflect the involvement of the resident in programming. In addition, most states require that attendance records be kept for nursing-home residents (Miller et al., 1995).

Assisted living requires no documentation regarding activities. Activity professionals should indicate in some way the involvement of the resident. Progress notes are an easy way to keep track of a resident's involvement in the life of the SCC. I recommend a progress note at least every 90 days. Some communities also develop a service plan that indicates programs a resident particularly enjoys. Families who are unable to visit often appreciate a letter explaining what their family member enjoys during the day. Families also enjoy pictures sent by staff of their loved one engaged in leisure programs. A picture may be worth a thousand words.

# December 1998

## *Life Enrichment Program*

| Sunday | Monday | Tuesday | Wednesday | Thursday | Friday | Saturday |
|---|---|---|---|---|---|---|
| November 98<br>S M T W T F S<br>1 2 3 4 5 6 7<br>8 9 10 11 12 13 14<br>15 16 17 18 19 20 21<br>22 23 24 25 26 27 28<br>29 30 | | **1**<br>10:30 AM Kitchen Creations<br>1:30 PM Golden Steppers Entertainment<br>2:30 PM Birthday Cake Marilyn<br>6:00 PM Reminisce<br>6:00 PM T.V. News<br>7:00 PM Word Games | **2**<br>10:30 AM Cheshire Dog Club<br>1:30 PM Readers Digest<br>2:30 PM Strength Training<br>3:30 PM Sing-A-Long<br>6:00 PM T.V. News<br>7:00 PM Bingo | **3**<br>10:30 AM Arts & Crafts Wreath<br>11:30 AM Big Band Music<br>1:30 PM Bingo<br>2:30 PM Movie & Popcorn<br>6:00 PM T.V. News<br>7:00 PM Music Social | **4**<br>10:00 AM Sara's Garden Picture Day<br>1:30 PM Exercise<br>3:30 PM Happy Hour<br>6:00 PM T.V. News<br>7:00 PM Music Social | **5**<br>10:30 AM Short Stories<br>1:30 PM Home Cooking<br>3:30 PM Nails & Details<br>6:00 PM T.V. News |
| **6**<br>10:30 AM Hymns & Bible Readings<br>1:30 PM Ice Cream Social<br>3:30 PM Sing-A-Long<br>6:00 PM T.V. News<br>6:30 PM Cards & Games | **7**<br>10:30 AM Current Events<br>1:30 PM Exercise<br>2:30 PM Scenic Drive<br>6:00 PM T.V. News<br>7:00 PM Monday Night Social | **8**<br>10:30 AM Kitchen Creations<br>1:30 PM Hymns w/Mrs. Benke<br>2:30 PM Afternoon Tea<br>3:30 PM Reminisce<br>6:00 PM T.V. News<br>7:00 PM Word Games | **9**<br>10:00 AM Culinary Arts Class<br>1:30 PM Readers Digest<br>2:30 PM Strength Training<br>3:30 PM Sing-A-Long<br>6:00 PM T.V. News<br>7:00 PM Bingo | **10**<br>10:30 AM Word Games<br>11:30 AM Big Band Music<br>1:30 PM Bingo<br>2:30 PM Movie & Popcorn<br>6:00 PM T.V. News<br>7:00 PM Trivia Challange | **11**<br>10:00 AM Catholic Mass<br>11:00 AM Rosary<br>1:30 PM Exercise<br>3:30 PM Happy Hour<br>6:00 PM T.V. News<br>7:00 PM Music Social | **12**<br>10:30 AM Short Stories<br>1:30 PM Home Cooking<br>3:30 PM Nails & Details<br>6:00 PM T.V. News<br>7:00 PM Music Social |
| **13**<br>10:30 AM Hymns & Bible Readings<br>1:30 PM Ice Cream Social<br>3:30 PM Sing-A-Long<br>6:00 PM T.V. News<br>6:30 PM Cards & Games | **14**<br>10:30 AM Current Events<br>1:30 PM Exercise<br>2:30 PM Scenic Drive<br>6:00 PM Boy Scouts Carols Lobby | **15**<br>10:30 AM Kitchen Creations<br>1:30 PM Hymns w/Mrs. Benke<br>2:30 PM Afternoon Tea<br>3:30 PM Reminisce<br>6:00 PM T.V. News<br>7:00 PM Word Games | **16**<br>10:00 AM Culinary Art Class<br>10:45 AM Aqua Turf Xmas Party<br>1:30 PM Readers Digest<br>2:30 PM Strength Training<br>3:30 PM Sing-A-Long<br>6:00 PM T.V. News<br>7:00 PM Bingo | **17**<br>10:30 AM Word Games<br>11:30 AM Big Band Music<br>1:30 PM Bingo<br>2:30 PM Movie & Popcorn<br>6:00 PM T.V. News<br>7:00 PM Trivia Challange | **18**<br>10:30 AM Arts & Crafts<br>1:30 PM Exercise<br>5:00 PM Resident/Family Holiday Party<br>7:00 PM Movie & Popcorn | **19**<br>10:30 AM Short Stories<br>1:30 PM Home Cooking<br>3:30 PM Nails & Details<br>6:00 PM T.V. News<br>7:00 PM Music Social |
| **20**<br>10:30 AM Hymns & Bible Readings<br>1:30 PM Ice Cream Social<br>3:30 PM Sing-A-Long<br>6:00 PM T.V. News<br>6:30 PM Cards & Games | **21**<br>10:30 AM Current Events<br>1:30 PM Exercise<br>2:30 PM Scenic Drive<br>6:00 PM T.V. News<br>7:00 PM Monday Night Social | **22**<br>11:00 AM Protestant Service<br>1:30 PM Hymns w/Mrs. Benke<br>2:30 PM Afternoon Tea<br>3:30 PM Reminisce<br>6:00 PM T.V. News<br>7:00 PM Word Games | **23**<br>10:00 AM Culinary Art Class<br>1:30 PM Sara's Garden Holiday Party<br>3:30 PM Holiday Carols<br>6:00 PM T.V. News<br>7:00 PM Bingo | **24**<br>10:30 AM Word Games<br>11:30 AM Xmas Music<br>1:30 PM Holiday Reminisce<br>2:30 PM Movie & Popcorn<br>6:00 PM T.V. News<br>7:00 PM Hot Coco & Cookies | **25**<br>10:30 AM Holiday Music<br>12:00 PM Holiday Meal<br>2:30 PM Holiday Reminisce<br>7:00 PM Movie & Popcorn | **26**<br>10:30 AM Short Stories<br>1:30 PM Home Cooking<br>3:30 PM Nails & Details<br>6:00 PM T.V. News<br>7:00 PM Music Social |
| **27**<br>10:30 AM Hymns & Bible Readings<br>1:30 PM Ice Cream Social<br>3:30 PM Sing-A-Long<br>6:00 PM T.V. News<br>6:30 PM Cards & Games | **28**<br>10:30 AM Current Events<br>1:30 PM Exercise<br>1:30 PM Hymns w/Mrs. Benke<br>2:30 PM Scenic Drive<br>6:00 PM T.V. News<br>7:00 PM Monday Night Social | **29**<br>10:30 AM Kitchen Creations<br>2:30 PM Afternoon Tea<br>3:30 PM Reminisce<br>6:00 PM T.V. News<br>7:00 PM Word Games | **30**<br>10:30 AM Culinary Art Class<br>1:30 PM Readers Digest<br>2:30 PM Strength Training<br>3:30 PM Sing-A-Long<br>6:00 PM T.V. News<br>7:00 PM Bingo | **31**<br>10:30 AM Word Games<br>11:30 AM Big Band<br>1:30 PM Bingo<br>2:30 PM Movie & Popcorn<br>6:00 PM New Years Eve Party | January 99<br>S M T W T F S<br>1 2<br>3 4 5 6 7 8 9<br>10 11 12 13 14 15 16<br>17 18 19 20 21 22 23<br>24 25 26 27 28 29 30<br>31 | |

**FIGURE 3.1.** Example of a calendar of activities at a special care center.

## ☐ Evaluation

In nursing facilities, the effects of increasing the amount of time during which the residents are involved in programming may be dramatic. Resident, family, and staff satisfaction increases if the lifestyle approach is used. As a consultant for a major healthcare provider, I coordinated a study to determine what changes had been noted in residents' condition since the implementation of the lifestyle approach. After I interviewed families, staff, and physicians, as well as observing the residents, it was apparent that residents smile more and are more alert and engaged in activities if this approach is used. In one facility in which I worked as a consultant, a physician updating charts at the nurse's station remarked how much quieter it was because residents were busy. Previously, residents had set the security system off as they tried to leave the floor, or they stood at the nurse's station asking repetitive questions. Prior to the lifestyle approach being incorporated into the daily programming, families would find their loved ones asleep in their rooms, or wandering in the hallway. Families now report that when they visit, their family member is busy and surrounded by others. Families also seem to perceive an increase in the level of care provided, because the residents are not sleeping in front of the nursing station or isolated in their rooms. Even the families of residents who are in the terminal stage of Alzheimer's disease are comforted by their loved one being in a room with others as opposed to being in bed. They are not alone.

In an SCC in which household tasks are part of the lifestyle approach, one family member walked into the country kitchen and observed his wife washing dishes. He began to cry. When asked what was wrong he replied that it had been years since he had seen his wife do anything "normal," something she had always felt was her job. He was so happy to see his wife smiling and feeling good about herself.

Staff members also have reacted positively to the lifestyle approach. Rather than feeling burdened that they have to take residents to programming, they enjoy seeing the residents have a good time. If they have finished their tasks, they often can be found participating in the program. Although more research needs to be undertaken regarding the satisfaction among staff members in SCCs, most facilities will verify that there is a significant decrease in staff turnover in SCCs using the lifestyle approach.

# ☐ Conclusion

The lifestyle approach, if incorporated into the admission process, assists the person with a memory impairment to adjust to the many changes in his or her life. With information from the lifestyle assessment, a typical day for the resident can be incorporated into the care provided from the first day that she or he comes to live in a new home. If the resident's leisure time is filled with familiar and meaningful leisure activities or household or work-related tasks, anxious behavior is minimized. Residents seem happier, families are satisfied, and staff members feel that they are making a positive difference in a resident's life. Oliver Sacks (1985) perhaps said it best in his book, *The Man Who Mistook His Wife for a Hat*: "People do not consist of memory alone. They have feeling, will sensibility, moral being. . . . It is here you may touch them and see a profound change."

## ☐ References

Alzheimer's Disease and Related Disorders Association. (1995) *Activity programming for persons with dementia: A sourcebook.* Chicago: Author.

Alzheimer's Disease and Related Disorders Association. (1996) *An exploration of the plight of the Alzheimer's caregiver.* Chicago: Author.

Alzheimer's Disease and Related Disorders Association. (1997) *Key elements of dementia care.* Chicago: Author.

Bell, V., & Bell, D. (1997). *The best friends approach to Alzheimer's care.* Baltimore, MD: Health Professions Press.

Brawley, E. C. (1997). *Designing for Alzheimer's disease: Strategies for creating better environments.* New York: John Wiley & Sons.

Cohen, D., & Eisdorfer, C. (1987) *The loss of self.* New York: Penguin Books.

Dehlin, O. (1990). Relocation of patients with senile dementia: Effects on symptoms and mortality. *Journal of Clinical Experimental Gerontology, 12,* 1–12.

Dempsey, M., & Baago, S. (1998, March/April). Latent grief: The unique and hidden grief of carers of loved ones with dementia. *American Journal of Alzheimer's Disease, 13*(2), 84.

Dowling, J. R. (1995). *Keeping busy: A handbook of activities for persons with dementia.* Baltimore, MD: The Johns Hopkins Press.

Hegland, A. (1993, June). Alzheimer's activities. *Contemporary Long Term Care, 16*(6), 72–75.

Hellen, C. R. (1997). *Alzheimer's disease: Activity focused care.* Boston, MA: Andover Medical Publishers.

Mace, N. L., & Rabins, P. V. (1991). *The 36-hour day: A family guide for caring for persons with Alzheimer's disease, related dementing illnesses, and memory loss in later life* (Rev. ed.) Baltimore: The Johns Hopkins University Press.

Manning, D. (1992). *When love gets tough: The nursing home decision.* Hereford, TX: In-Sight Books.

Morton, A. (1995, July). Camouflaging. *Contemporary Long Term Care,* 40.

Sacks, O. (1985). *The man who mistook his wife for a hat and other clinical tales.* New York: Summit Books.

Thomas, W. H. (1996). *Life worth living: How someone you love can still enjoy life in a nursing home—the Eden alternative.* Acton, MA: VanderWyk & Burnham.

Melitta K. Maddox
Theressa Burns

# Adapted Work Program:
# A Sheltered Workshop
# for Patients with Dementia

The Geriatric Research, Education, and Clinical Center (GRECC) at the Minneapolis Veterans Administration Medical Center has been conducting longitudinal studies in dementia for the past two decades. The GRECC Adapted Work Program (AWP) was initiated in 1989 as a research project to develop and test new approaches for the care of persons with early to moderate Alzheimer's disease. Over the years the program has been able to accommodate those with more severe deficits and identify a wide range of tasks and activities tailored to the progressive deficits of those with dementia (Doble et al., 1997; Maddox & Burns, 1997).

Based on the sheltered-workshop model, the program provides meaningful jobs and a small salary for veterans struggling with loss of memory and thinking. With increased professional and public awareness, the diagnosis of Alzheimer's disease is being made earlier, and with the advent of new medications there is promise that the disease can be stabilized in the early stages for longer periods of time. Most individuals with dementia continue to live in the community for several years. Younger patients often have been forced to leave their previous occupations because of errors made on their jobs or inability to carry out complex responsibilities. Difficulty in planning and initiating activities accompanies the memory problems of early dementia, making it difficult to find meaningful ways to occupy time at home. Feelings of frustration and boredom, loss of self-esteem, and mood and behavior changes can become problematic for both the individual and family (Barnes, Raskin, Scott, & Murphy, 1981; Gwyther & George, 1986; Zarit & Zarit, 1985).

Few community resources are available to meet the needs of those in the early stages of dementia. Early-stage victims of the disease may become uncomfortable in their usual social groups and become unable to volunteer their services in community projects that entail independent responsibilities. But typical day care programs may be unacceptable to those who have only mild impairment and are physically quite healthy. Caregiver stress and the need for respite, however, may be present already.

The AWP has come to serve the needs of both patients and their families and has evolved to provide a continuum of care through the middle and up to the late stages of the disease process. The staff of the program has been a resource for the family (Maddox & Burns, 1997). As a result, family members have learned to carry out some of the strategies that facilitate patients' participation in other activities and manage mood and behavior changes in the home situation. This chapter explores the AWP in terms of the theoretical framework and the process for establishing a sheltered work program adapted for those with progressive cognitive impairment.

## ☐ Relevant and Current Research

The major goal of the AWP is to find a way to improve the quality of life for those with early and moderate dementia. A therapeutic program must address the emotional needs of the participants and manage the behavioral difficulties that often accompany the cognitive decline. Numerous studies have reported the prevalence of depression and anxiety (Jarvik & Trader, 1988; Reifler, Larson, & Hanley, 1989). Lazarus et al. (1987) found that depressed patients with dementia often demonstrated anxiety, low self-esteem, helplessness, and hopelessness. Fear of failure and withdrawal from former activities often occurs in the person repeatedly experiencing difficulty and frustration in trying to perform once-familiar tasks (Ebbitt, Burns, & Christensen, 1989). Cooley, Sewell, and Rich (1985) reported that shared mealtimes and cooperative tasks could facilitate social interaction for those with disabilities. Reingold (1964, 1966) reported a sheltered workshop designed to offset "role discontinuity" in two separate studies of nursing-home residents.

The program continues to serve as a laboratory for students and researchers, who spend time in the program learning to assess the functional abilities of those at various stages of dementia. Comparisons are made between the testing and assessments of various disciplines and the differences between self-report measures and standardized observational testing (Burns, Mortimer, & Mechak, 1994; Diehl, 1998; Guralnik, Seeman, Tinetti, Nevitt, & Berkman, 1994; Spector & Fleishman, 1998).

# ☐ Conceptual Model

From the earliest years of the profession, occupational therapists recognized the therapeutic aspects of work (Barton, 1919). Bodily action and regularity could divert the mind, exercise the body, and relieve the monotony and boredom of illness. Work can be seen as employment for compensation, but it also can include all forms of productive activity. Society values a person's productivity and rewards workers with salaries. A regularly scheduled program provides structure, and purposeful, useful activity can enhance self-esteem and meet the needs of the impaired person for a meaningful role.

The nursing self-care model of Dorothea Orem (1980) has guided the strategies to facilitate optimal function of the individual and compensate for deficits. This compensatory model serves as a resource for a person who, without reminders and cues, experiences excess disability. The appropriate environmental and interactive support enables the impaired person to participate in activities that he otherwise would not initiate or accomplish (Dawson et al., 1986). The progressively lowered stress threshold described by Hall has provided a model for predicting and preventing anxiety and escalating agitation with the progressive decline (Hall & Buckwalter, 1987). These nursing models have merged synergistically with the Allen cognitive disabilities framework of occupational therapy (Allen, 1988; Allen & Allen, 1987). Assessing functional abilities directs clinicians to design strategies that allow full use of the remaining capabilities. If the functional deficits are identified, clinicians can provide the appropriate assistance to compensate for the person's losses. This theory is able to address the changes in performance as the progressive disease causes increasing disability. Six performance levels describe normative function at the highest functional level (6) through the profoundly disabled lowest level (1). The abilities and deficits described for each level provide guidelines for the adaptations that are needed for care and activities.

The basic work skills required for production identified by Mosey (1973) include willingness to engage in a task, acceptance of supervision, ability to sustain interest, appropriate use of supplies, acceptable rate of performance, appropriate attention to detail, ability to follow directions, and ability to organize tasks in a logical manner. Obviously, adaptations have to be made for each level of dementia. Tasks that require more than minimal reading, writing, or alphabetizing are too complex and need to be excluded. For each level the tasks need to be challenging enough to make use of the remaining abilities. Task analysis allows the occupational therapist to match the person's assets and limitations to an available job.

Other theoretical models also are used to facilitate efficiency and worker satisfaction. Burns and Buell (1990) describe the integration of theories and approaches that were used to operationalize a realistic work program that could adapt to the declining function and emotional needs of participants with dementia. Object-relations theory suggests that workers may prefer duties that closely resemble their previous occupations (Mosey, 1973). A former office manager may be asked to collate and staple brochures. Sensory-integration theory (Ayres, 1974) guides the use of proprioceptive and kinesthetic input to assist those with apraxia. Working as part of a pair to fold blankets, an apraxic worker can mirror the actions of a partner. Division of labor, chaining, and the breakdown of complex tasks are necessary to accomplish complicated jobs and provide appropriate work for those of different functional levels (Burns & Buell). One paid hospital employee may inspect, fold, and stack towels for the operating room. In the AWP a level 5 worker may inspect the towels for stains; a level 4 worker may fold and stack them. If a task requires multiple steps such as stuffing and sealing envelopes, a worker may be directed to stuff all of the envelopes and then seal them. Repeating the same motor action facilitates training and maximizes efficiency and accuracy. Gross motor tasks may foster concentration for workers who demonstrate hyperactivity.

## Therapeutic Milieu

The therapeutic program of the AWP addresses both the cognitive and emotional needs of the participants. Careful assessment of cognitive function is made so that they can be assigned jobs in which they can be successful. Welcoming and accepting attitudes provide reassurance for newcomers. Although most are anxious coming into the program, a few successes and encouragement from other workers promote comfort. Particularly for lower-functioning workers, the familiarity of a repetitive task seems to provide a sense of security. Many have favorite jobs they seem to take ownership of, boasting to others or to their families of the work they do. Jobs range from relatively complex tasks to very simple repetitive activities. The jobs and supervision are structured so that the staff give directions at the level of the person's understanding. Individual attention and support, hints, and reminders given at the right time all help the person know what to do. Actual objects and samples of work are much more helpful than pictures or signs for orienting workers. Stress and frustration usually are avoided because the staff members step in quickly with cues if the person is confused about what to do next. Jobs are adjusted so the person is challenged enough to feel accomplishment but comfortable and at ease with a task he or she enjoys doing.

The activity rooms are large so that work spaces are adequate and participants have ample room to move about. Large windows provide pleasant and interesting stimulation and diversion if a break is needed from repetitious tasks. Tables and chairs are at the proper height for the work to be done. Clutter is kept to a minimum. Lunch is served in a separate room.

Volunteers are an important part of the program. They are chosen and trained to encourage socialization and initiate conversations among the participants. They escort patients to areas outside the department and help provide close supervision for the lower-level workers who need frequent direction. They share general interests and foster humor and camaraderie. They sometimes help complete tasks or join in to help motivate workers.

All staff members provide flexible approaches to meet workers' needs. Decaffeinated coffee and tea are available for informal breaks and can be suggested if diversion is needed. Subtle adjustments in assignments or work stations are made if disagreements occur or intolerance is noted between workers. Support, reassurance, and praise are used freely to build confidence and self-esteem.

The importance of the therapists' skills in matching the task to the functional capability of the individual cannot be overemphasized. The task adaptation must be within the person's range of ability. Sample products, repeated demonstrations, ample practice time, and staff patience are the keys to learning new tasks. The therapists use matter-of-fact approaches to demonstrate and give concrete instructions. Placing items in the positions in which they are to be used helps to avoid confusion. Therapists watch an individual's actions to determine if adaptations can be made to help the person perform better. For example, if a worker folds a towel lengthwise instead of cross-wise, the towel can be turned so that she or he automatically folds it the other way. For stuffing envelopes, the envelope's opening should be facing the items, and the items should be positioned in the direction that fits into the envelope. A box should be placed beside the arm holding the envelope so the finished work can be stacked as the last step of the task.

## Application of the Cognitive-Disabilities Theory

### The Theoretical Framework

The six hierarchical levels of cognition described by Allen (1985) measure the severity of disability in terms of a person's ability to process information. The deficits are the consequence of the disease process. The occupational therapist identifies what sensory cues the individual uses to perform voluntary motor actions while doing a purposeful task. The need for specific cues is similar across all types of activities. This framework describes the abilities and deficits at six levels of cognitive function that occur as the disease progresses. If we know that the person has specific deficits we can predict what precautions we should take. We can provide specific assistance to prevent problems and allow function to continue. Level 6, the highest ability level, is normal function without cognitive disability. Level 5 describes the mild functional decline of early dementia. The person has the beginnings of deficits in abstract thought processes. At level 4 deficits of the person with moderate dementia extend from abstract to concrete thought processes. Level 3 shows severe functional decline with loss of awareness of task goals and need for increased cues and assistance. Level 2 shows severe impairment in purposeful activity or ability to recognize or use objects. Level 1 shows only limited awareness or response to the environment.

## Assessment Instruments

The assessment tools used to determine the functional level of AWP participants include the following:

- *The Allen cognitive level test* is a standardized screening tool to determine a subject's ability to perform three increasingly complex leather lacing stitches (Allen, 1985). Each stitch correlates with a specific level of function. The test has empirical support and provides the therapist with an initial screening of the person's capability for new learning.
- *The Cognitive Performance Test* identifies the functional level through standardized observation of performance of six specific tasks (Burns et al., 1994). This test is used in conjuction with the Allen cognitive level test in patients with Alzheimer's disease. It offers additional information concerning familiar tasks that vary in complexity.
- *The Routine Task Inventory* gives level-specific, behavioral descriptions of performance in abilities to follow directions, maintain pace, perform simple versus complex tasks, and get along with coworkers (Heimann, Allen, & Yerxa, 1989). These items can be completed periodically to track decline in work performance in relation to functional and cognitive decline with disease progression.
- *Comprehensive Occupational Therapy Evaluation* scales rate 25 observable general, interpersonal, and task behaviors (Brayman & Kirby, 1982). The scales can be used to assess day-to-day work behaviors. Items of special interest include concentration, interest in activity, frustration tolerance, following directions, problem solving, and initial learning.

- *Time studies* can be used to track the amount of time spent in work, social interaction, breaks, or nonproductive or disruptive behavior. These can be beneficial in comparing work habits of persons at the various levels, determining staffing needs, and determining amounts and types of jobs appropriate for current participants.

## Profiles and Work Plans

Tables 4.1 through 4.3 illustrate the general characteristics and plans for workers at Allen cognitive levels 5, 4, and 3. Each table identifies the performance assets and limitations, describes the adaptations that must be made, and gives examples of tasks that can be done successfully at the particular functional level. Of course, individuals' scores may fall between levels, and participants will experience gradual decline from one level to the next. Continued assessment and task adaptation occurs as needed. Individual preferences and enjoyment of particular jobs always are considered, as well as workers' compatibility with each other, general stress levels, and fluctuations from day to day.

By level 2 individuals no longer understand the concept of work or meaningful activities. They are unable to focus on or use objects purpose-

**TABLE 4.1.    The level 5 worker: Profile and work plans**

| Performance Assets | Performance Limitations | Task Adaptations | Adapted Work Program Tasks |
|---|---|---|---|
| Uses cause and effect concepts | Decreased ability to use abstract information | Give concrete demonstrated directions with repetition for new tasks | Inspecting, sorting, stacking surgical towels |
| Able to do some problem solving | Decreased ability to plan task strategies | Demonstrate potential problems and solutions | Portioning and wrapping salads |
| Can judge quality | | | Collating written materials |
| Has geographic orientation | Trial and error approach to problem solving | Allow additional time for learning new tasks | Engraving name tags |
| Can do 3 to 5 steps at a time | Memory deficit | Allow additional time to complete tasks | Picking up and delivering to hospital departments |
| | Task repetition needed for independent performance | Spot check to assist with problems | Assisting a level 4 worker |
| | | Post concrete signs to aid memory | Doing any level 4 task |

**TABLE 4.2. The level 4 worker: Profile and work plans**

| Performance Assets | Performance Limitations | Task Adaptations | Adapted Work Program Tasks |
|---|---|---|---|
| Can direct visual attention to achieve visible goals | Typically cannot use abstract information | Provide specific set-up for each task (limited supplies, clear boundaries) | Folding blankets, towels, brochures |
| Can learn specific tasks with training | Requires tasks with visible sequence and outcome | Give only 1 to 3 steps at a time | Filling salad bowls |
| | Problem-solving abilities are impaired | Give concrete demonstrated directions with repetition | Rolling and binding bandages |
| | Has difficulty with cause and effect concepts | Allow additional time for learning a task (may need repeated directions at beginning of each day) | Stuffing, labeling, sealing envelopes (one task at a time) |
| | May focus on irrelevant task components | | Simple collating |
| | Requires extra time to learn a specific task | May need tasks that do not require precision | Crushing cans |
| | Learning does not generalize easily | Needs frequent spot checks to solve problems | Assist with deliveries to hospital departments |
| | Geographic orientation is variable | Give visual cues (objects, sample product) to aid memory | |
| | Memory deficit increases | | |

fully and cannot follow directions to perform tasks. Day programs in which participants are free to move about safely with supervision are important, but it is no longer appropriate to attempt to engage these persons in work activity. Appropriate stimulation can be provided through less structured programs that include movement, sounds, and comfortable surroundings; activities such as walking, dancing, exercise movements, music, and poetry; objects of various colors, temperatures, and textures; and one-to-one attention during meals and personal care.

## ☐ Pilot Study

With consideration for the multiple losses and role changes experienced by those with progressive dementia and the importance of the work role

**TABLE 4.3. The level 3 worker: Profile and work plans**

| Performance Assets | Performance Limitations | Task Adaptations | Adapted Work Program Tasks |
|---|---|---|---|
| Can continue to do some jobs learned at level 4<br><br>Can perform actions on objects and repeat simple sequences<br><br>Can follow simple 1-to-1 directions | Grasps and uses objects but has difficulty focusing on task goals or outcomes<br><br>May not attend to quality or accuracy<br><br>Is easily distracted<br><br>Requires intermittent and ongoing direction<br><br>Unable to solve problems<br><br>May attempt to leave the area without frequent direction to task<br><br>Beginning difficulty locating or using the bathroom<br><br>May be confused about the bag lunch | Take 1 to 3 steps at a time<br><br>Give concrete, demonstrated directions with repetition<br><br>Hand objects to get the person started<br><br>Refocus to task as necessary, spot check to solve problems<br><br>Offer reminders to keep going, to stop<br><br>Use visual cues (sample products) to aid memory<br><br>Alternate any repetitious sitting tasks with gross motor activities that allow the person to move about<br><br>Have the person stand at a raised table facing a wall for reduced stimulation<br><br>Supervise for safety and assist with self-care activities<br><br>Set up for each task (limited items, clear boundaries) | Rolling and binding bandages or belts<br><br>Crushing cans<br><br>Folding blankets, towels, brochures<br><br>Pushing a cart to other departments (with an escort) |

in our society, a small pilot study was initiated in 1988 by the staff at the GRECC to determine the feasibility of a sheltered work program as an alternative to traditional day care. The goals of the pilot study were to determine the types of tasks that would be appropriate, the staffing and environmental needs, the therapeutic effects of such a program, and the acceptance by patients and families. The interests and preferences of families surveyed led to the structure of the program. The occupational therapists chose to use the Allen cognitive disabilities theory as a model for identifying work tasks and task adaptations for various levels of impairment (Allen, 1985; Ebbitt et al., 1989). Jobs were sought from various hospital departments, and tasks were screened for safety and complexity. Jobs that could be done within each department and would be available on a regular basis were chosen.

Special effort was made by the staff to minimize stress and anxiety and promote success and enjoyment. The first step was a careful assessment of the patient—functional abilities and deficits, mood, and interests. Jobs were chosen that fit with cognitive and functional abilities. Appropriate instructions and supervision were provided, with ample time for learning and adjusting to the routine. Praise and positive feedback were considered important during the tasks. Several measures were put in place to normalize the work situation and reinforce the meaning and value of the work. Because the tasks being done were essential work that would otherwise be done by paid employees or volunteers, the workers were paid a small wage for the hours of work. Hospital employees expressed their appreciation when the workers delivered the finished products to the various hospital services.

A large activity room with adjoining kitchen and toilet facilities was used as a site for the program. An occupational therapist managed the program with the help of a volunteer approximately the age of the participants. Because of potential hazards related to driving, a policy was established that transportation must be provided by family members or available transportation services for handicapped persons. Car pooling was arranged by some, and workers brought sack lunches. Socialization was encouraged by staff during scheduled coffee and lunch breaks. Participants were met at the door in the morning and escorted to wait for their rides at the end of the program. Workers were observed carefully during the program for their tolerance and response to the activities. Flexibility allowed for time-out periods and shifts from an activity that became stressful. The occupational therapist's objective of focusing each worker's attention on enjoyable tasks within his or her capabilities helped participants to succeed and to feel a sense of accomplishment and increased self-confidence.

## ☐ Funded Research Project

This setting was ideal for studying the changes in thinking and function during the progression of dementia. During the 6-month pilot study the staff continued to refine its assessment of skills and abilities at each level of dementia as well as to develop more specific techniques and approaches. Funding was obtained for a 12-month formal study of a structured work project. This study, supported by the GRECC and the National Alzheimer's Association, evaluated the work behaviors and work tolerance of the participants, the appropriateness of tasks, and the task adaptations needed for individual workers. Instruments also assessed the effect of participation on mood, self-esteem, and the maintenance of skills over time. Assessment of the family members included caregiver burden, caregiver depression, and social and activity levels.

A total of 14 individuals (aged 56–77 years) with diagnoses of possible or probable Alzheimer's' disease according to Alzheimers' Disease and Related Disorders Association–National Institute for Neurological Communication Diseases and Stroke criteria and mild to moderate impairment consistent with stage 3, 4, or 5 on the Global Deterioration Scale (Reisberg, Ferris, DeLeon, & Crook, 1982) whose caregivers were willing to participate in the study were enrolled in the program. Their varied previous work roles included pharmacist, high-school teacher and coach, heavy-equipment operator, salesman, engineer, computer analyst, musician, office manager, and produce manager. The original participants all were men. The prevalence of men in the program was mostly because of the fact that the overwhelming percentage of veterans are men, but also possibly because women of that age group were less likely to work outside the home and so felt less desire to participate in a job outside the home. (Women have successfully participated in the program in recent years, however. The program offers a wide array of jobs, and task preferences seem not to be gender-specific). Prior to entrance into the program participants were given the Allen cognitive level test (Allen, 1985) and the Cognitive Performance Test (Burns et al., 1994) to determine the level of task performance. Additional assessments consisted of the Mini-Mental State Examination (Folstein, Folstein, & McHugh, 1975), the Geriatric Depression Scale (GDS) (Yesavage et al., 1983), and the Self-esteem Scale (Rosenberg, 1965). All instruments were used every 3 months during the study. Staff members completed a daily mood evaluation for each participant, and the GDS was administered monthly. In addition, the occupational therapist performed ongoing assessments of all work-program participants during the work day. The Routine Task Inventory (Heimann et al., 1989) and the Comprehensive Occupational Therapy Evaluation scales

(Brayman & Kirby, 1982) were used to evaluate work behavior and socialization.

Caregivers were interviewed prior to their relative's enrollment in the program regarding the participant's mood, behavior and functioning at home. The caregivers completed the caregiver burden interview (Zarit et al., 1985), the GDS (both for themselves and as informants for the participants), the Memory and Behavior Problems Checklist (Zarit, Anthony, & Boutselis, 1987) and the Physical Self-maintenance Scale and Instrumental Activities of Daily Living Scale (Lawton & Brody, 1969). Twelve patients, matched for age and stage of disease, and their caregivers followed in the dementia outpatient clinic served as control subjects. The control-group members were evaluated with the same measures at entry and 6-month intervals during the study.

Participants attended the program 3 days each week for 4 hours. The program was staffed by a registered occupational therapist (OTR), a certified occupational therapy assistant, and a volunteer. A clinical nurse specialist was available to assist with health or behavioral concerns, maintain contact with caregivers, and assist with data-collection interviews.

Twelve of the 14 participants completed the full year of the program. MMSE scores on entry into the project ranged from 11 to 25. Typical deficits that affected work performance included impairments in problem solving, following directions, and new learning. Deficits in memory, orientation, visual-spatial abilities, and language as well as judgment and reasoning varied among the participants. To compensate for these deficits, appropriate task selection and adaptation were essential. The cognitive disabilities theory (described elsewhere in this chapter) provided the frame of reference for identifying workers' ability levels and for adapting tasks accordingly. Tasks were selected based on complexity, portability, and ongoing availability. Sample tasks included collating and stapling printed materials, labeling envelopes, inspecting and sorting surgical towels, folding blankets, and food portioning and wrapping for the cafeteria. Repetition and manual demonstration of work tasks proved to be essential for teaching and learning in the population and helped compensate for memory deficits. Mildly impaired participants generally could perform tasks with minimal adaptations, because no complex jobs were accepted for the AWP. Moderately impaired workers benefited from demonstrated instructions, visual cues, and concrete steps. Assessments of worker productivity suggested a slow decline in rate of performance over time, although acceptable quality was maintained.

Study results demonstrated a positive effect on participants' mood as measured by the GDS. This 30-point instrument has been validated for use with persons with early to moderate dementia as well as the general geriatric population. A cohort of patients ($n = 7$) whose mean GDS scores were 10.4 at entry declined to a mean score of 5.2 after 15 months of participation. The control group, with a similar initial mean score of 11.1, demonstrated a decline of only 0.9 points. A second cohort of workers ($n = 7$) whose entry GDS scores of 4.2 did not indicate depression remained basically stable throughout the study. Participant self-esteem scores exhibited only minimal improvement during the course of the study, but staff noted that comprehension and declining ability to make comparisons seemed to make this test increasingly difficult for impaired individuals. However, the majority of subjects clearly enjoyed the opportunity to be active and productive. Likewise, caregiver burden was not substantially relieved by participation, although caregivers were enthusiastic about the respite time provided and their spouses' positive responses to the program. Interview comments by both participants and spouses expressed benefits that indicated the program's positive impact on quality of life. Benefits included achieving success in task performance, the continuation of the work role and a useful activity, and maintenance of social relationships.

## ☐ Current AWP Program

The investigators believed the concepts merited expansion and further evaluation. The GRECC at the Minneapolis Veterans Adminstration Medical Center has continued to include the AWP as one of its primary clinical, education, and research programs. There always has been a strong interest from individuals with early dementia and their families. More and more hospital departments have supplied work willingly and reported satisfaction with the quality of work produced by the program. (Close supervision with gentle directions and subtle corrections by staff during or after the work ensures accuracy.) Veterans' groups enthusiastically have taken on the support of the workers' salaries. The clinical experience of the staff members and their research projects have continued to refine the assessments and programming for participants. Further adaptations of tasks and behavioral strategies have allowed the program to accommodate those with increasingly impaired function. Most enrollees now stay in the program until their families are no longer able to care for them because of increasing needs for physical care or behavioral disruptions at home. In some situations continuing attendance has been able to provide continuity for a person through the adjustment period of a nursing-home admission. Transportation to and from the nursing home is arranged so that the person can work for a period of time until she or he becomes comfortable with the new environment and activities of the facility.

Families continue to appreciate the respite time for themselves and report various benefits they feel the workers derive from their participation. Family members feel free to call the AWP staff for advice, knowing that the staff knows the person well and seems to manage the idiosyncratic problems. Staff members spend time discussing problems and teaching family caregivers to use some of the strategies and techniques for home care difficulties.

The program has served as a laboratory for multidisciplinary student learning. Students, interns, and residents observe the behavioral and functional changes of the progressive illness. Students participate in assessments, plan strategies, interact with patients and caregivers, and design projects that enhance the program's ability to improve and serve the community.

## ☐ Program Effectiveness

As part of ongoing evaluation the staff has kept track of both the participants' and their caregivers' moods as well as the participants' job functioning. Participants' comments invariably revolve around "liking to be busy" and their "enjoyment of each other." Comments include "I like all the jobs here," "We're busy, that's the main thing," "This is a neat program; the guys are great," "I have a place to come and work and talk to other people," and "This sure beats staying home with the TV." Staff members observe a lot of joking and laughing. One person's sense of humor seems to be picked up quickly by others. Staff members are amazed at the relaxed manner and sometimes candor with which the men talk to each other about their forgetfulness and difficulty with their everyday problems.

The family caregivers always have been enthusiastic about the positive responses they see in their loved ones. These responses often include a decrease in depression, an increased interest in doing things, and increased self worth, especially in terms of having a job to go to and earning money. Formal study of the workers' depression over a 1-year period demonstrated significant decrease in depression scores. The AWP is often the first resource the families use after the diagnosis of Alzheimer's disease is made. Spouses appreciate the respite the program provides them during the hours the veterans spend at work, but their own feelings of burden are not necessarily lessened. Early dementia is a time in which families are just beginning to realize what this illness entails and what it means to be a caregiver for a person with Alzheimer's disease. The close contact with the program staff is an additional support for families as the disease progresses. Staff members continue to develop both formal and informal support and education for families.

The middle stages of Alzheimer's disease are perhaps the most frustrating for the individual and most definitely so for the caregiver. With the loss of memory and thinking ability, there is loss of control over much of one's life. Even if aware of the changes, the individual can do nothing about it. There may be great anxiety and depression in struggling to continue even familiar tasks and activities. Repeated failures with even basic daily routines cause loss of self-esteem and much of the enjoyment and happiness that life can provide.

Although productivity is high and the workers are amazingly dedicated and focused on their work, the goal of the staff is to provide a meaningful and enjoyable experience for participants. Over time as the enrolled patients have progressive decline, the program is able to accommodate lower and lower functional levels. Very straightforward, one-step tasks such as rolling or stacking objects, alternating with activities such as pushing carts, can engage those who have very short attention spans but are interested in handling objects. Caregivers are encouraged to provide similar activities at home in order to focus the person's attention away from disruptive behavioral problems. As the care becomes too strenuous for the family caregiver and the person is admitted to a nursing home, the work program sometimes has allowed continuation of the AWP for a period of time to promote easier adjustment to the nursing home. At the time of placement a cognitive functional evaluation is done and a summary of the person's current abilities and deficits is provided to the institution. Nursing homes often welcome suggestions for how to continue some of the simple activities after the person's placement.

The theoretical model used in the AWP allows the staff to learn more precise information about the changes in thinking that occur as the disease progresses. The program looks at the individuals' responses to the disease and the approaches and techniques that allow them to function optimally and comfortably as long as possible. Healthcare professionals of all disciplines can apply the concepts and adapt the approaches used in this program. The occupational therapy assessment tools and task adaptation techniques are taught to occupational therapy students. Workshops and presentations frequently are given by the staff. The model can be replicated in other day care or long-term care settings.

## ☐ Developing a Work Program

Any day care program serving patients with dementia may use the AWP model. An existing day care might choose to develop a work program for patients with dementia who have difficulty accepting or attending to group activities they can no longer comprehend. Even without a separate program, these patients might be given work tasks based on an assessment of their functional levels. In some programs it might be practical to set aside part of the day (preferably the morning, when alertness and energy level are usually highest) for a work program and to schedule more leisurely activities for the afternoon. The program is also ideal for long-term care facilities, in which patients with dementia are often disruptive to other residents during activities that they no longer are able to understand. Appropriate approaches that match functional capabilities can go a long way to maintain interest and prevent disruptive behaviors. Establishing work programs in assisted-living facilities is being considered, as the need for structured activity for residents who become demented is recognized and addressed. Establishing an AWP involves setting aside space, hiring and preparing staff, finding jobs, identifying and assessing participants, and planning the task adaptations. Policies and design of the program, of course, depend on the organizational setting and participants to be involved.

It is advisable to plan details carefully and start with a small, somewhat heterogeneous group of higher-functioning individuals. Staff and participants alike need time to adjust to the program and become acquainted with each other and the routines. The skillful assessment and task planning by the occupational therapist is an essential element for a smooth orientation period. Starting with a group of six to eight is manageable in terms of supervision and provides comfortable socialization as well as one-to-one attention. As the participants' functional abilities gradually decline, the tasks can be adjusted. Introducing new participants to the group gradually is important. Staff members need to give adequate attention to a new person and to encourage other workers to welcome and help new members. However, some participants become anxious or agitated by the "intrusion" of too many unfamiliar people or sudden changes in routines. New participants may be quite anxious about starting a new endeavor. Even those in early dementia have a great deal of anticipation anxiety if they are uncertain of what to expect or if they fear failure or embarrassment in a situation they face. Every effort needs to be made to assess participants carefully and provide support and reassurance during the early contacts and the learning period.

## Reasons for Starting a Program

Reasons for starting an adapted work program include:

- To improve the quality of life for dementia patients
- To provide structured, meaningful activity in a supportive environment

- To reintroduce a familiar role and the rewards that go with it (a sense of accomplishment, wages and praise, and identity as a productive member of society)
- To optimize function through matching of tasks to the ability and skill level
- To provide an acceptable alternative day care program
- To provide short-term respite for family caregivers

## Space Requirements

The space requirements depend on the type of work to be done and the number of participants. The majority of the work activities in the original program take place in a 23 × 33 room of approximately 760 ft². This space has been adequate for 10 to 12 workers and two to three staff members and volunteers. It is probably not advisable to have more than 12 participants working in one room. Small numbers promote socialization and familiarity and help keep noise and stimuli at tolerable levels for the those with dementia. A second adjoining kitchen area (approximately 620 ft²) is available for food-preparation tasks and the workers' lunch time, periodic testing, or interviews. Both rooms offer natural daylight and a pleasant view that the men often comment about or wander toward during breaks. Easy access to bathrooms is essential.

## Equipment Needs

The following equipment is necessary:

- Labeled coat hooks are important for participants' outdoor clothing to help minimize confusion and prevent loss.
- Name badges with large letters are important to identify workers with the program.
- Work tables or counters for performance of various tasks are essential. (Hydraulic work tables that adjust to different heights for different tasks are ideal and encourage good body mechanics.)
- Comfortable, sturdy chairs for doing tasks at the table are necessary.
- A supply cabinet or shelves can be used for storage of equipment and unfinished tasks.
- A small refrigerator and microwave are helpful.
- Assorted office supplies are needed for the staff's administrative duties as well as for use by the workers to carry out various tasks.

## Staffing Needs

A *registered occupational therapist* is responsible for the overall administration of the program. The tasks include procurement and organization;

initial and ongoing evaluation of participant functioning; training and direct supervision of the workers, staff, and volunteers; adaptation and assignment of tasks; and overseeing the set-up and clean-up, the escort service, attendance records, social programs, and behavioral interventions as needed.

A *certified occupational therapy assistant* works with the day-to-day activities of the participants and assists the registered occupational therapist with administrative duties as needed.

A *registered nurse* may assist with healthcare issues and behavioral changes and communicate with family members regarding home care management of the participants. A clinical nurse specialist has assumed this role in the AWP and has provided referrals to the program and done initial screening of participants. The nurse and occupational therapist may confer jointly to develop policies and procedures that govern the operation of the program.

*Volunteers* are an integral part of the AWP. They are oriented to the needs of persons suffering from dementia and the objectives of the program. Volunteers of retirement age can relate well to the workers and find it rewarding to help with the program. They assist the staff with set-up of tasks, supervision of workers (particularly with one-to-one assistance for level 3 workers), escort duties, and errands. Their most valuable role is in facilitating socialization—initiating conversations among the workers, bringing up topics of interest, and maintaining a sense of camaraderie in the group.

## Policies and Procedures

Administrative decisions must establish policies to be followed and procedures for the operation of the program. Some areas to consider include the following.

### Criteria for Participants

These include the number of workers that can be accommodated and screening criteria (functional levels, health status, behavioral history).

### Family Communication

This involves orientation meetings and support programs, day-to-day assistance with home care issues, and advice regarding behavioral concerns

### Safety Concerns

These include transportation, medication administration, lost workers, injuries or illness during work hours, disruptive behaviors, and compliance with facility regulations. If food-preparation tasks are used, workers may need the tests for food handlers required by the health department.

## Job Procurement

In large facilities there are many opportunities for work. Departments and services solicited need to be given detailed information about the types of jobs that are appropriate, the time frame and details for pick-up and delivery, and the supervision and quality control of the work. Careful planning is important to estimate the types of jobs and amount of work that participants can handle and complete in a reasonable time period. In some situations contracts might be arranged so that income can be obtained for the amount of work done. In small facilities arrangements or contracts can be sought with other organizations such as churches, volunteer organizations, or other private businesses. All staff members need to assume responsibility for maintaining good relations with departments that provide jobs for the participants. Community programs may have opportunities to offer cooking, gardening, or cleaning tasks that participants find familiar and enjoyable.

## Budget

Costs of the program include the space available for the program, the staff salaries, and the equipment and supplies that are needed. In already established programs, most of these may be in place. Decisions must be made about whether or not to offer salaries for the workers. Our program was fortunate to have research funding and then volunteer organizations who recognized the value of the program to the participants and provided the salaries. The workers take pride in the fact that they receive a salary for their work and seem to have little awareness of the small amount they actually make. One participant occasionally talked about asking for a raise; others joined in with strategy suggestions such as "talk to the boss" or "you should write your congressman." Families, of course, must pay fees for participation in community day care programs. It might still be possible to find creative ways to reward workers in order to keep this aspect of the productive activity. If money is not possible, some other tangible reward might be created, particularly if the offer of a job is in addition to an ongoing program in which not all participants are working.

## Evaluation and Research

Initial and periodic assessments are necessary to determine the functional level of each participant and to adjust task expectations according to changes. Evaluation of mood and behavior changes, interests, and abilities should be tracked and communicated to the family. Concerns should be discussed among the program staff and adjustments made in the approaches or tasks. Sudden changes or progressive problems that do not respond to interventions may need to be brought to the attention of the healthcare provider.

Staff members also must track the effectiveness of their approaches and make adjustments in the environment and interactions to improve participants' experiences. Quality assurance and continuous improvement projects should be ongoing. Suggestions for evaluations include appropriateness and adaptation of tasks; work behavior and tolerance; effectiveness of the program on mood, self-esteem, and skill maintenance; and family response or involvement.

The work program is a virtual laboratory for learning about the changes in progressive dementia. Staff members learn from the patients if we watch their responses to their disease and to our attempts to help them. We need to be sensitive to their reactions and find creative ways to help them enjoy as much as they still can.

## ☐  A Typical Day

An early morning visitor to the AWP likely will find the staff setting up work stations—placing supplies and preparing sample items so that workers will be able to begin their jobs. A coffee pot and plate of cookies (sent by a worker's spouse) sit on a cart near the doorway. As workers arrive, a few at a time with a volunteer escort, they hang their coats on wall hooks below their names. Lunches are placed in the refrigerator, and they gather at the table and converse over coffee about the trip in, the weather, or something interesting that comes to mind. The visitor watches the smooth beginning of the day as staff members introduce each worker to a job and give the instructions needed. The first job of the day is usually a familiar one with which the person is comfortable. Most workers are enthusiastic and anxious to get to work. Higher-functioning workers often start the day by going to the laundry for carts of blankets and towels. They see themselves as helping to get the others started with their work. They are the ones who greet the visitor and ask questions, boast about their great program, and begin to tell about the work here. Soon each worker is busy with a task. Some work in pairs—one more impaired individual who can mirror the actions of the other and feel an equal sense of accomplishment that he or she never could attain on his or her own. Most workers stay busy at their tasks; some need reminders or gentle corrections. Others finish a chore quickly and need to be given a new task before they become anxious or restless. More able participants are able to carry on conversations with staff members or each other as they work. Some who regularly work side-by-side develop friendships, chatting through the morning about fishing trips, the war years, or their wives and how things go at home. Lower-functioning workers usually work quietly at their repetitious tasks. They are unable to attend to both work and conversations at the same time and may be quite content to continue with a familiar task for long periods of time. Staff members make a point of monitoring their responses and encouraging a break or change of pace if restlessness develops.

The smooth, casual atmosphere belies the amount of attention and synchronization it requires of the staff to keep ahead of each worker. The staff must have the appropriate jobs lined up for each worker but be flexible and able to make changes in plans if needed. There is continuous setting up, instructing, reminding, checking, and gently or subtly correcting. There is also a cooperative effort to watch for anxiety, boredom, building tensions, need for time out, separation of certain participants, or changes in the direction of conversation.

At all levels participants seem to focus diligently on their work tasks. Attitudes are overwhelmingly positive. Families often report that participants arrive home in very good spirits but cannot say what they did— only that they "worked hard" or "got a lot done today." Caregivers also report that workers come home tired and need little additional activity that day. They do put great effort into their work and seem to be guided not only by the staff and volunteers but by the "peer pressure" they feel to "measure up" to the accomplishments of other workers.

This competitive spirit spurs cooperation and possibly prevents behavioral acting out by individuals. Awareness of others seems to foster their ability to maintain social graces and self-control. Laughter and joking often is initiated by workers and encouraged by staff and volunteers. The same stories are enjoyed over and over, and the workers are easily able to laugh at themselves and their own situations. At the same time, it is amazing to see how comfortably the participants are able to discuss their concerns about their memory problems and anxieties with each other. They are aware that they all are "in the same boat," that they all are in the program because of dementia, and they express appreciation for each other and for the staff members who help them. Although some have more insight than others, no one seems uncomfortable during discussions. Rather they seem to have a sense of understanding each other in a way that they cannot in their usual social groups. Common comments include: "Sometimes I can't get the word out that I'm dying to say." "I get mad at myself a lot." "This is a great place to come and work and talk." "This sure beats sitting home at the TV." " I don't like any one job more than another, they're all good. We're busy, that's the main thing." "This takes me away from my wife so she can go do the things she wants to."

As the disease progresses and function declines, jobs are tailored accordingly. Jack, for example, who began the program 5 years ago, has slipped from functional level 5 to level 3. He used to pick up and deliver laundry, inspect linen for stains, and portion and wrap salads. A volunteer now sits beside him to lay out bandages for him to roll by hand. He still can fold blankets with a volunteer partner to guide his actions. He still has his sense of humor as he responds to comments directed towards him, and his wife reports that he still talks to the children about his "work."

## ☐ Conclusion

People with dementia have many remaining abilities, but someone must compensate for their deficits so they can enjoy participating in meaningful activities and derive a sense of accomplishment if they succeed and are recognized. The AWP has proved to be not only a feasible alternative to traditional activity programs but also a truly successful program for the institution, the staff, and the participants and their families. Usual behavioral approaches are combined with specific strategies to enhance an individual's participation and self-esteem. Staff satisfaction levels stay high when members are able to see the capabilities of the workers realized. Those providing jobs for the program have been satisfied with the quality and timeliness of the work produced. Families overwhelmingly praise the program, not only for the respite it provides them, but for the changes they see in the person's mood and attitudes.

Sheltered or adapted work programs can be an enhancement to many existing day care or long-term care facilities. They are an exciting possibility for community agencies and for the ever-expanding assisted-living environments. The assessments and strategies can provide a continuum of care from the very earliest stage of dementia until the very late stages are reached.

## ☐ References

Allen, C. K. (1985). *Occupational therapy for psychiartic disease: Measurement and management of cognitive disabilities.* Boston: Little, Brown.

Allen, C. K. (1988). Occupational therapy: Functional assessment of the severity of mental disorders. *Hospital and Community Psychiatry, 39,* 140–142.

Allen, C. K., & Allen, R. E. (1987). Cognitive disabilities: Measuring the social consequences of mental disorders. *Journal of Clinical Psychiatry, 48*(5), 185–190.

Allen, C. K., Blue, T., & Earheart, C. A. (1995). *Understanding cognitive performance modes.* Ormon Beach, FL: Allen Conferences.

Ayres, J. (1974). *Sensory integration and learning disorders.* Los Angeles, CA:Western Psychological Services.

Barnes, R. F., Raskin, M. A., Scott, M., & Murphy, C. (1981). Problems of families caring for Alzheimer's patients: Use of a support group. *Journal of American Geriatric Society, 29,* 80–85.

Barton, G. E. (1919). *Teaching the sick: A manual of occupational therapy as re-education.* Philadelphia: WB Saunders.

Brayman, S., & Kirby, T. (1982). The comprehensive occupational therapy evaluation. In B. Hemphill (Ed.), *The evaluation process in psychiatric occupational therapy.* Thorofare, NJ: Slack.

Burns, T., & Buell, J. (1990). The effectiveness of work programming with an Alzheimer population. *Occupational Therapy Practice, 1*(2), 64–73.

Burns, T., Mortimer, J. A., & Merchak, P. (1994). Cognitive performance test: A new approach to functional assessment in Alzheimer's disease. *Journal of Geriatric Psychiatry and Neurology, 7,* 46–54.

Cooley, E. L., Sewell, D. R., & Rich, C. I. (1985). Job and interpersonal need satisfaction: An assessment of disabled workshop employees. *Journal of Rehabilitation, 51*(4), 38–40.

Dawson, P., Kline, K., Wiancko, D. C., & Wells, D. (1986). Preventing excess disability in patients with Alzheimer's disease. *Geriatric Nursing, 7,* 298–301.

Diehl, M. (1998). Everyday competence in later life: Current status and future directions. *The Gerontologist, 38,* 422–433.

Doble, S. E., Fisk, J. D., MacPherson, K. M., Fisher, A. G., & Rockwood, R. (1998). Measuring functional competence in older persons with Alzheimer's disease. *International Psychogeriatrics, 9,* 25–38.

Ebbitt, B., Burns, T., & Christensen, R. (1989). Work therapy: Intervention for community-based Alzheimer's patients. *American Journal of Alzheimer's Care and Related Disorders, 4,* 7–15.

Folstein, M., Folstein, S., & McHugh, P. (1975). Mini-mental state: A practical method for grading the cognitive state of patients for the clinicians. *Journal of Psychiatric Research, 12,* 189–198.

Guralnik, J. M., Seeman, T. E., Tinetti, M. E., Nevitt, M. C., & Berkman, L. F. (1994). Validation and use of performance measures in a non-disabled older population: MacArthur Studies of Successful Aging. *Aging Clinical Experimental Research, 6,* 410–419.

Gwyther, L. P., & George, L. K. (1986). Caregivers for dementia patients: Complex determinants of well-being and burden. *Gerontologist, 126,* 245–247.

Hall, G. R., & Buckwalter, K. C. (1987). Progressively lowered stress threshold: A conceptual model for care of adults with Alzheimer's disease. *Archives of Psychiatric Nursing, 1,* 399–406.

Heimann, N. E., Allen, C. K., & Yerxa, E. J. (1989). The Routine Task Inventory: A tool for describing the functional behavior of the cognitively disabled. *Occupational Theapy Practice, 1*(1), 67–74.

Jarvik, L. F., & Trader, R.W. (1988). Treatment of behavior and mood changes. In M. K. Aronson (Ed.), *Understanding Alzheimer's disease.* New York: Scribner.

Lawton, M. P., & Brody, E. (1969). Assessment of older people: Self-maintaining and instrumental activities of daily living. *Gerontologist, 9,* 179–186.

Lazarus, L. W., Newton, N., Cohler, B., Lesser, J., & Schweon, C. (1987). Frequency and presentation of depressive symptoms in patients with primary degenerative dementia. *American Journal of Psychiatry, 139,* 623–626.

Maddox, M. K., & Burns, T. (1997). Positive approaches for dementia care in the home. *Geriatrics, 52*(Suppl. 12), 554–558.

Mosey, A. (1973). *Activities therapy.* New York: Raven Press.

Orem, D. (1980). *Nursing concepts of practice* (2nd ed.). New York: McGraw Hill.

Reifler, B. V., Larson, E., & Hanley, R. (1982). Coexistence of cognitive impairment and depression in geriatric outpatients. *American Journal of Psychiatry, 139,* 623–626.

Reingold, J. (1964). Octogenerians work for a living in three-year health-morale study. *Journal of American Hospital Association. 38,* 59–65.

Reingold, J. (1966). The establishment of a sheltered workshop in a home for the aged: Some initial considerations. *Journal of Jewish Community Services, 42,* 269–273.

Reisberg, B., Ferris, S. H., DeLeon, M. J., & Crook, T. (1982). The global deterioration scale for assessment of primary degenerative dementia. *American Journal of Psychiatry, 139,* 1136–1139.

Rosenberg, M. (1965). *Society and the adolescent self-image.* Princeton, NJ: University Press.

Spector, W. D., & Fleishman, J. A. (1998). Combining activities of daily living with instrumental activities of daily living to measure functional disability. *Journal of Gerontology: Social Sciences, 53B,* 546–557.

Yesavage, J. A., Brink, T. L., Rose, R. L., Lum, D., Huang, V., Adey, M., & Leirer, V. D. (1983). Development and validation of a geriartic depression screening scale: A preliminary report. *Journal of Psychiartic Research. 17,* 37–49.

Zarit, S. H., Anthony, C. R., & Boutselis, M. (1987). Interventions with caregivers of dementia patients: Comparison of two approaches. *Psychology and Aging, 2*(3), 225–232.

Zarit, S., Orr, N., & Zarit, J. (1985). *The hidden victims of Alzheimer's disease: Families under stress.* New York: University Press.

## 5

**CHAPTER**    Scott A. Trudeau

# Prevention of Physical Impairment in Persons with Advanced Alzheimer's Disease

One of the hallmarks of Alzheimer's disease is progressive physical decline. This decline is manifested in both decreased ability to perform activities of daily living and deterioration of neuromotor function. The degeneration of motor function may be caused by rigidity, decreased strength and endurance, impaired sensory awareness, or apraxia, singularly or in any combination. In spite of the often profound limitations of motor performance and functional ability in persons with Alzheimer's disease, little attention is paid to their need for rehabilitative care. This lack of attention frequently is written off as obvious in light of a pervasive belief that persons with advanced Alzheimer's disease do not possess any rehabilitative potential. Buy, are physical deformity and immobility inevitable consequences of this disease process? This chapter reviews the issues of impaired functional performance and decreased mobility and outlines some possible strategies to intervene to improve quality of life.

## ☐ Background

### Functional Decline and Staging in Alzheimer's Disease

Functional deterioration as a result of Alzheimer's disease is well established in the literature (Corey-Bloom et al., 1995; Geldmacher &

**80**

Whitehouse, 1996; Reisberg, Ferris, & Franssen, 1985; Volicer, Hurley, & Mahoney, 1995). Furthermore, there are those who argue that functional decline occurs predictably, in the reverse order of normal development. Many of the scales developed to track stages of Alzheimer's disease rely on this as a basic assumption (Cohen-Mansfield et al., 1996). Reisberg et al. have done much of the work in this area, seeking to define the process of deterioration in functional terms.

In their earlier work, Reisberg, Ferris, DeLeon, and Crook (1982) developed the Global Deterioration Scale. This scale was later incorporated into the more comprehensive Functional Assessment Staging Tool (FAST; Reisberg et al., 1985). For purposes of this discussion the FAST tool is highlighted; the reader needs to keep in mind that the stages identified were defined initially in the Global Deteriation Scale. In other words, the seven stages of the Global Deteriation Scale were expanded into seven stages with nine substages in the FAST, for a total of 16 possible levels. The FAST ranges from 1 (no impairment) to 7f (loss of consciousness). The following is a summary of the functional status at each of Reisberg's FAST stages:

1. No impairment
2. Difficulties finding words
3. Impaired job performance
4. Assistance required with complex tasks (finances etc.)
5. Assistance required selecting proper clothing
6a. Assistance required donning clothing
6b. Assistance required with bathing
6c. Assistance required with toileting
6d. Urinary incontinence
6e. Fecal incontinence
7a. Speech decrease to approximately a half dozen intelligible words
7b. Speech decrease to one intelligible word
7c. Inability to ambulate
7d. Inability to sit up
7e. Inability to smile
7f. Loss of consciousness

Nolen (1988) provides statistical support for Reisberg's notion that activity of daily living functions are lost in reverse order of the developmental acquisition of these skills in children. In more recent work, Cohen-Mansfield, Werner, and Reisberg (1995) explored these principles of functional decline within a general nursing-home population. This work sought to further investigate the order in which these functions are lost, and to correlate this to losses in cognition. This work correlates with previous findings that there is a definitive order in which activity of daily living abilities are lost. Understanding the magnitude and sequence of this decline in functional ability is necessary to guide professional interventions; however, it appears to over simplify the issues one deals with clinically.

Clinically, there is a need to consider the unique circumstances of each person with Alzheimer's disease. Most individuals do not fit neatly into scales such as the FAST. In working with an individual with advanced Alzheimer's disease, it may be easier to perceive his or her status in terms of a given level, but this may give too much power to the disease process and blind the clinician to opportunities for intervention. Clinicians may reach a point at which all functional decline is attributed to the disease progression, rendering them helpless and hopeless to intervene.

A more general conceptual framework of function may be indicated in persons with advanced Alzheimer's disease. Leidy (1994) maintains that functional status is a multidimensional concept lacking a uniform definition. She proposes that functional status encompasses an individual's ability to perform the necessary activities to fulfill the demands of one's usual routine. Thus, there is a significant contextual component to functional status. Functional status is further defined in her framework by an interplay between functional performance (what one does) and functional capacity (one's maximum potential).

No matter how function is conceptualized in persons with advanced Alzheimer's disease, the losses and changes that occur are profound and warrant closer scrutiny. It is essential to understand some of the neuropathological changes that may occur as the disease progresses.

## Neuromotor Deterioration

Souren, Franssen, and Reisberg (1997) look more specifically at functional loss in terms of neuromotor changes in persons with Alzheimer's disease. These authors describe *paratonia*, an involuntary rigidity response to passive movement. Paratonic rigidity, also called *gegenhalten*, is differentiated from Parkinsonian rigidity by the absence of cogwheel effect and inconsistency throughout the arc of passive movement. This rigidity may recede suddenly only to resume moments later. Paratonia continues to increase in severity throughout the progression of Alzheimer's disease and may result in generally flexed posture, labile balance, and falls. As these involuntary changes occur, it is imperative for caregivers to adapt interventions and the environment to compensate for the effects of this rigidity. Souren et al. speculate that paratonia may be a significant contributor to the development of contractures in late stages of

Alzheimer's disease, because loss of balance and frequent falls often lead to immobility.

Impairments in mobility frequently occur as a part of the aging process. Decreased visual and auditory acuity, limited endurance and strength, and changes in coordination and flexibility have all been associated with "normal" aging. In addition to the obvious neuromuscular influences that may limit mobility, issues of disuse must also be considered. Disuse can result in the debilitating effects of inactivity including a generalized state of physical deconditioning for the elder (Bottomley, 1994).

Losses of muscle mass, strength, and flexibility all have been linked to inactivity. It has been estimated that full bed rest may result in as much as a 3% decrease in strength per day (Payton & Poland, 1983). The issue of inactivity is especially poignant for the individual with advanced Alzheimer's disease. As noted previously, functional and behavioral changes that occur as part of the disease process may predispose individuals with advanced Alzheimer's disease to profoundly limited activity levels. Consequently, persons with Alzheimer's disease endure the double jeopardy of falls and immobility (Alexander et al., 1995).

Morris, Rubin, Morris, and Mandel (1987) suggest that impaired ambulation and potential for falls may increase the rate of institutionalization three-fold for persons with Alzheimer's disease as compared with cognitively intact elders. Institutionalization clearly complicates matters for the person with Alzheimer's disease. Carlson, Fleming, Smith, and Evans (1995) describe the phenomenon of *excess disability*, which is the difference between functional performance and functional capacity. Therefore, behavioral and functional problems that are disproportionate to the level of cognitive impairment may be attributable to iatrogenic effects of the institutional setting (Post & Whitehouse, 1995).

Satin (1994) labels these iatrogenic factors "health care–produced disabilities." He warns that intervention, however well intended, may be more disruptive than helpful to an elderly person. Some common iatragenic effects of healthcare for persons with Alzheimer's disease may include loss of autonomy; depression; dependence in activities of daily living; decreased self image; compromised dignity; inactivity, which can lead to muscle atrophy; and altered awareness caused by medications (Post & Whitehouse, 1995; Satin, 1994).

All of these risk factors are magnified further for individuals with advanced Alzheimer's disease in long-term care settings if physical restraints are used. Post and Whitehouse (1995) reflect this sentiment, outlining the hazards of restraint use including strangulation, immobility, and physical deconditioning. Although restraints often are employed to enhance safety, there is limited evidence supporting this rationale.

The body of literature exploring the effects of restraint-reduction programs with the elderly has grown since the Omnibus Budget Reconciliation Act (1987). These regulations were implemented in October of 1990. Part of their mandate specifically addresses that nursing-home residents have the right to be free of physical or chemical restraints, other than those required to treat "medical symptoms" (Department of Health and Human Services, 1989).

Evans and Strumpf in 1989 attempted a comprehensive review of the literature on physical restraint of the elderly and found that most citations centered around auto-safety devices, restraint use in psychiatry, and laboratory animal-immobilization techniques. These researchers estimated a prevalence of restraint ranging from 25% to 85% in nursing homes.

Tinetti, Liu, Marrotoli, and Ginter (1991) describe physical (mechanical) restraints as devices applied to impede or limit movement. These authors studied 12 nursing homes, caring for 1756 residents over the age of 60 years. Of this sample a full 66% experienced physical restraint over the course of the 1-year study. Unsteadiness or risk for falls and disruptive behaviors were cited as the most common explanations for restraint.

In a related project, Tinetti, Liu, and Ginter (1992) explored the impact of mechanical restraints on fall-related injuries. These authors report no decrease in falls or serious injury among residents receiving restraints as compared with nonrestrained residents. They speculate that changes in strength and balance as a result of immobility may have contributed to this finding.

Neufeld and Dunbar (1997) report that in the 7 years since the implementation of the Nursing Home Reform Act, the prevalence of restraint use in nursing homes has decreased from 40% to 19%. In a series of articles, these authors and colleagues describe a multistate intervention and education strategy targeted at direct-care and administrative long-term care personnel. They implemented a multidisciplinary education session (2 days), followed by quarterly on-site consultation. Their team consisted of a nurse, physician, occupational therapist, and physiatrist. The homes studied experienced a 90% decline in restraint use, from 41% to 4%. They strongly advocate the multidisciplinary nature of developing restraint alternatives, especially the use of occupational and physical therapists to assess mobility, prevent falls, and promote proper positioning (Cohen, Neufeld, Dunbar, Pflu, & Breuer, 1996; Neufeld & Dunbar, 1997; Neufeld, Libow, Foley, & White, 1995).

Similarly, in their review article, Evans and Strumpf (1989) advocate rehabilitative therapies as integral in the establishment of alternatives to restraint. Alternative environmental adaptations, such as redesigning furniture or introducing appropriate assistive devices, also are prevalent in this literature.

Addressing the multiple losses and challenging behavioral issues that the individual with Alzheimer's disease may present can be an awesome task. In spite of the fact that Alzheimer's disease is irreversible, it is important to recognize opportunities for intervention that may impact the individual positively. One of the most obvious areas for intervention, yet often overlooked, is the environment supporting the individual with Alzheimer's disease.

Kiernat (1982) describes the environment as "the hidden modality" in light of the impact it may play in the care of older adults. Lawton (1983) acknowledges the implicit and explicit demands the environment places on an individual to function. Skolaski-Pellitteri (1983) and Corcoran and Gitlin (1991) address more specifically the role the environment can play in dementia care. Two critical areas that the environment can influence significantly are safety of the individual with Alzheimer's disease, and promotion of maximal function.

## ☐ Intervention Strategies

Because the scope of the neuromotor changes in question is so broad and often variable, so must the programs be to treat them. The single most important requirement of any intervention is that it must be individualized to meet the needs of the specific person in question. Unfortunately, there is no quick-fix approach to this issue. Further, in order to ensure the best outcome, an interdisciplinary approach to treating functional and mobility losses is a requirement of any intervention. This approach must include and respect the expertise of rehabilitative staff (occupational or physical therapy), nursing, physicians, pharmacists, and so forth.

Interdisciplinary approaches can be achieved best through the collaborative inception and development of an idea. There are currently many intervention strategies being tested at a veteran's hospital in the northeastern United States, to address the functional and mobility needs of dementia special care unit residents. As further definition of the precise neuropathological losses involved in Alzheimer's disease occurs, this repertoire is subject to change and expansion.

Prior to initiation of any intervention strategy, comprehensive and complete assessment must be performed. This patient assessment is best accomplished through an interdisciplinary team process that extracts multiple perspectives on the root cause of the immobility and functional decline. Once the assessment determines that there is a need for intervention, careful discussion as to the best strategy for the individual is key.

Intervention strategies can be as simple as encouraging nursing staff to assist the individual with ambulation as much as possible throughout the day. If more specific rehabilitative needs are present, the person is likely to fit into one of the following categories:

- *Acute change in ambulatory status (less than 1 month)*: This is often the result of intercurrent infection and immobility from short-term bed rest, orthopedic injury, or an acute cerebrovascular accident. In these cases rehabilitative potential is generally relatively good.
- *Long-standing immobility*: This may be the result of prolonged bed rest or confinement in a chair. Rehabilitative potential is greatly influenced by the individual's motivation and mental status.

In considering the rehabilitative potential of an individual, it is imperative that one consider the implicit and explicit influences from the environment. The success of any intervention is correlated directly with nursing-staff investment. Thus, interdisciplinary collaboration and communication are again essential.

The following is a case example of a patient who represents the first category, acute-onset immobility:

Mr. G is an 81-year-old, married White male who is newly admitted to a dementia special care unit from home, where he resided with his wife. Within 14 days following his admission, significant functional decline is observed and noted. He no longer ambulates, and both of his lower extremities are experiencing significant edema. He transfers from bed to chair with moderate to maximal assistance from caregivers. He is placed in a large geriatric chair in a reclined position to elevate his edematous legs. He is becoming increasingly agitated and vehemently complains of being confined in the chair. There is an increase in pharmacologic interventions to control this agitation.

Discussions with the nurse practitioner and the physician reveal no significant precautions; thus, a fairly aggressive rehabilitation plan commences. This includes daily occupational therapy to increase endurance and independence with self-care activities and improve functional mobility. Inherent in this plan is the ongoing education of nursing staff as to strategies to help Mr. G maximize his independence. After 3 weeks of this intervention, Mr. G is able to assist with most of his morning care tasks including walking to the bathroom with minimal assistance and standing at the mirror to shave independently. Although he has shown significant improvement, his walking endurance is still compromised, and his sense of being confined in a chair is a source of great frustration for Mr. G.

At this time it becomes clear that Mr. G is a candidate for assistive devices, but which? Here staff initiates two strategies. First, in a collaborative effort physical therapy and occupational therapy fit Mr. G to a personal wheelchair. The chair is fitted so that it is low to the ground with a slight anterior angle to the seat to facilitate Mr. G's ability to self-propel the chair with his feet. He readily accepts this device and quickly is maneuvering about the environment.

Second, Mr. G is introduced to the Merry Walker (Merry Walker Corp., Richmond, IA), which allows him opportunities to stand and walk without direct assistance from staff.

The case of Mr. G clearly presents the fluidity and complexity of the assessment and intervention processes. Two of the interventions described previously are noteworthy and are described further—first, the physical and occupational therapy collaboration and intervention for fitting wheelchairs. At this VAMC setting, the physical therapy area is far removed from the dementia special care unit. For many demented patients the stress of leaving the unit, and the safety risks that may be involved, in the past prohibited them from accessing services. To rectify this, a specialized wheelchair clinic has been established on the dementia special care unit. Further, this has provided the opportunity for direct collaboration between physical and occupational therapies.

Second, the Merry Walker is a steel-constructed walker on four wheels. This walker includes a built-in seat behind the individual that enhances safety by limiting falls. This assistive device was essential in the case of Mr. G to allow him continued mobility in an upright position. The walker also compensated for his decreased endurance, allowing him to safely walk with modified independence, and he quickly learned to sit down if fatigued.

This case also reflects intervention strategies related to other areas of physical loss for Mr. G, specifically self-care deficits. It would have been easy to attribute his inability to perform activities of self-care as merely an inevitable consequence of his advanced Alzheimer's disease. However, upon careful consideration of this case, it became clear that these functional losses were more acute in nature, and thus rehabilitative potential was apparent.

Occupational therapy interventions focused on familiar activities of daily living, as a means to both increase physical mobility and endurance and restore functional independence. This patient was able to reclaim abilities to assist with dressing and grooming tasks, much to the surprise of direct-care staff.

## ☐ Walking and Quality of Life

The need for persons with Alzheimer's disease to retain some sense of purposeful activity may be evidenced in the frequently described persistent wandering of some patients. Whether anxiety-driven or not, the need to move seems to be retained late into the disease. The deeply ingrained nature of walking is consistent with the FAST scoring of loss of ambulation ability into the last quarter (12th out of 16 items) of the scale (Reisberg et al., 1985). Lawton, Devoe, and Parmelec (1995), Teri and Logsdon (1991), and Albert et al. (1996) laid the groundwork for consideration of the consequences of seemingly insignificant daily activities on quality of life. In fact, within the context of the profound losses experienced in Alzheimer's disease, it may be a misnomer to label *any* activity "insignificant."

One study in a general nursing-home population attempted to measure the effect of a walking program on general physical condition and quality of life. These researchers provided 12 weeks of an individualized walking program at a resident-selected pace. They found that the frail elderly involved were able to adhere to the rigors of the program and significantly increase their walking endurance capacity, without any adverse effects (e.g., falls or cardiovascular incidents) being reported. Although these results do not directly reflect quality of life, they support the notion that even chronically ill, frail elders can tolerate and benefit from increased ambulation (MacRae et al., 1996)

Friedman and Tappen introduced Alzheimer's disease patients to a "planned walking" intervention in 1991. This pilot study investigated the effect that walking had on the communication skills of demented individuals. Thirty subjects (15 in each group) participated in this study at two long-term care sites. Half the subjects received the walking intervention with conversation for 30 minutes three times per week for 10 weeks. The second group received a conversation-only intervention for the same amount of time for 10 weeks. The results supported the hypothesis that walking could improve communication performance for persons with Alzheimer's disease.

In a recent study (Trudeau, Volicer, & Biddle, 1998) the impact that enhancing ambulation status has on quality of life of persons with advanced Alzheimer's disease was explored. This study intervened using the Merry Walker with persons with Alzheimer's disease who required assistance walking. Although the sample size was small ($n = 6$), the findings were quite promising.

The study used a cross-over design with 2-week intervals, such that subjects served as their own controls. The results of the data analysis included significant improvement of observed mood and environmental engagement, increased walking, increased interaction with others, decreased daytime sleeping, and decreased agitation as a result of using the walker during the observation period (Trudeau et al., 1998).

# ☐ Conclusion

The inherent need for persons with Alzheimer's disease to continue to move is a powerful force. In conjunction with this, it is apparent that the meaning associated with walking and mobility is deep rooted. There are many academic scholars who may argue that individuals in the moderate to late stages of Alzheimer's disease could not possibly learn to use or benefit from assistive devices such as custom wheelchairs or Merry Walkers. Further, there is often a presumption made that persons with Alzheimer's disease do not possess any rehabilitative potential, and thus rehabilitative services often are inadequately available. There is strong research and clinical anecdotal evidence to contradict these beliefs. Not only can persons with advanced Alzheimer's disease benefit from such interventions, their quality of life depends on them.

# ☐ References

Albert, S. M., Del Castillo-Castaneda, C., Sano, M., Jacobs, D. M., Marder, K., Bell, K., Bylsma, F., LaFleche, G., Brandt, J., Albert, M., & Stern, Y. (1996). Quality of life in patients with Alzheimer's disease as reported by patient proxies. *Journal of the American Geriatrics Society, 44,* 1342–1347.

Alexander, N. B., Mollo, J. M., Giordani, B., Ashton-Miller, J. A., Schultz, A. B., Grunawalt, J. A., & Foster, N. L. (1995). Maintenance of balance, gait patterns, and obstacle clearance in Alzheimer's disease. *Neurology, 45,* 908–914.

Bottomley, J. M. (1994). Principles and practice of geriatric rehabilitation. In D. G. Satin (Ed.), *The clinical care of the aged person* (pp. 230–280). New York: Oxford University Press.

Carlson, D. L., Fleming, K. C., Smith, G. C., & Evans, J. E. (1995). Management of dementia-related behavioral disturbances: A nonpharmacologic approach. *Mayo Clinics Proceedings, 70,* 1108–1115.

Cohen, C., Neufeld, R., Dunbar, J., Pflug, L., & Breuer, B. (1996). Old problem, different approach: Alternatives to physical restraints. *Journal of Gerontologic Nursing, 22,* 23–31.

Cohen-Mansfield, J., Reisberg, B., Bonnema, J., Berg, L., Dastoor, D. P., Pfeffer, R. I., & Cohen, G. D. (1996). Staging methods for the assessment of dementia: Perspectives. *Journal of Clinical Psychiatry, 57*(5), 190–198.

Cohen-Mansfield, J., Werner, P., & Reisberg, B. (1995). Temporal order of cognitive and functional loss in a nursing home population. *Journal of the American Geriatric Society, 43,* 974–978.

Corcoran, M., & Gitlin, L. N. (1991). Environmental influences on behavior of the elderly with dementia: Principles for intervention in the home. *Physical and Occupational Therapy in Geriatrics, 9,* 5–22.

Corey-Bloom, J., Thal, L. J., Galasko D., Folstein, M., Drachman, D., Raskind, M., & Lanska, D. J. (1995). Diagnosis and evaluation of dementia. *Neurology, 45,* 211–218.

Department of Health and Human Services. (1989). Medicare and Medicaid: Requirements for skilled nursing facilities. *Federal Register, 54,* 5363.

Evans, L. K., & Strumpf, N. E. (1989). Tying down the elderly: A review of the literature on physical restraint. *Journal of the American Geriatric Society, 37,* 65–74.

Friedman, R., & Tappen, R. M. (1991). The effect of planned walking on communication in Alzheimer's disease. *Journal of the American Geriatric Society, 39,* 650–654.

Geldmacher, D. S., & Whitehouse, P. J. (1996). Evaluation of dementia. *New England Journal of Medicine, 335,* 330–336.

Kiernat, J. M. (1982). Environment: The hidden modality. *Physical and Occupational Therapy in Geriatrics, 2,* 3–12.

Lawton, M. P. (1983). Environment and other determinants of well being in older people. *Gerontologist, 23,* 349–357.

Lawton, M. P., DeVoe, M. R., & Parmelee, P. (1995). Relationship of events and affect in the daily life of an elderly population. *Psychology and Aging, 10,* 469–477.

Leidy, N. K. (1994). Functional status and the forward progress of merry-go-rounds: Toward coherent analytic framework. *Nursing Research, 43*(4), 196–202.

MacRae, P. G., Asplund, L. A., Schnelle, J. F., Ouslander, J. G., Abrahamse, A., & Morris, C. (1996). A walking program for nursing home residents: Effects on walk endurance, physical activity, mobility, and quality of life. *Journal of the American Geriatric Society, 44,* 175–180.

Morris, J. C., Rubin, E. H., Morris, E. J., & Mandel, S. A. (1987). Senile dementia of the Alzheimer's type: An important risk factor for serious falls. *Journal of Gerontology, 42,* 412–417.

Neufeld, R. R., & Dunbar, J. M. (1997). Restraint reduction: Where are we now? *Nursing Home Economics, 4*(3), 11–15.

Neufeld, R. R., Libow L. S., Foley, W., & White, H. (1995). Can physically restrained nursing-home residents be untied safely? Intervention and evaluation design. *Journal of the American Geriatric Society, 43,* 1264–1268.

Nolen, N. R. (1988). Functional skill regression in late-stage dementias. *American Journal of Occupational Therapy, 42,* 666–669.

Omnibus Budget Reconciliation Act. (1987). Subtitle C. Nursing Home ReformAct, PL100–203.

Payton, O. D., & Poland, J. L. (1983). Aging process: Implications for clinical practice. *Physical Therapy, 63,* 41–48.

Post, S. G., & Whitehouse, P. J. (1995). Fairhill guidelines on ethics of the care of people with Alzheimer's disease: A clinical summary. *Journal of the American Geriatric Society, 43,* 1423–1429.

Reisberg, B., Ferris, S. H., DeLeon, M. J., & Crook, T. (1982). The global deterioration scale for assessment of degenerative dementia. *American Journal of Psychiatry, 139,* 1136–1139.

Reisberg, B., Ferris, S. H., & Franssen, E. (1985). An ordinal functional assessment tool for Alzheimer's type dementia. *Hospital Community Psychiatry, 36,* 593–595.

Satin, D. G. (1994). Emotional and cognitive issues in the care of the aged. In D. G. Satin (Ed.), *The clinical care of the aged person* (pp. 62–107). New York: Oxford University Press.

Skolaski-Pellitteri, T. (1983). Environmental adaptations which compensate for dementia. *Physical and Occupational Therapy in Geriatrics, 3,* 31–44.

Souren, L. E. M., Franssen, E. H., & Reisberg, B. (1997). Neuromotor changes in Alzheimer's disease: Implications for patient care. *Journal of Geriatric Psychiatry and Neurology, 10,* 93–98.

Teri, L., & Logsdon, R. G. (1991). Identifying pleasant activities for Alzheimer disease patients: The Pleasant Events Schedule–AD. *Gerontologist, 31,* 124–127.

Tinetti, M. E., Liu, W. L., & Ginter, S. F. (1992). Mechanical restraint use and fall-related injuries among residents of skilled nursing facilities. *Annals of Internal Medicine, 116,* 369–374.

Tinetti, M. E., Liu, W. L., Marrotoli, R. A., & Ginter, S. F. (1991). Mechanical restraint use among residents of skilled nursing facilities: Prevalence, patterns, and predictors. *Journal of the American Medical Association, 265,* 468–471.

Trudeau, S. A., Volicer, L., & Biddle, S. (1998). *Enhanced ambulation and quality of life for persons with advanced Alzheimer's disease.* Unpublished manuscript.

Volicer, L., Hurley, A. C., & Mahoney, E. (1995). Management of behavioral symptoms of dementia. *Nursing Home Medicine, 3*(12), 300–306.

# SPECIALIZED
# APPROACHES

Scott A. Trudeau

# Bright Eyes: A Structured Sensory-Stimulation Intervention

Activity programming is an essential consideration in seeking strategies to enhance quality of life for persons with Alzheimer's disease and other related causes of dementia (Mace, 1987). Although it may seem obvious, what people do with their time has great impact on perceptions of themselves and the environment around them. As dementia progresses to the point that an individual requires institutionalization, the need for purposeful activity persists despite the fact that the individual's surroundings have become unfamiliar.

Persons with dementia lose their ability to communicate wants and needs and may no longer be capable functionally of pursuing once-familiar hobbies and interests. Thus, providing for the activity needs of persons with advanced dementia is an extremely complex and often daunting task. As the disease progresses, individuals often are unable to initiate meaningful activity (Volicer, Hurley, & Mahoney 1995), rendering them dependent on others to provide opportunities for purposeful outlets.

This chapter explores the development and implementation of the Bright Eyes group at a veterans hospital in the northeastern part of the United States. Tne Bright Eyes protocol was developed by an occupational therapist, for patients with probable dementia Alzheimer's type residing in dementia special care units. The title of the program reflects its initial purpose: to spark recognition in the often vacuous stare of people with advanced dementia.

# ☐ Background

## Functional Impairment

Functional impairment is an inevitable primary consequence of dementia and is required in order for a clinical diagnosis of Alzheimer's disease to be made. According to Volicer et al. (1995), the core problem of dementia results in functional impairment, delusions, and depression that can lead to processes of spatial disorientation, anxiety, dependence in self-care activities, and lost ability to initiate meaningful activity. As patients lose the ability to recognize and articulate their needs, it becomes imperative for care providers to remain flexible and creative with regards to activity programming. Therefore, defining "meaningful activity" becomes the responsibility of the caregiver, often without the subjective input of the individual with dementia. Meaning is, after all, an individual perception, and this issue may represent the first of many challenges for the service provider.

Macdonald (1986) proposed three levels of activity intervention as Alzheimer's disease progresses. Initially, in the early stage of the disease, therapeutic group intervention focuses on motor, verbal, and self-care activities. Next, in middle to late stages, group tasks include simpler fine- and gross-motor, verbal, and sensory activities. Last, in late stages of Alzheimer's disease, passive involvement in verbal or activity groups may be possible, but sensory stimulation is the primary intervention.

Mace (1987) asserts that activity programs must emphasize meaningful tasks, pleasure, and dignity, and restore familiar role and functional performance. Socialization and friendships also should be an anticipated byproduct of activity interventions. Activities should be structured, short-lived, and concrete in nature, offering opportunities for positive reinforcement and interaction (Macdonald, 1986). In addition, infantile activities must be avoided, and selected activities need to be extremely flexible within a given time frame (Griffin & Matthews, 1986).

Group treatment of the elderly is encouraged and in fact is becoming a necessity. As demands on limited staffing persist, group treatment represents a cost-effective intervention. This fact, coupled with the fact that group intervention offers a powerful tool to address the social and cognitive needs of demented patients, makes group work an increasingly viable treatment option for a dementia population (Levy, 1987).

## Sensory Stimulation

Striking a balance between preventing sensory deprivation and avoiding sensory overload is the goal of sensory-stimulation interventions

(Macdonald, 1986). Skolaski-Pelletteri (1983) and Davis (1986) describe the phenomenon of environmental press which is pertinent to this issue. *Environmental press* refers to the complexity of the demands that are imposed externally on the person with Alzheimer's disease. Because the individual with Alzheimer's disease is no longer able to regulate and initiate activity, it is the responsibility of the care provider to structure the environment to provide the "just right" challenge. If this balance is not established, frustration, increased anxiety and confusion, and even catastrophic reactions may result (Skolaski-Pelletteri, 1983).

Equally as devastating as sensory overload are the effects of sensory deprivation. The sensory-stimulation approach seeks to increase the overall level of sensory stimulation in the environment, so as to avoid the adverse effects of sensory deprivation (Bowlby, 1993; Levy, 1987). Bower (1967) showed that the course of irreversible dementia could be altered by providing persons with an enriched environment over a long period of time. In Bower's research, patients were exposed to 4.5 hours of sensory-rich programming 5 days a week for 6 months. Activities included grooming, exercise, crafts, music, and games. Results showed that half of these subjects improved on all scales, with sustained improvements noted in half of this group at the 6-month follow-up (Bower, 1967).

Richman (1969) conceptualized sensory training as an intervention for working with geriatric patients who were unresponsive to more traditional procedures. Facilitating the regressed patient's reconnection with the environment through the stimulation of all sense receptors is the goal of sensory training (Richman, 1969; Rogers, Marcus, & Snow, 1987).

Richman (1969) emphasizes the importance of kinesthetic, tactile, olfactory, auditory, and vision senses; others include gustatory senses with these necessary senses (Bowlby, 1993; Ernst, Badash, Beran, Safford, & Kleinhauz, 1977; Maloney & Dailey, 1986; Paire & Karney, 1984; Rogers et al., 1987). Bowlby (1993) acknowledges that a body of well-controlled data describing the effectiveness of sensory stimulation for persons with Alzheimer's disease does not exist because it scarcely has been tested.

## ☐ Sensory-Stimulation Treatment Strategies

The Bright Eyes group protocol used for this treatment intervention is based on the work of Bowlby (1993); therefore her approaches to sensory stimulation are expanded upon further here. She espouses that one use sensory-stimulation interventions for persons with cognitive impairment who have difficulty in relating or responding to their environment. Meaningful and familiar smells, movements, feels, sights, sounds, and tastes are presented in a structured and systematic manner that can be understood by the individual. The parallel group format allows the patient to focus on each sensory cue, explore materials, and relate to familiar past experiences. The group leader then is able to elicit adaptive responses from members. This intervention can be considered compensatory in limiting the effects of sensory deprivation that persons with Alzheimer's disease may experience.

## Sensory Deprivation

Bowlby (1993) reports that sensory deprivation can increase the dysfunction of individuals with Alzheimer's disease. The absence of stimulation leads to deterioration of the person's physical status, decreased social participation, and impaired intellectual performance (Ernst et al., 1978). Persons in dementia special care units are especially vulnerable to sensory deprivation for the following reasons:

- Age-related losses of sensation
- Impaired reasoning, perception, and judgment, and inability to interpret and act on sensory cues caused by Alzheimer's disease
- Potential for over- or understimulation imposed by the institutional environment

These risk factors magnify and compound each other. Bowlby describes this cyclical influence with deprivation limiting activity, which leads to further reduced opportunities for sensory stimulation. Sensory-stimulation intervention helps "eliminate excess disability through building on an asset, since the primary sensory areas of the brain remain relatively untouched by Alzheimer's disease" (Bowlby, 1993; p. 276).

Rogers et al. (1987) poignantly report the devastation caused by sensory deprivation and institutionalization in their case report of Maude. Maude, a 90-year-old woman, had regressed in all areas of functional performance during her 5 years as an institutionalized resident of a nursing home. At pretest Maude was described as totally dependent for self-care tasks, nonambulatory, nonverbal, and markedly disoriented. An individual, intensive sensory-stimulation intervention strategy was implemented for 5 weeks. Afterwards, testing revealed marked improvement in orientation, attention, concentration, self-feeding, mobility, communication, and cooperation with caregivers.

## Group Goals

Bowlby (1993, p. 282) states "The overall goal of the group is to provide organized, understandable, sensory stimulation to enable environmental awareness and responsiveness." Thus, the intervention capitalizes on the assets of sensory receptors and compensates for the inability to initiate and organize activities, while enhancing the individual's quality of life. In addition to the increased environmental engagement, quality of life can be enriched through effective socialization, emotional expression, and fostering self-esteem by eliciting adaptive responses to the sensory materials. Therefore, improved awareness, understanding, and responsiveness to the environment lay the foundation for a multiplicity of individual goals.

## Group Protocol

In order to maximize the structure and organization of the group format, sensory cues are presented to each participant in isolation, in a parallel group format. Upon presenting each sensory cue, the group leader attempts to elicit a related adaptive response to the cue. For instance, if the olfactory cue is a fresh flower, the leader may encourage each group member to reach for it and bring it to his or her nose. Bowlby (1993) emphasizes the need to organize and plan cues around a specific theme or focus. Seasonal themes often help the group leader determine cues to be used, and they offer orientation cues to group members (see Table 6.1).

**Table 6.1. Sample Bright Eyes sessions**

| Sense | The Beach | Trains | Baseball | Fishing | Gardening |
|-------|-----------|--------|----------|---------|-----------|
| Olfactory | Coconut suntan lotion | Ground coffee | Fresh-cut grass | Sardines | Garden fresh tomato |
| Kinesthetic | Beachball toss | Balloon volley | Soft baseball toss | Casting with rod and reel | "Digging" with shovel |
| Tactile | Terrycloth towel | Conductor's cap | Felt baseball hats | Fishing flies (feather and thread) | Potting soil and trowel |
| Visual | Photos from a Hawaiian calendar | Black & white train photos | Photo of local ballpark | Calendar of trout flies | Seed catalogs |
| Auditory | Ocean-waves tape | "Atchinson Topeka and the Santa Fe" | "Take Me out to the Ballgame" | Seagull sounds | Tape of crickets at dusk |
| Gustatory | Cold lemonade | Chocolate cookies | Nonalcoholic beer | Sardines on saltine crackers | Peeled tomato |

Further, the sensory cues are organized into a defined hierarchy for presentation in the following order:

1. Olfactory (smell)
2. Kinesthetic (movement)
3. Tactile (touch)
4. Visual (seeing)
5. Auditory (hearing)
6. Gustatory (taste)

General arousal and alertness are highlighted first in smell and gross-motor activities. Touch, visual, and auditory cues provide increasing complexity and require higher-level interpretive skills. The taste experience is used to end the group because of its rewarding and reinforcing effect, and it encourages informal socialization. All sensory cues are selected to be pleasurable and novel. Although noxious olfactory cues such as ammonia may promote arousal, the potential to elicit agitation outweighs their usefulness, and they should be avoided.

Developing a repertoire of group themes and related sensory cues is the first chore for effective implementation of this protocol. It is at this stage that the creativity of the therapist is directly challenged. Although there is no recipe book to develop group activities, there are some guidelines that may be helpful to consider:

- Know your audience. Themes should center around familiar experiences for individuals in the group. Gender, age, and cultural backgrounds must be considered in designing cues. For instance the veteran population is predominantly male, which is quite different than many community nursing home groups; activities must reflect these differences.
- Make it easy on yourself. Use current events or seasonal attributes to develop themes. Again, cultural sensitivity is crucial in introducing holiday themes, ensuring that group members are treated with the respect they deserve.
- Know your setting. Determine the optimal set-up for the group to happen with minimal distractions. Many long-term care facilities do not have the benefit of extra space for groups. Structuring whatever space you do have will go a long way to supporting the therapeutic process.
- Physical status of each participant also should be considered. Varying levels of support and assistance from the leader necessitates planning ahead. Know the strengths and limitations of your group members.
- Establish specific goals for the intervention, but be realistic.
- Be prepared to think on your feet and stay flexible. Be real and have fun.

In this day of budgetary cutbacks it is important to note that cues are best if they are familiar objects and often can be relatively inexpensive. This is actually an unforeseen benefit to this protocol. For instance, large, glossy photographs from outdated calendars can be very useful as visual cues and obtained free of charge (if you tell all your friends you need them at the end of the year). Household objects from the kitchen or the workbench often elicit the best responses, as they appear to tap recognition in group members.

## ☐ Evaluation

There are many success stories that come to mind in reviewing the 3 years that this protocol has been in use at the Veterans Administration Medical Center. These successes have ranged from major awakenings of regressed and withdrawn individuals to simple functional responses to sensory cues.

Mr. C, for instance, had been in the group twice a week for approximately 3 months. Although he was mute and unable to walk, he typically passively attended the group and often would use engrained pattern responses of catching and throwing to participate in the movement activity. One morning, the group gathered as usual and the leader prepared the olfactory cue, warm gingerbread muffins. As the leader presented this individual the cue, Mr. C turned his head, making direct eye contact, and stated, "There is molasses in these, isn't there?" This extraordinary level of involvement and verbalization was maintained throughout that session, but only recurred one other time before his death. Both of these episodes centered around the group activity, raising the question of whether they would have occurred without the group intervention.

In another scenario, Mr. W had a tendency to keep his eyes tightly closed most of the time. It was a goal to get him to open his eyes and tolerate the sensory experiences of the group session. This goal often was achieved. At the end of one such successful session, one of the aides arrived to walk him. He looked at her, smiled, and got up, walking out of the room. The success of this walking intervention appeared to be positively impacted by the fact that the patient had just participated in the sensory-stimulation intervention.

In an effort to quantify some of these anecdotal observations, a formal research project was conducted on one of four dementia special care units of a Veterans Administration Medical Center in the northeastern United States.

## Research Question

This project explored the question: Does sensory stimulation group treatment have an impact on activity of daily living task performance? The decision to explore the carryover effect to this performance was based on the observed positive clinical effect this intervention had on seemingly unrelated functional behaviors such as walking, as well as the findings of Rogers et al. (1987) described previously.

It was hypothesized that the experimental group either would display improved functional performance or would show less functional deterioration than the control group as a result of the group sensory-stimulation intervention.

## Research Method

This study was designed to incorporate both quantitative and qualitative methodology. Quantitative design included random assignment to control or experimental group, and repeated measures of functional performance by a blind evaluator before, during, and after the manipulation period. Manipulation consisted of three 1-hour sensory-stimulation group treatment sessions per week for 6 weeks, conducted according to the protocol outlined previously.

Qualitative data were collected in the form of detailed field notes maintained by the group leader for each treatment session. These data included both the sensory cues employed and the individual patient responses to each session.

## Data-Analysis Methods

Using descriptive statistics and repeated-measures analysis of variance (ANOVA), the quantitative data were analyzed. Pretest scores on the Functional Independence Measure (FIM; Hamilton, Laughlin, Fiedler, & Granger, 1994)), the Short Portable Mental Status Questionnaire (SPMSQ; Lewis & McNerney, 1994), and three subtests of the Refined Activity of Daily Living Scale (RADLS; Tappen, 1994) were compared using $t$ tests to insure that the groups were equivalent with regards to functional status at the start of the study.

The field notes were reviewed repeatedly to extract pertinent data elements. A coding scheme was developed based on the performance areas that emerged. Observations were categorized under four general headings: verbal social function; physical social function; physically disruptive behavior; and verbally disruptive behavior.

For each session, separate index cards for each patient were created, noting pertinent behavioral observations. The cards then were clustered under the headings, and trends were noted.

## Sample

The study included 13 patients, from a dementia special care unit, who had not been included previously in the occupational-therapy sensory-stimulation program called Bright Eyes. After discussion with the researchers, the nurse manager identified which patients might be appropriate for the study. There were only two exclusionary criteria used: inability to maintain an upright posture for the 1-hour session, and inability to tolerate the session without excessive disruptive behavior. These criteria were purposefully vague, so as not to exclude any subject who had the potential of benefiting from the intervention.

Upon receipt of informed consent from the appropriate next of kin, these patients were assigned randomly to control or experimental groups. Baseline assessment was completed including the FIM, the SPMSQ, and the three subtests of the RADLS. These initial data were compared to insure that the groups were matched for functional levels.

Initially 16 patients were potential subjects for this research. Of this group, one was excluded because of acute illness, and one lacked appropriate consent. Further, one subject assigned to the control group became ill and passed away during the data-collection phase; thus, his data were not included in the analysis.

The total sample included 12 male veterans and one female veteran, ranging in age from 60 to 85 years old. The control group included six of these subjects, ranging in age from 65 to 80 years, all of whom were male. The remaining seven subjects made up the experimental group, ranging from 60 to 85 years of age, six male and one female. Of the experimental group, 58% ($n = 4$) fell into the 80- to 85-year-old age range, as compared with 0% of the control group.

## Instrumentation

The dependent variable was measured using the RADLS (Tappen, 1994). Because it was hypothesized that the sensory-stimulation intervention would improve functional performance, three subtests of the 14-task scale were selected including hand washing, hair combing, and upper-extremity dressing. As noted previously the evaluator was blinded to the subjects' group assignment, to limit bias. Tappen supports the use of a sampling of separate tasks for assessment of function.

The RADLS was developed by analyzing self-care tasks to define the individual sequential steps necessary for task completion. Scoring focuses on the level of assistance the individual requires for task success. Five levels of assistance are defined: no assistance, verbal prompt, nonverbal prompt, physical guiding, and full assistance. Each of the component steps of the task are scored and a total sum score for each task is derived. The RADLS was administered during a pretest phase into the first week of the study, and then on a weekly basis for the remaining 5 weeks. As much as possible the evaluator made efforts to perform the evaluation on the same day of the week at the same time of day; over the course of the study, however, for practical reasons this was not always possible. Posttesting was completed 5 weeks after the group intervention was discontinued, to determine carryover effect.

The leader of the sensory-stimulation group intervention recorded stimuli presented, group attendance, and participant response to the intervention in a free-flowing narrative format in the field notes.

## Results

Initial *t*-test results indicated that the control and experimental groups were matched for functional level. An ANOVA compared each interval of measurement against the pretest scores and indicated that the groups' scores were essentially equal to the pretest throughout the study. Further ANOVA compared just the pretest and posttest scores for the RADLS hand-washing, hair-combing, and upper-extremity dressing activities. Between subjects and within subjects, there were no differences shown between treatment and control groups.

The qualitative data analysis revealed that more than two thirds of the instances of intervention included some notation of patient engagement in the group process. Engagement included verbal and nonverbal participation and was described by the researcher as a positive state for the subject.

Throughout the field notes words such as "responsive," "alert," and "connected" reflect this finding. Eye contact, smiling, and verbal interaction noted in the field notes also are considered relevant to this finding; for example:

> In for the full session . . . napped only briefly once . . . easily re-engaged. Seemed to respond well to a bit of extra attention. Quite verbal as to [country] fair attendance. Recognized that photos must be "from the old days" . . . because he spotted a straw hat on one of the men in the photo.

In another case the following entry was made after the first experimental session:

Noted for frequent wandering—staff initially uncertain if he'd tolerate the process. He did well! Spoke with appropriate 1–2 word responses twice, drank lemonade independently—handshake with good eye contact at the end of the session. Napped in chair briefly once—easily arousable and engaged.

In both these excerpts, the behaviors noted are quite different from the way these individuals were expected to perform by staff. For most of these subjects, the nursing staff questioned whether or not they would even tolerate the group session.

Capacity for adaptive responses within the group emerged in more than half the observations. These responses took the form of relatively simple behaviors such as smelling a flower or more complex behaviors such as reaching for and eating the gustatory stimuli.

Overall, in the vast majority of the observations, all subjects displayed the capacity to tolerate the multisensory stimuli with a minimum of disruptive behavior. Further, there were no adverse responses to the intervention that were noted (Trudeau & Jones, 1998).

## Discussion

This study has demonstrated that institutionalized patients with Alzheimer's disease successfully engage in and benefit from sensory-stimulation group activities. In addition, adaptive responses throughout the intervention indicate an ability for patients to perform better with optimal levels of stimulation and structure. The levels of engagement and functional response within the group context were greater than clinically anticipated.

Although the hypothesis that this intervention would impact the functional performance of persons with Alzheimer's disease was not proven statistically, there was an increase in hand-washing and hair-combing scores in the experimental group that was not seen in the control group at week 6. This finding may represent a cumulative effect of the treatment intervention. This observation raises the question of whether the intervention may have ended prematurely.

Upon analysis of the means plotted for each group throughout the duration of the study, there is definite fluctuation in performance. This finding may be reflective of the disease course more than study design. However, if functional performance naturally fluctuates as a result of Alzheimer's disease, then a single pretest score is insufficient to use as baseline. This issue must be considered more fully in future designs. Baseline performance may need to be assessed over time and averaged in an effort to control for this fluctuation.

Consistent with the qualitative results in this study, Paire and Karney (1984) concluded that sensory stimulation "forestalled deterioration and rekindled interest in the environment." Their study looked at a more intensive intervention (four sessions per week, two leaders per five patients) of 12 weeks' duration, with a sample of geropsychiatric patients. The intensity and duration of the present study may have limited the effectiveness. Related studies typically have had greater leader/subject ratios and longer durations. Because the experimental group demonstrated its best performance in week 6, the cumulative effect of the intervention must be considered.

The groups were functionally equivalent at the start of this study, but the demographic data analysis reveals a discordance in the average age and average length of stay between experimental and control groups. For instance, nearly 60% of the experimental group was 80 to 85 years old. No subject in the control group was in this category. Comparison of length of stay reveals that 42% of the experimental group had been institutionalized for more than 1 year, but only 17% of the control group had resided in the institutional setting for more than a year.

The significance of institutionalization is difficult to quantify but clearly has an impact on these findings. Tappen (1994) reports that recent studies of nursing-home staff provide evidence that the usual assistance is not modified to match the individual needs of the resident. Further, independence is perceived as atypical or inappropriate. Tappen argues that daily tasks that are carefully graded to the individual can decrease the excess disability found in institutionalized patients with Alzheimer's disease. The longer an individual is exposed to an environment that promotes dependence, the more difficult it becomes to decrease the excess disability. There is undoubtedly a tendency for well-intentioned nursing staff to provide too much assistance with self-care activities. Clearly the ability of a sensory- stimulation intervention to influence activity of daily living function will be thwarted if the environmental expectations are for dependence in activities of daily living..

Quality of life is reflected clearly in the behavioral observations of engagement. Lawton (1994) acknowledges that researchers must rely on behavioral observations to extrapolate quality of life in later stages of dementia. Using eye contact, facial expressions, and verbal output, this study reflects a direct improvement in quality of life for patients participating in this sensory-stimulation program.

## ☐ Conclusion

Structured sensory-stimulation experiences, such as the Bright Eyes program, represent hope for persons with advanced Alzheimer's disease by playing a key role in preserving quality of life. Providing opportunities for meaningful activities to persons with advanced Alzheimer's disease poses a significant challenge for caregivers, especially as the disease progresses. So significant is this challenge that some might argue it is futile. As caregivers it is essential that we not succumb to these feelings of futility.

Functional losses incurred by patients with the disease must be balanced with the individuals' needs to engage in meaningful activity. This need for meaning remains significant throughout the disease course. Structured-sensory stimulation intervention can fulfill this inherent need for purposeful activity and must be a core of activity programs for persons with advanced Alzheimer's disease.

# ☐ References

Bower, H. M. (1967). Sensory stimulation and the treatment of senile dementia. *The Medical Journal of Australia, 1*, 1113–1119.

Bowlby, M. C. (1993). *Therapeutic activities with persons disabled by Alzheimer's disease and related disorders.* Gaithersburg, MD: Aspen Publishers.

Davis, C. M. (1986). The role of the physical and occupational therapist in caring for the victim of Alzheimer's disease. *Physical & Occupational Therapy in Geriatrics, 4*(3), 15–28.

Ernst, P., Badash, D., Beran, B., Safford, F., & Kleinhauz, M. (1978). Isolation and the symptoms of chronic brain syndrome. *The Gerontologist, 18*, 468–474.

Griffin, R. M., & Matthews, M. U. (1986). The selection of activities: A dual responsibility. *Physical & Occupational Therapy in Geriatrics, 4*(3), 105–112.

Hamilton, B. B., Laughlin, J. A., Fiedler, R. C., & Granger, C. V. (1994). Interrater reliability of the 7-level Functional Independence Measure (FIM). *Scandinavian Journal of Rehabilitation Medicine, 26*, 115–119.

Lawton, M. P. (1994). Quality of life in Alzheimer's disease. *Alzheimer's Disease & Associated Disorders, 8*(suppl. 3), 138–150.

Levy, L. L. (1987). Psychosocial intervention and dementia, part I: State of the art, and future directions. *Occupational Therapy in Mental Health, 7*(1), 69–107.

Lewis, C. B., & McNerney, T. (1994). *The functional tool box: Clinical measures of functional outcomes.* Washington, DC: Learn Publications.

Macdonald, K. C. (1986). Occupational therapy approaches to treatment of dementia patients. *Physical & Occupational Therapy in Geriatrics, 4*(2), 61–72.

Mace, N. L. (1987). Principles of activities for persons with dementia. *Physical & Occupational Therapy in Geriatrics, 5*(3), 13–27.

Maloney, C. C., & Dailey, T. (1986). An eclectic group program for nursing home residents with dementia. *Physical & Occupational Therapy in Geriatrics, 4*(3), 55–80.

Paire, J. A., & Karney, R. J. (1984). The effectiveness of sensory stimulation for geropsychiatric inpatients. *American Journal of Occupational Therapy, 38*, 505–509.

Richman, L. (1969). Sensory training for geriatric patients. *American Journal of Occupational Therapy, 23*, 254–257.

Rogers, J. C., Marcus, C. L. & Snow, T. L. (1987). Maude: A case of sensory deprivation. *American Journal of Occupational Therapy, 41*, 673–676.

Skolaski-Pelletteri, T. (1983). Environmental adaptations which compensate for dementia. *Physical & Occupational Therapy in Geriatrics, 3*(1), 31–44.

Tappen, R. M. (1994). Development of the refined ADL Assessment Scale for patients with Alzheimer's and related disorders. *Journal of Gerontologic Nursing, 20*(6), 36–42.

Trudeau, S. A., & Jones, J. (1998). *The effect of sensory stimulation on functional performance of persons with advanced Alzheimer's disease.* Unpublished manuscript.

Volicer, L., Hurley, A. C.,& Mahoney, E. (1995). Management of behavioral symptoms of dementia. *Nursing Home Medicine, 3*(12), 300–306.

Barbaranne J. Benjamin

**CHAPTER 7**

# Validation:
# A Communication Alternative

Validation therapy provides a coherent framework for staff-patient inter-action, which may result in improved quality of life for the patient and reduced stress for the healthcare worker. Although group validation therapy should be conducted by a trained professional, the principles of validation therapy are incorporated easily into the daily routine of the long-term care facility as all staff members interact with the elderly pa-tient with moderately severe to severe dementia. The central tenant of validation therapy is that communication can be used to affirm the dig-nity of the patient and the humanity and humaneness of the healthcare professional.

Most healthcare professionals have chosen their profession because they care about people. Although other reasons may be involved in choosing a career or employment in healthcare, commitment to the welfare of oth-ers is the critical ethical foundation for professionals, paraprofessionals, and aides alike. Consequently, the principles and techniques of valida-tion therapy resonate with their need to relieve suffering and respect the individual's worth and dignity and support their empathetic understand-ing of human interaction and communication.

## ☐ Need for Validating Communication

Long-term care facilities often provide an impoverished communication environment for patients (for summary, see Kaakinen, 1995; Lubinski,

1995). This environment is further reduced if the patient is considered difficult because of personality, disorientation, agitation, or behaviors associated with dementia.

For example, in a geriatric hospital in Canada, Jones (1992) reported on communication between nurses and patients with dementia during morning and evening care periods, times of day at which the level of communication was considered to be high. Communication was limited, with an average of 26 words spoken between nurse and patient in the 2-hour period under investigation. Nurses averaged five commands, two statements, and 1.5 questions in the time period. Fewer than half of the questions asked by either nurse or patient were answered.

These results are consistent with findings that confused residents were unengaged 85% of the time and that communication interaction was limited primarily to directives and correctives regarding daily living activities (for a summary, see Orange, Ryan, Meredith, & MacLean, 1995.) Such impoverished communication environments contribute to the isolation patients experience in long-term care facilities.

These impoverished communication environments are exacerbated further by sensory impairment. For instance, visual acuity of 20/50 or less in the better eye affects approximately 30% to 35% of persons older than age 69 years. In addition, significant hearing loss affects 60% to 90% of elderly persons in long-term care facilities (Corbin & Eastwood, 1986). Such sensory impairments serve to further isolate the patient by restricting awareness of the environment and by contributing to a reduction of communication and interaction opportunities.

The restricted communication environment and the sensory deterioration combine to isolate the individual from opportunities for meaningful communicative contact. Reduced contact with others in the environment and lack of perceived external stimulation result in a limited contact with the external world and allow the patient to focus on internal mental images. Consequently, the patient may be involved in reverie and oblivious to the muted, nonstimulating environment that surrounds him or her. If the external environment impinges on the internal reverie, the individual must make the transition from mental reverie to the external here and now.

The ease with which the individual, lost in reverie or reminiscence, is able to make the transition from the sharp, clearly focused internal world of memory to the external, perceptually muted world of the present reflects the level of intact cognitive facility including the ability to easily shift attention. The patient whose cognitive abilities have been reduced by the dementing disease has a difficult time in rapidly shifting from the internal to the external world and, thus, may appear "misrepresentational" or "psychotic." Reminiscing disorientation theory suggests that such disoriented behavior in the person with dementia may be the result of decreased sensory perception, reduced social stimulation, and limited cognitive capability for attentional shifts and informational processing rather than indicative of underlying psychotic disassociation (Jones & Burns, 1992).

## ☐ Description of Validation

In 1963, Naomi Feil began the development of validation therapy for persons with late-onset disorientation caused by dementia who did not respond to reality-based orientation. Today, over 500 facilities throughout the world use validation therapy (Morton & Bleathman, 1991). Validation therapy has been described by Feil in articles (1984, 1989, 1990, 1995), in book chapters (1991, 1992), and in book-length detail (1982, 1993). When inevitable deterioration caused by dementia can no longer be addressed through reality orientation, behavior modification, or other approaches, validation therapy provides a humane alternative that relies on validating the worth of the individual through communication.

All communication relies on the cooperation of communication partners to adapt to each other's knowledge level, attitudes, and emotional states. Communication partners must make assumptions about mutually shared knowledge, understanding, feelings, and intentions. With the onset of dementia in a person, a greater burden is placed on communication partners to assume responsibility for the course of the communication interaction. Too often, the communication partners resort to directives, commands, or even argument in an attempt to direct the course of communication to accomplish a specific task.

Validation therapy provides the healthcare professional with an alternative method for communicating with very elderly, confused, disoriented patients. Rather than directing the communication into safe, reality-based topics, the professional, aide, or family member responds to the topic that concerns the patient. The topic may be a reminiscence; it may be related to feelings of loss. Acknowledging such feelings validates the legitimacy of the feelings and, subsequently, the worth of the individual. Acceptance of the patient's feelings provides the basis for validation therapy and permits the patient to find resolution to achieve final ego integrity (see Babins [1986] and Feil [1982, 1984] for the theoretical bases of validation therapy).

In validation, the healthcare professional or other communication partner accepts the topic of conversation selected by the individual with dementia. For instance, rather than attempting to lead the patient back to reality, the communication partner may discuss recipes with the patient who started the conversation about making supper for her husband who loves liver and onions. Using validation allows the communication partner to ignore the fact that the husband is dead and focus on the topic of conversation, which validates the patient's worth and self-esteem as a cook and homemaker.

## Types of Validation

Validation is both a therapy and an approach. As a therapy, it is formalized, studied, and conducted by professionals who are trained in the method. As an approach, it is an institutional philosophy that permeates communication interactions between professionals, staff, or family members and residents or patients.

Validation-therapy groups are conducted by certified validation therapists. The validation approach is more inclusive than validation therapy and can be applied by validation workers, staff, or family members who interact with the patient on a daily basis to provide a validating environment. For the early stage in which the patient is confused and defensive, guidelines suggest 5- to 10-minute individual sessions three times per week in long-term care institutions or twice daily in acute-care hospitals (Feil, 1992).

Others have suggested that staff members use validation techniques whenever appropriate during the course of their interactions throughout the day. Because this method integrates validation as a normal part of the patient's day, it gives the staff ample opportunity to validate the patient's feelings. In addition, the philosophy of patient worth and dignity is reinforced throughout the day and becomes self-perpetuating. Such an atmosphere of concern and respect can result in reduced stress for staff, decreased staff turnover, and an increase in patient quality of life. Alprin (as cited in Feil, 1992) provided quantifiable data on positive behavior for both staff and patients. In addition, the costs of formal validation therapy could be eliminated "if validation therapy were conducted by all personnel as an integral part of clients' treatment plans" (Robb, Stegman, & Wolanin, 1986, p. 116).

## Validation for the Stages of Disorientation

Validation-therapy techniques are adapted to the individual's stage of disorientation. Malorientation, the first stage, is characterized by defensiveness. Succeeding stages include time confusion, repetitive movement, and the final vegetative state. The healthcare professional must determine the stage of disorientation before selecting the appropriate validation techniques to be used with a patient. Because each stage of disorientation has certain typical characteristics, it is relatively simple to determine a patient's stage of disorientation. Table 7.1 provides a summary of the major characteristics of disorientation stages.

## Stage 1: Malorientation

Patients in this first stage of disorientation are occasionally confused but become defensive in situations that are perceived as fluctuating and transforming into hostile environments. These patients rationalize the perceived changes and inconsistencies in their environments by blaming others and by taking defensive actions such as complaining or hoarding (Feil, 1982, 1993).

Patients in this first confusional stage are anxious and tense; they are attempting to maintain normality in a world that they perceive is deteriorating. Physically, the tension is seen in narrowed eyes, which are focused and alert for suspicious behavior in others; breathing is shallow and movements are purposeful and somewhat abrupt. The muscles of face and body reflect the tension of uncertainty and the fear as patients face a world that is becoming unfamiliar and strange. Patients may fold their arms to create a barrier between themselves and the world, or they

**Table 7.1. Summary of confusional stages**

|  | Malorientation | Time Confusion | Repetitive Motion |
|---|---|---|---|
| Focus | Externally focused | Unfocused | Internally focused |
| Behaviors | Purposefully clutching personal object | Muted, limited range of motion | Stereotypical repetitive pacing, moaning |
| Physical manifestations | Physical tension, narrowed eyes | Relaxed movements, clear unfocused eyes | Stooped posture unaware of incontinence |
| Verbal manifestations | Harsh, whining | Vague words | Slow |
| Emotional/ cognitive manifestations | Feels threatened, denies feelings | Confused as to time, person, place | Uninhibited emotion |
| Communication topics | Blames others | Misidentification | Does not initiate |
| Physical contact | Anathema | Derives comfort | Notices |

may clutch a personal object for security (Feil, 1982). These maloriented patients are the ones who hide their favorite nightgowns, forget where they put them, and blame the nurses' aides for stealing their valuable property. They may accuse staff of trying to poison them, blame the doctors for causing their spouse's death, or charge family members with stealing their money and home.

To deny the feelings of increasing confusion and to alleviate fears of losing control of their mental facilities, these patients adopt a rigid set of social standards. Often, they do not want to associate with persons who display confusion or disorientation; they do not want to be touched nor do they want to touch others. They appreciate routines that help them understand their environments and their roles and provide stability in a world they can no longer trust.

To validate the feelings of defensive, maloriented patients, the healthcare provider should be as nonthreatening as possible. This includes refraining from touching maloriented patients as an indication of concern or support. These patients do not want sympathy but do appreciate tacit acknowledgment of their concerns. They want to be respected as individuals; they want their statements and communications given due consideration by the important people in their environment. To provide nonthreatening communication interactions for maloriented patients, feelings should not be addressed directly. At a time at which they are feeling most insecure, patients in the malorientation stage do not want to acknowledge their feelings but need to have their concerns, whether real or imaginary, given consideration. If authentically felt although imaginary concerns are dismissed by the healthcare workers, maloriented patients become more emphatic in an attempt to have their concerns taken seriously.

Validation therapy for the maloriented patient is designed to reduce patient anxiety by using the patient's remaining intellectual capability to explore the perceived problem and perhaps to identify coping strategies that have been used successfully in the past. To validate the statements and concerns of the maloriented patient, the caregiver need only ask probing questions to continue the conversation—on the patient's terms. Rather than deny the accusations and subsequently dismiss the reality of the underlying insecurity and fear, the healthcare professional can request further information: Asking for additional information validates the patient and the concerns without necessitating that the healthcare worker actually believe that the accusations are true. Requests for additional information should be limited to questions of *who, what, where, when,* and *how.* Questions of *why* are threatening and should not be used. These questions require use of cognitive ability that is deteriorating in these patients and may be associated with past reprimands by parents.

If the staff or family member is uncertain of the patient's meaning, repetition or paraphrasing is useful. In addition, using the patient's preferred sense helps build a feeling of trust. If the patient describes the scene, the caregiver can paraphrase or question further about the visual aspects, how things appeared, what they looked like. If the patient describes a noise, the caregiver can use auditory questions about the sound and its characteristics. If the patient describes a kinesthetic sense, the caregiver can use such questions as: How does it feel? Where does it hurt?

For instance, with a patient who is unable to find a favorite nightgown and suspects that someone stole it, the caregiver may ask the patient to describe the nightgown. Often, the patient's description reveals underlying values and feelings that will become more important as the cognitive-deterioration dementia progresses. The caregiver further explores the topic by asking when the patient last saw the nightgown, where it was located, and so forth. When the topic has been explored sufficiently to authenticate the patient's concerns, the caregiver can use three techniques to guide the patient to more positive feelings.

*Polarity*, the first technique, explores the extreme by asking the patient to describe specifically the problem at its worst. For example, the patient may respond by indicating that the aide sneaks into her room at night and steals her nightgowns; she says she is afraid she will have nothing to wear to bed at night.

The second technique is to *reminisce* about related memories in the past. For instance, the caregiver redirects the patient to remembering a favorite article of clothing or possession. During the discussion, the caregiver finds that the patient's sister "borrowed" her clothing and often did not return favorite items. The caregiver asks the patient what she did when confronted with this related problem to discover coping strategies successfully employed in the past.

Finally, the caregiver asks the patient to *imagine the opposite* of the problem to focus on positive situations and feelings. In this example, the patient decided that having a special nightlight would deter the thief from stealing her nightgowns; but she also decided to keep her extra nightgowns under her pillow at night.

## Stage 2: Time Confusion

Patients in the second stage are increasingly disoriented as to time, place, and person. The patients who are time-confused are no longer anxious but rather are unfocused. This lack of focus is reflected in the patients' physical appearance. Muscle tone is relaxed; facial muscles are smooth without strain; bladder control is relaxed, with incontinence often occurring in patients in this stage. Eye contact occurs with partners, but the eyes are generally are unfocused, although bright (Feil, 1982, 1991).

The lack of focus extends through the cognitive domain and is reflected in social interaction, language use, and orientation to person, place, and time. Reduced focus on social mores results in patients who may be uninhibited; social conventions are optional. Consequently, these patients are difficult to motivate and often will not conform to the expectations of family and staff.

The lack of focus also is exhibited in the patients' use of language; there is a reduction in the number of specific nouns and an overuse of vague words and unidentified pronouns. Consequently, the topic of an utterance may be unclear to the conversation partner. The tenses of verbs vary from present to past, further contributing to the uneasiness that is felt when engaging time-confused patients in interactional communication. Without warning, time-confused patients alter their conversational topics by unexpectedly jumping from present to past, often in consecutive sentences (Feil, 1993).

The defining characteristic of patients in this stage is the inability to remain focused in the present. Time-confused patients cannot differentiate consistently the present from memories of the past. They easily misidentify persons in their immediate environment as individuals from past memories. The disorientation and confusion become more pervasive as patients progress deeper into this stage.

To gain the attention of the time-confused patient, the healthcare professional should utilize touch to promote a bond between caregiver and patient. Unlike the maloriented patient of stage 1, the time-confused patient is uninhibited and appreciates the human contact and support of physical touch. Touch provides this patient with a gentle anchor to present reality; touch conveys caring and comfort.

The bond created by physical touch can be strengthened further by use of eye contact. Eye contact is not supplementary to interactional communication but primary. The caregiver can assume that the patient's visual ability is impaired. Consequently, it is important to approach the patient from the front to gain the patient's attention. To be seen, the caregiver must get close to the patient so that eye contact can be established. This closeness implies reduced physical distance, face-to face communication with the patient, and similar eye levels between caregiver and patient. Closeness also implies an emotional genuineness in which the caregiver respects the patient; this unfeigned closeness will be reflected in the concern and regard apparent in the close eye contact.

Similarly, the caregiver must consider the patient's probably reduced hearing sensitivity. The caregiver's voice must be clear and moderately loud to surmount the typical reduction in hearing sensitivity associated with aging and any additional impediment caused by hearing loss sustained by the patient. To assure maximum comprehension of the spoken message, the caregiver should use simple words in short sentences with a slow rate of speech.

To illustrate the nonverbal aspects of communication with the time-confused patient, May, an aide, alerts the patient to her presence by approaching from the front and saying the patient's name: "Good morning, Mrs. C. How are you this morning?" As the patient focuses attention, May provides a comforting touch to the patient's forearm and aligns herself for level eye contact by partially kneeling to the front and side of Mrs. C's wheelchair. May proceeds to talk at a level that is sufficiently loud to be heard by Mrs. C, but she is careful not to offend by speaking too loudly or by allowing the tension of speaking loudly to show as strain in her face.

To validate patients who are time-confused, the caregiver can use simple words to describe emotions the patient presents. Universal feelings of loss of love (of parent, of spouse), loss of esteem (of social role), and loss of usefulness (of job) are reflected in the time-disoriented episodes experienced by the patient. After identifying the underlying emotion reflected in the memory that triggered the confusion, the healthcare professional uses simple language to comment on the inherent feelings. For instance, if the patient is cradling her arm and humming lullabies, the healthcare professional may comment on missing the baby, the love felt for a baby, or the fact that babies are comforted by singing. If the meaning of the patient's comments or actions are unclear, the professional can resort to ambiguous pronoun usage, vague questions, and generalized comments related to the emotions probably felt by the patient. Validation techniques can be used to explore the significance of the expression to determine the underlying emotion. In an example from the literature, a patient pointed his finger and counted to 30 constantly. Using vague language, the validation worker responded with, "That is hard work . . . Does it take a long time to finish?" The patient, who worked in a cannery, responded appropriately to the validation worker: "Yup! Thirty cans in 30 minutes" (Feil, 1992, p. 212). Obviously, the underlying feelings of self-worth and the importance of a job well done are feelings that the staff continued to validate.

## Stage 3: Repetitive Motion

Patients in the third stage are focused increasingly internally, with repetitive behaviors a prominent characteristic. Patients primarily engage in repetitive actions or vocalizations, resulting in decreased contact with the external environment. The internal focus, based on emotion and feelings, blocks the patients' awareness of external experiences such as personal incontinence. The overall picture of patients in the repetitive motion stage is one of collapsing in upon one's self.

Patients in stage 3 are withdrawn from social contact; they are often unaware of their environments and oblivious to others in their surroundings. Eye contact is further reduced from that of stage 2 patients because of a stooping posture that results in a lowered head position. Contact with the environment is minimal and rarely initiated by patients in this stage (Feil, 1991).

The defining characteristic of patients in this stage is the pervasive employment of a stereotypical repetitive motion that appears disconnected with the meaningful environment. The repetitive motion may be realized as repetitive behavior such as continual pounding, tapping, rocking, or pacing; the repetitive motion may be verbal with repetition of a single word or phrase, constant moaning, singing, humming, or repetitious clucking, "tsk-tsking," or mouth popping (Feil, 1982, 1993).

At this level of deterioration, the number of possible effective techniques is reduced. Nevertheless, the healthcare professional is able to connect with the patient for brief periods of time. Any meaningful contact in which the patient is engaged contributes to improving the patient's quality of life.

To connect with the patient who displays repetitive motion, the healthcare professional must be sensitive to the emotional meanings underlying the repetitive behaviors. These feelings, related to universal needs, provide the caregiver with avenues for comforting interaction. Family members and case histories also may provide insights into the meaning of repetitive behaviors.

To validate the stage 3 patient who displays repetitive motions, the staff member must be positioned to be accessible, on a level with patient; in this way, the staff member minimizes the isolating impact of sensory deficits and is available for communicative interaction. The caregiver proceeds to imitate the patient's repetitive movements in time with the patient's movements. This reflection of nonverbal repetitive movement acts as a validation of that movement and of the underlying feelings or needs. If the patient becomes aware of the person and the reflected movement, the patient may engage in a brief interaction. This temporary awareness provides a momentary connection with another human being, who affirms the worth of the patient and validity of his or her feelings. The patient's quality of life has been improved momentarily, and the healthcare worker has the satisfaction of appreciably improving the patient's well-being for a brief period.

For the patient who is verbally repetitive, the caregiver should attempt to engage the patient through auditory or verbal means. Although the patient still may understand single words and short phrases, these isolated, fleeting utterances do not make an impact on the patient in the repetitive-motion stage. Sustained, repetitive auditory stimulation can gain the patient's attention. The most significant and engaging auditory stimulus is music; music that is remembered, meaningful, and relevant to the individual. Consequently, simple songs sung in childhood, songs that were popular during early adult years, or lullabies that mothers sing to infants are potentially engaging for the stage 3 patient. The family may provide songs that were especially meaningful to the individual or songs that are appropriate for patients of a particular culture or ethnic background.

### Stage 4: Vegetative

The final state of mental and physical dissolution, vegetative, is realized when the patient further withdraws from interaction with the environment. The patient ceases movement, often assuming a fetal position. The eyes generally are closed and the breathing is shallow. During this stage, only touch and music have been shown to elicit an occasional response.

## ☐ Case Examples

These case studies provide descriptions of typical patients in various stages of disorientation and illustrate the use of validation as a response in certain common situations.

Differentiating patients who are maloriented from those who demonstrate more consistent confusional states is necessary before appropriate intervention can occur. The anxious maloriented patient is defensive and highly sensitive to skepticism and does not want to be touched. Patients who are time-confused or in the repetitive-motion stage appreciate the comfort of touch but differ in their cognitive abilities and what they can understand of the caregiver's conversation. Figure 7.1 provides a flow chart in selecting appropriate validation techniques for disoriented patients.

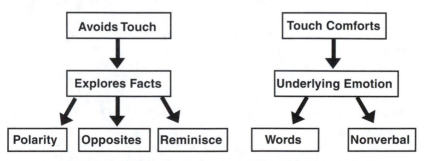

**FIGURE 7.1.** Flow chart of appropriate intervention strategies.

## The Maloriented Patient

Mrs. G, aged 82 years, recently had been admitted as a patient in the long-term care facility because of a broken hip. Before her accident, her niece reported that she was a crotchety old lady who had alienated all of her friends and relatives. Mrs. G blamed her niece for the broken hip she had sustained. According to Mrs G, she would not have broken her hip if Susan had brought her groceries on time.

Mrs. G's blaming expanded to include the doctors who treated her in the hospital and the staff in the nursing home. She was not popular with either the staff or residents. She began to accuse the nurses of stealing her food, nighties, and pictures of her late husband. Mrs. G began hiding things so "those thieving nurses couldn't steal them." Nightgowns, oranges, tissue, and other things were stuffed under her mattress, in her bedclothes, or behind the night stand.

In a partial attempt to validate Mrs. G's concerns, the staff refrained from confronting her with the hidden objects, arguing that no theft took place, or defending each other from her accusations. Refraining from confrontation was not validating and resulted in Mrs. G becoming more insistent in her accusations. Most of the staff members continued to ignore the accusations or changed the subject, but one aide resolved to apply validation techniques when Mrs. G began blaming others. No particular time for validation was set aside; rather, validation occurred when Mrs. G began blaming others.

In a typical interaction, as Tasha, the aide, helped her get dressed, Mrs. G. lowered her voice and confided that "those nurses are stealing my things every night." Tasha did not dismiss the accusation, ignore the statement, or change the subject but validated Mrs G's concern by exploring the problem. Asking a probing question—"What was missing?"—resulted in the response of, "My nighty and my picture of my husband." Because the picture implied a visual sense, Tasha continued to probe by asking for a description of the items, eliciting Mrs. G's preferred sense of vision. Mrs. G responded with, "My best nighty, the one with the pink flowers. It has a little bow, right here."

Tasha turned to the next step, polarity, and asked Mrs. G to imagine the extreme by asking, "When is it worse?" Mrs. G responded, "At night. They come in. They think I'm asleep, but I'm not. They steal my things."

Tasha then applied the next step by asking the opposite: "Is there a time when your things weren't stolen?" This question tapped into Mrs. G's unhappiness being in the nursing home: "No one ever stole from me when I was home."

Rather than dwell on unhappy feelings, Tasha diverted Mrs. G's thoughts to reminiscing in an attempt to identify coping mechanisms that Mrs. G had used successfully in the past: "You had all your things at home?" Mrs. G responded with, "Yes, and they were safe. Everything had a place." Tasha and Mrs G continue talking as the conversation evolved from treasured objects to the need for organization to run a home to efficient methods for house cleaning.

The entire exchange took nearly 6 minutes from Mrs G's initiation of the subject. During that time, Mrs. G's dressing was completed and she was settled in her wheelchair. After the validation and dressing session, Mrs. G was involved in reminiscing about household duties and continued on this conversational topic at breakfast with another resident patient. By midmorning, the staff noticed that she had reverted to her customary blaming behavior.

This case study of validating the patient in the malorientation stage demonstrates the ease with which validation can occur in conjunction with daily tasks. Tasha discovered that she need not limit her communication to directing Mrs. G's behavior while helping her dress; the physical cues inherent in the process and the habit of the daily ritual were sufficient to lead Mrs. G though the dressing process without the customary directives to keep her on task. Consequently, the concurrent conversation addressed Mrs. G's emotional concerns, while the staff attended to her physical needs.

## The Time-Confused Patient

Mrs. A, aged 85 years, sat in the lobby with three other patients, all aged more than 80 years. Conversation was minimal, with each patient slouched in her chair focused on her own thoughts. Mrs. A had been a resident of the long-term care facility for 3 years. Her husband had died over 20 years ago, and her grown children were dispersed throughout the Midwest. One adult daughter who lived locally had been taking care of her mother. Home healthcare, meals-on-wheels, and community partners had supplemented the daughter's frequent visits. When Mrs. A had partially turned on the gas jets, burned a tea pot, and put her safety in jeopardy, her daughter had insisted that she sell the house and reside in the facility, where she could receive appropriate care. Mrs. A had agreed to the move but fluctuated in her acceptance of her status as patient rather than homeowner.

Michele, a local college student participating in a long-term classroom assignment, was designated to provide validation to five residents for 5 minutes a minimum of three times per week. Michele greeted the four residents seated in the lobby and went to sit next to Mrs. A. She repositioned her chair so that she was in Mrs. A's line of sight. Leaning forward to touch Mrs. A's hand, Michele greeted her and identifed herself: "Good morning, Mrs. A. Remember me? I'm Michele."

Mrs. A raised her bowed head and looked questioningly at Michele saying, "Take me home?" Michele responded to the underlying feeling by saying, "You miss your home." Mrs. A nodded and repeated, "Yes, yes, miss home." With more energy and focus than usual, Mrs. A continued with, "Go home. Go home. Have to make dinner." Rather than attempting to orient Mrs. A to the actual time of day or the fact that she no longer has a home, Michele explored the implicit emotions with, "You like to cook?" "Oh, yes," replied Mrs. A, "He likes my cooking. He's a meat and potatoes man." She then shifted her weight in an aborted attempt to get out of her chair as she said, "I have to go. He'll be mad if it isn't ready. Harriet, you know how he is."

Although Michele had no idea who Harriet was, she suspected that the "he" who will be angry was the husband who died 20 years ago. Michele ignored Mrs. A's confusion regarding person and picked up on the vague pronoun; she redirected Mrs. A's attention as she asked, "He likes your cooking, huh? What's his favorite food?" Mrs. A smiled as she settled back into the chair and said, "Dandelion stew." Michele asked what dandelion stew was, and Mrs. A, with startling clarity, provided her with detailed directions for cooking dandelion greens with bacon and onions. Although the sentences Mrs. A used were short, they were meaningful. In continuing the description (a procedural narrative), Mrs. A began to use the past tense in talking about her husband. The conversation continued and, within a few minutes, Mrs. A was telling Michele about her husband's funeral.

For a brief period, Mrs. A was oriented as to time and place and was communicating with Michele as one competent individual to another. While the validation session lasted, Mrs. A was animated and communicative. Although she became more focused for the brief period of the validation therapy, Mrs. A quickly tired and returned to her revelries. Validation therapy was not a cure but provided the patient with meaningful, nonthreatening interaction and contact with another human being.

## The Repetitive-Motion Patient

Patients most in need of validation are those who have unresolved emotional issues from the past. Although such issues are denied in the maloriented patient and underlie the disoriented statements of the patient in the time-confused stage, patients in repetitive motion have deteriorated to a point at which their only expression of these unresolved issues is through nonverbal means.

Before admission to the local nursing home, Mr. W's middle-aged grand-daughter would check in on him daily. He was receiving meals at home from the local church, and he and his neighbor from the apartment next door kept an eye on each other. When Mr. W began wandering outside without a coat in subzero temperatures, the family decided they could no longer care for him sufficiently. They had endured his difficult behaviors and accepted his confusion, but now his safety was in jeopardy. Although the support system of nieces, grandchildren, church members, and social services was extensive, Mr. W had deteriorated to a point at which constant care was needed.

In the nursing home, Mr. W continued to wander. He rather quickly deteriorated, with his wandering restricted to slowly pacing back and forth while murmuring under his breath, "Gotta go." Although Mr. W was compliant and would allow himself to be led to a chair to sit, he would resume his slow pacing and murmuring almost immediately. His cooperation saved him from the physical or chemical restraints that are often used, but the frequency of the behavior kept increasing. When asked where he was going, Mr. W either would ignore the questioner completely or turn to him or her, and, with unfocused gaze, continue to repeat, "Gotta go; gotta go."

In an attempt to make meaningful contact with Mr. W, a speech-language pathologist tried validation for the first time. She had returned from a workshop and was intrigued with the concept of validation but was skeptical that it would work.

To validate Mr. W and his behavior, Marty, the speech-language pathologist, mirrored his pacing; she walked next to him as he paced back and forth. After a few turns, she slowly said, "You've got to go," as she walked. Mr. W continued pacing but turned his head slightly in her direction. She continued, "You've got to go, huh?" As this point, Mr. W stopped pacing and looked directly at Marty. Having captured his attention, Marty asked, "Where are you going, Mr. W?"

Shocking Marty, Mr. W responded, "Get to work."

Marty was unprepared, she could not remember what type of work Mr. W had done. In a panic, she commented on the topic striking on the emotion underlying Mr. W's words. "Work's important, huh?"

Mr. W responded, "Can't be late."

Marty responded with, "You worked hard."

"Oh, yes," said Mr. W, "Get to work."

Marty suspected that Mr. W might have worried about being punctual for his job, but she had no idea if this was a particularly important or particularly troublesome issue in his life.

Mr. W seemed to lose focus. Marty led him over to a chair by a window. As they looked out the window together, Marty commented on the beauty outside, but Mr. W just quietly stared. The period of lucidity was brief, but the focus of attention and the number of coherent utterances was greater than Mr. W had produced in months. Although Mr. W was in the later stages of repetitive motion, he was able to communicate with Marty and cease his relentless movement for a time.

# ☐ Effectiveness of the Technique

Although validation therapy has been used with disoriented, confused elderly patients for over 35 years, few controlled studies have been conducted to determine the efficacy of the approach. Many anecdotal reports in the literature confirm the effectiveness of the validation approach applied to individual patients; healthcare professionals who have used the techniques of validation with patients attest to the dramatic, although transitory, effectiveness of the approach. Although the underlying philosophy of validation therapy resonates with the belief systems of healthcare professionals, their personal experiences in using validation therapy with specific patients make them advocates for adaption of validation as the basis for a productive, affirming approach for staff when interacting with patients.

The few published studies of the effectiveness of validation therapy focused on the impact of group-therapy sessions on patients' behaviors. The impact of a validation approach, used as a pervasive mode for interacting with patients throughout the day, has not been examined formally or systematically.

## Anecdotal Reports

Many healthcare professionals, including the author, have used validation-therapy principles in their dealings with specific patients who were particularly problematic. Professionals, although not conducting systematic investigations of the effectiveness of validation techniques on particular identified behaviors, have documented noticeable changes in patients' behaviors when they are engaged in validating interactions. Clinical evidence and the expert judgment of working professionals should not be dismissed. Anecdotal evidence, although not rigorously controlled, offers testimony of the effectiveness of validation in temporarily reducing the confusion and disorientation of elderly patients in the later stages of dementia.

A literature review provides reports of case studies and anecdotal evidence supporting the effectiveness of validation. Jones (1985) presented a description of her first use of the validation approach and the immediate impact on her patient. Feil's (1982, 1993, 1995) publications abound with case studies and anecdotal evidence of the immediate effectiveness of validation on the quality of communication between patient and worker. The empathic listening inherent in validation was found to be effective for three confused patients who were adversely affected by a reality-orientation approach (Dietch, Hewett, & Jones, 1989). Individual cases (Gouldie & Stokes, 1989) and cases from group therapy (Bleathman & Morton, 1992) also are described in the literature.

## Effectiveness of Validation Therapy

Several studies have been published that investigate the impact of formal validation therapy on selected patient behaviors during and following therapeutic sessions. Limiting the investigation of the effectiveness of validation therapy to encapsulated therapeutic sessions ignores the impact that could occur if validation is used by the staff throughout the day.

Data collected during validation therapy sessions have shown that patients increase their talking in the group; the number of smiles, touches, and eye contact; and the level of physical participation (Babins, 1988; Babins, Dillion, & Merovitz, 1988). In a study reported by Fritz (cited in Feil, 1992), significant increases in fluency and lucidity were found in the speech patterns of maloriented and time-confused patients who participated in validation sessions.

Although statistical significance was not obtained, patients participating in validation-therapy groups improved mental status and morale; control-group patients decreased in these areas (Robb et al., 1986). Carryover into daily interactions occurred as validation patients increased communication by making a greater number of requests. The carryover of communicative behaviors was not viewed as totally positive because the staff, which was untrained in the philosophy and principles of validation, considered the unexpected attempts at communication by the patients to be burdensome. These results underscored the need to involve the entire facility in the validation philosophy. The researchers examined validation-therapy groups in financial terms and suggested that the permeation of validation techniques into all staff interactions with patients on an ongoing basis would prove more cost-effective than provision of validation in a formalized group-therapy session.

In a comparative investigation of validation and reality orientation, 7 of 10 patients involved in validation therapy showed qualitative improvements in behavior; only three of eight patients in a reality-orientation group improved (Peoples, 1982). In a comparative study of the effects of validation therapy and reminiscence therapy on interactions in the daily environment, two of three patients increased their frequency of initiation of communication and the length of their communications following validation-therapy sessions; one patient increased communication following reminiscence-therapy sessions (Morton & Bleathman, 1991). In a long-term study comparing the effectiveness of group validation therapy with group sessions devoted to social contact, nurses reported that patients receiving validation therapy were less physically and verbally aggressive, less depressed, but more nonphysically aggressive in terms of increased wandering, pacing, and repetitive movement (Toseland et al., 1997).

# ☐ Conclusion

Validation therapy has been practiced in certain long-term care facilities for 35 years. Although anecdotal and small-sample studies have demonstrated the impact of validation on the behavior of elderly confused patients, major investigations of the efficacy of the approach are lacking. Consequently, validation, which is grounded in a philosophy of humanitarianism, has not been adopted widely.

A validation approach, if used by all staff in their daily contact with patients, can make a significant contribution to the quality of life of both disoriented patients and nursing home staff. Validation offers a practical system for dealing with the disruptive behaviors of demented patients and provides a means for interaction that acknowledges the worth and dignity of the patient.

# ☐ References

Babins, L. (1986). A humanistic approach to old-old people: A general model. *Activities, Adaptation and Aging, 8,* 57–63.

Babins, L. (1988). Conceptual analysis of validation therapy. *International Journal of Aging and Human Development, 26,* 161–168.

Babins, L. H., Dillon, J. P., & Merovitz, S. (1988). The effects of validation therapy on disoriented elderly. *Activities, Adaptation and Aging, 12,* 73–86.

Bleathman, C., & Morton, I. (1992). Validation therapy: Extracts from 20 groups with dementia sufferers. *Journal of Advanced Nursing, 17,* 658–666.

Corbin, S. L., & Eastwood, M. R. (1986). Sensory deficits and mental disorders of old age: Causal or coincidental associations? *Psychological Medicine, 16,* 251–156.

Dietch, J. T., Hewett, L. J., & Jones, S. (1989). Adverse effects of reality orientation. *Journal of the American Geriatric Society, 37,* 974–976.

Dreher, B. B. (1988). Breaking up rigid attitudes. *Journal of Applied Gerontology, 7,* 121–124.

Feil, N. (1982). *V/F validation.* Cleveland, OH: Edward Feil Productions.

Feil, N. (1984). Communicating with the confused elderly patient. *Geriatrics, 39,* 131–132.

Feil, N. (1989). Validation: An empathic approach to the care of dementia. *Clinical Gerontologist, 8*, 89–94.

Feil, N. (1990, December). Validation therapy helps staff reach confused residents. *Provider*, 33–34.

Feil, N. (1991). Validation therapy. In P. K. H. Kim (Ed.), *Serving the elderly: Skills for practice.* New York: Aldine de Gruyter.

Feil, N. (1992). Validation therapy with late-onset dementia populations. In G. M. M. Jones & B. M. L. Miesen (Eds.), *Care-giving in dementia: Research and application* (pp. 199–218). London: Routledge.

Feil, N. (1993). *The validation breakthrough.* Baltimore, MD: Health Profession Press.

Feil, N. (1995). When feelings become incontinent: Sexual behaviors in the resolution phase of life. *Sexual and Disability, 13*, 271–283.

Jones, G. M. M. (1985, March). Validation therapy: A companion to reality orientation? *The Canadian Nurse*, 20–23.

Jones, G. (1992). A communication model for dementia. In G. M. M. Jones & B. M. L. Miesen (Eds.), *Care-giving in dementia: Research and application* (pp. 77-99). London: Routledge.

Jones. G., & Burns, A. (1992). Reminiscing disorientation theory. In G. M. M. Jones & B. M. L. Miesen (Eds.), *Care-giving in dementia: Research and application* (pp. 57–76). London: Routledge.

Kaakinen, J. (1995). Talking among elderly nursing home residents. *Topics in Language Disorders, 11*(2), 36–46.

Lubinski, R. (1995). State-of-the-art perspectives on communication in nursing homes. *Topics in Language Disorders, 15*(2), 1–19.

Morton, I., & Bleathman, C. (1991). The effectiveness of validation therapy in dementia: A pilot study. *International Journal of Geriatric Psychiatry, 6*, 327–330.

Orange, J. B., Ryan. E. B., Meredith, S. D., & MacLean, M. J. (1995). Applications of the communication enhancement model for long term care residents with Alzheimer's disease. *Topics in Language Disorders, 15*(2), 20–35.

Peoples, M. M. (1982). *Validation therapy versus reality orientation as treatment for disoriented institutionalized elderly.* Unpublished master's thesis, College of Nursing, University of Akron, OH.

Robb, S. S., Stegman, C. E., & Wolanin, M. O. (1986). No research versus research with compromised results: A study of validation therapy. *Nursing Research, 35*, 113–118.

Toseland, R. W., Diehl, M., Freeman, K., Manzanares, T., Naleppa, M., & McCallion, P. (1997). The impact of validation group therapy on nursing home residents with dementia. *Journal of Applied Gerontology, 16*, 31–50.

**8**

CHAPTER

Lois Camberg
Patricia Woods
Kevin McIntyre

# SimPres®: A Personalized Approach to Enhance Well-Being in Persons with Alzheimer's Disease

Helen developed Alzheimer's disease in 1982 and survived 8 years of disease progression, 6 years of which were in a nursing home. The nursing staff reported that she often was withdrawn and appeared distressed if her family was not present. Her son observed, however, that Helen could participate in and enjoy conversations and visits with her family members and only became depressed and distressed if no one she loved and trusted was present. The son developed an audiotape by talking into a microphone as if he were having one of his usual conversations with his mother, discussing positive and meaningful family events, in a positive and affirming manner. The audiotape was introduced to Helen by the nursing staff using a portable tape player. The goal was to "simulate the presence" of the family if they were unable to be present. Helen interacted with the audiotape; she seemed to perceive the conversation as a telephone call; and she appeared delighted. Nursing staff reported to the son that Helen experienced a noticeable enhancement in her quality of life during and after listening to a tape. The nursing-home staff and family members also felt less burdened by her distress.

As the saying goes, necessity is the mother of invention, and so simulated presence (SimPres) was born. The son in the story realized that his mother had a need that could not be filled within the existing system, and so he developed his own intervention to address her need. Helen represents the existence of a great many Alzheimer's disease sufferers.

During the latter stages of the dementing illness the loss of cognitive abilities results in an inability to interpret environmental information (Hall & Buckwalter, 1991). This decline in cognitive functioning often is associated with a variety of behaviors that are believed to indicate a lack of psychological well-being. Two general categories that have been used to describe these behaviors are *agitation* and *withdrawal*, representing the active and passive manifestations of negative well-being. We observe these behaviors in the person who repeatedly asks, "Where is my mother?" as well as in the person who watches her own wringing hands as she moans quietly, the person who screams, and the person who appears dazed most of the time.

Because persons with Alzheimer's disease have trouble interpreting their environment, they require assistance in one way or another to help make a meaningful connection. This need to connect with their environment can be met by family members who by their mere presence or their conversations can recreate environments from times passed, or by staff members in the nursing-home environment who can comfort, redirect, and help focus the person within the current environment. But neither visitors nor nursing staff can be constantly available, and without directed stimulation, the person with Alzheimer's disease often suffers from discomfort, frustration, or isolation. Furthermore, persons with Alzheimer's disease may experience secondary negative impacts because certain behaviors they may exhibit can also alienate staff and family members (Ryden & Feldt, 1992).

Stress and burden associated with Alzheimer's disease is experienced not only by the patient but also by nursing-home staff and family members. A globally effective therapy is one that positively impacts the patient, first and foremost, but also provides some relief of burden to nursing staff and family members. This concept is illustrated as a therapeutic triangle (Figure 8.1) on which the person with Alzheimer's disease, the nursing staff, and the family are all included.

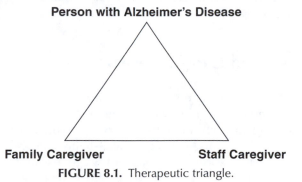

FIGURE 8.1. Therapeutic triangle.

Personal attention from nurses, although perceived as desirable and useful, is highly demanding on the overburdened nursing teams found in a great majority of nursing homes. Although empirical data are limited, it is commonly thought that challenging behaviors contribute to increased staffing needs, burnout of staff caregivers, and increased staff turnover (Heine, 1986). Ryden and Feldt (1992) reported that nursing assistants feel a sense of hopelessness and a lack of a consistent plan to manage challenging behaviors. Moreover, the use of chemical and physical restraints in nursing homes is now limited by the 1987 Omnibus Budget Reconciliation Act, which has led to a growing interest in defining alternative strategies to manage behavior problems.

Regarding family, a strong bond often exists between elders and family caregivers (Smith & Bengston, 1979). Many family members experience guilt and anguish as they observe the physical and mental decline of their loved one. Few families view nursing-home placement as a rationale to abandon responsible involvement (Caroff & Dobrof, 1974). Although most family-based interventions are focused on home care of the dependent elder, the contribution of family members to the care of their institutionalized relative with Alzheimer's disease is seldom recognized (Linsk & Keigher, 1988). Consequently, interventions to reinforce family involvement or improve their visits have received little attention. Both Smith (1979) and York and Calsyn (1977) reported that family members of institutionalized patients were uncertain of their roles, perceived little support from physicians and nursing-home staff in dealing with their relative, and indicated that they would welcome programs to help them become more involved and make their visits more meaningful.

The purpose of this chapter is to introduce the reader to SimPres, as an intervention that can help persons with Alzheimer's disease make a connection to a familiar environment, thereby improving their psychological well-being. In this chapter we describe existing knowledge and research that relates to this type of intervention, the specific conceptual assumptions underlying SimPres, its practical application, and the evaluative research on SimPres that has been conducted to date.

## ☐ Relevant and Current Research

As mentioned in Chapter 1, measuring quality of life among individuals with advanced dementia is highly challenging. Most of the existing measures of quality of life rely on self-assessment, which is impossible for severely demented persons. Aspects of well-being that can be observed objectively are facial expression, bodily movements, and verbalization. Interpretation of these phenomena as positive, negative, or neutral is driven necessarily by the nondementia perspective. Therefore, we believe smiling is better than frowning, pleasant conversation is better than screaming, purposeful activity is better than nondirected motion, and calm—no motion—is better than agitated or aggressive movements. But is an upturned mouth in a demented person the same as in a nondemented person, and does a neutral expression indicate contentment or lack of happiness? Further, does wandering signify restlessness or a desire to move and explore the environment? If a person rubs or taps a table top, is this a way of expending energy and connecting with something outside of oneself, or is it an indication of discomfort? When is a person calm versus withdrawn? Moreover, there are some behaviors that reflect problems more for the caregiver than for the person with dementia, such as wandering or perhaps even repetitive questions (because the person with Alzheimer's disease is not aware of the repetition).

Another major research challenge is designing intervention studies that are rigorous enough to sufficiently reduce threats to internal validity (i.e., to be confident that the result is really associated with the intervention of interest) but that can be feasibly implemented in a real-world environment. The demands of research are difficult to comply with if interveners are already burdened by caregiving responsibilities.

Given these research challenges, it is not surprising that the vast majority of the literature on interventions used with individuals with Alzheimer's disease and related dementias is descriptive, and research documenting statistically significant positive outcomes is limited, possibly because of small sample sizes and measures insufficient to detect sensitive changes in behavior. Moreover, the literature cites few interventions that even anecdotally have been successful in modifying or reducing secondary symptoms of dementia.

## Reminiscence

Reminiscence is the current therapeutic technique that is conceptually closest to SimPres and it has been implemented in the forms of story telling, conversation, music, and video. It is a process of recalling pleasurable memories and usually occurs in a group setting (Butler, 1961). Props and retrieval cues often are used to stimulate the reminiscence activity. The amount and richness of cognitive support has been associated with improved recall among patients with dementia (Ebersole, 1978). Anecdotal evidence supports the view that reminiscence therapy is associated with positive mood, higher self-esteem, and enhanced life satisfaction, but many of the studies are methodologically weak. In three studies using reminiscence group techniques in confused elderly persons, improvements were observed on measures of social behavior and spontaneous recall, but objective assessments were not made and there were no comparison groups (Namazi & Haynes, 1994; Rentz, 1995; Sandel, 1978). In another study, Goldwasser, Auerbach, and Harkins (1987) reported that no significant effects on cognitive or behavioral functioning were found among demented residents assigned to either reminiscence group therapy, supportive group therapy, or a "no treatment" group. Although reminiscence therapy seemed to have a positive effect on level of depression, the self-report instrument was deemed inappropriate for the more cognitively impaired patients.

## Video and Audio Technology

Two recent interventions have employed activity-based videotapes and audiotapes to distract and stimulate patients with dementia. Preliminary results indicate that while a person with Alzheimer's disease participated in watching a videotape, caregivers received some respite (Lund, Hill, Caserta, & Wright, 1995). In a small number of severely demented nursing-home residents, the use of environmental "white noise" resulted in a 23% reduction in verbal agitation (Burgio, Scilley, Hardin, Hsu, & Yancy, 1996).

## Communication

The literature on communication techniques is particularly relevant to SimPres. Evidence suggests that specialized communication techniques and styles may be effective in reducing negative patient behaviors (Mintzer et al., 1993; Ryden & Feldt, 1992), enhancing the functioning of the patient, and creating a more positive environment for individuals with dementia (Bourgeois, 1990). Cognitively impaired individuals retain some ability to create meaning from individual interactions and to make meaningful responses (Buckwalter et al., 1995). Bourgeois (1992) reports that the use of memory aids and a memory wallet improves the conversational content of patients with dementia. Wright (1991) found that patients with dementia respond positively to spousal contacts characterized by individual warmth. Caregiver speaking style is a personal and unique resource that often is overlooked as a tool to enhance communication (Beebe & Giles, 1984; Tannen, 1986). Burgener and Chiverton (1992) reported that patients with dementia show significantly improved functional status and calm behavior if caregivers smile and relate to the patients in a relaxed and flexible manner.

It is widely advocated that making certain speech and communication accommodations such as adopting a slower speaking rate, using a warm tone, simplifying sentences, and incorporating individualized and meaningful content can improve communication with dementia patients (Kemper, Aragnapoulas, & Heberlein, 1994; Waters, Caplan, & Rochon, 1995). On the other hand, overaccommodation can be counterproductive. Persons with dementia still remain emotionally sensitive to messages received and can distinguish speech patterns that sound patronizing or not genuine (Wingfield, Lahar, & Stine, 1989).

## ☐ SimPres: A Description

### Conceptual Framework

SimPres is based on the premise that preserved memory and positive emotions are the most valuable assets of individuals with dementia, and their effective presentation by a family member or surrogate can enhance psychological well-being. Memories are highly personal. Some memories are positive, others are negative. It is important to explore and mine each person's memory bank to identify those that bring her a feeling of positive familiarity, pleasure, and joy. As Figure 8.2 illustrates, SimPres uses each person's existing assets, which for most people in the middle stages of Alzheimer's disease include the presence of long-term memories, preference for familiarity, and experience of emotions. We have observed

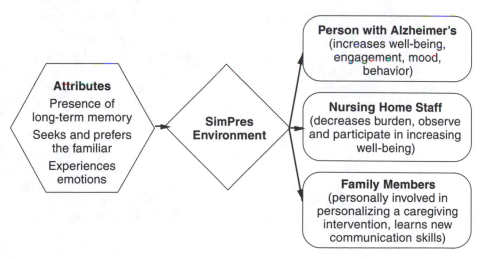

**FIGURE 8.2.** SimPres model.

that the SimPres environment leads to positive outcomes not only for the person with Alzheimer's disease but also for formal and informal caregivers in nursing homes and other sites, as well as for other family members involved in the SimPres process. Nursing-home staff and other direct caregivers have a new tool that helps them to have a meaningful role in increasing the well-being of the person with Alzheimer's disease and thereby decreasing their own physical and emotional burdens. Family members also feel empowered because they have contributed in the development of the intervention and have learned new skills that they can continue to use in conversations with their loved ones.

To the caregiver or other observer, SimPres appears as an audiotape that includes a caller's side of a conversation. The tape ranges from 5 to 7 minutes in length. Because people with Alzheimer's disease have recent memory defects, audiotaped messages can be played repeatedly and yet be perceived as a fresh conversation each time. The audiotape can be played through a recording device that looks like a telephone, or using a headset and an autoreverse tape player enclosed in a hip pack. The telephone device simulates a real telephone call; the tape player allows for the natural mobility of the individual wearing it. Clinical indications for use of SimPres include apathy, agitation, boredom, sadness, difficulty with activities of daily living, sleeplessness, and caregiver respite.

## ☐ The SimPres Development Process

The development of the SimPresence audiotape involves a specialized process and telephonic recording module. The process involves seven steps:

1. SimPres staff members work with family members who identify pleasant memories from the client's distant past (e.g., a special person or place, a favorite hobby).
2. SimPres staff members work with the client to prioritize the memories that elicit the most positive responses from the client.
3. A "qualified caller," preferably a family member, is trained in communication skills (including content and presentation) that have proven to produce a high level of engagement with individuals who have Alzheimer's disease.
4. The qualified caller calls the client on the telephone (prescheduled) and uses the selected memories and communication skills in a "spontaneous" conversation that is recorded on the SimPresence telephonic recording module.
5. SimPres staff members evaluate client responses using SimPres quality-control criteria.

6. SimPres staff members select the units of conversation to which the client responded best.
7. SimPres staff members produce the SimPres therapeutic audiotape.

The resulting SimPres audiotape is a one-sided simulated telephone call using the edited units of conversation (those that produced the best responses) and natural pauses that occurred in the live conversation to allow the client to respond after each unit. To reach therapeutic effectiveness, each tape must meet SimPres quality-control standards. Quality-control standards relate to the adherence to communication skills taught by SimPres staff, such as speaking clearly and slowly, introducing pretested memories in a warm and caring manner, and using techniques to keep the caller engaged and focused. Calls that positively engage persons with advanced Alzheimer's disease reach at least a score of 20 out of 28 on the quality-control assessment. Those that fall short usually can be improved with individual coaching.

## ☐ SimPres in Practice

Over the course of developing SimPres, hundreds of individual trials and observations have been conducted and assessed. SimPres has been effective under a wide range of circumstances. The term *effective* refers to the therapeutic triangle mentioned previously. That is, SimPres is most effective if it enhances the well-being of the person with dementia, facility caregivers, and family members.

To optimize its therapeutic impact, SimPres should be incorporated into the resident's care plan. This involves a careful assessment of the resident's behaviors and identified times of the day at which the resident is agitated or withdrawn.

In general, for agitation, introducing SimPres before a resident's behavior escalates is most effective. Often, individuals get agitated at the same time each day. SimPres can be used to distract attention until that time period passes or to prepare the individual for the next activity. As described in the subsequent cases, SimPres has been used to encourage individuals to attend to tasks that previously were difficult, such as bathing. For individuals who are withdrawn, SimPres has increased their sociability with both staff and other residents and improved their willingness to engage in other activities.

Following are three case studies that illustrate different circumstances in which SimPres was successful: a predictable behavior (e.g., focused on reducing a difficult behavior that occurs at the same time each day), a target behavior (e.g., focused on encouraging a specific desired behavior), and a withdrawn behavior. Each case is discussed in relation to its effectiveness within the conceptualized therapeutic triangle.

## Case 1: Using SimPres for a Predictable Behavior

Every morning after breakfast, Betty, a 75-year-old woman on an Alzheimer's disease special care unit, shouted for staff to help her get dressed. Nursing staff often still were feeding other residents and were unable to meet Betty's demands. Her screaming was disruptive to the other residents and stressful to staff. Betty's daughter usually stopped in to visit her mother on her way to work in the morning and witnessed her mother's distress. She often left feeling helpless and upset. During a resident-care conference, the SimPres staff recommended that the audiotape be used at 8:00 AM, when Betty was likely to be agitated. The goal was to intervene before Betty's behavior escalated and ultimately to see whether her behavior could be prevented.

Nursing staff documented that Betty's response to the SimPres was excellent. She responded positively to it 57 out of 60 times. Their comments included, "She was smiling and talking to the tape," and, "It calmed her. It worked like a medicine."

For the staff, Betty's positive response to SimPres changed the tone on the unit. Staff members were more relaxed and better able to tend to the needs of the other residents.

Betty's daughter felt involved in her mother's care. While working with the SimPres staff, Betty's daughter recalled her mother's love of poetry and identified her favorite poems. These were used to construct a familiar and comforting environment for Betty. Betty's daughter felt relieved that the mornings were calmer for "everyone on the unit."

## Case 2: Using SimPres for a Target Behavior

Millie, a 78-year-old woman, refused morning care. Staff tried everything possible to get Millie to the bathtub. Millie's son knew how difficult it was for the staff to get Millie bathed and dressed. In fact, staff members often had to wait until he arrived before approaching Millie. Millie's son developed a tape that included a statement, "Now, go get bathed and I'll talk to you again when you're done."

Millie listened to the tape each morning and began to comply with her bathing. Out of 20 observations prior to her morning bathing and dressing, she complied 19 times. Staff reported an "excellent" response as she smiled and conversed with the tape.

SimPres enabled the staff to perform the necessary activities of daily living routine with a cooperative, rather than combative, person. Staff members were surprised at the effectiveness of this intervention, because nothing else seemed to work.

Millie's son could not help but feel guilty that his mother was acting so "difficult" with the nursing staff. He could not believe how much his mother's mood changed after listening to the tape and how willing she was to cooperate with staff. He was greatly relieved by the success of the intervention. It alleviated his guilt.

## Case 3: Using SimPres for Withdrawn Behavior

John was a 74-year-old man who had been a resident on a dementia unit for 7 months. He frequently was observed sitting on the edge of his bed with a forlorn look, fidgeting with his hands and staring at the floor. He was alone much of the day except if a staff member or a unit volunteer asked how he was doing. He rarely left his room or participated in scheduled activities. Although John was not considered a "problem patient," staff members felt helpless in trying to improve his quality of life. John's granddaughter made the SimPres audiotape. She talked about John's love of baseball and also asked him to say a prayer that he taught her when she was a child.

When John received the SimPres audiotape, his face lit up. With a smile he listened attentively and responded verbally. He listened and interacted with the tape for as long as 30 minutes. Afterward, he was more social with staff members and even interacted with other residents. Out of 44 observations, staff reported that he responded positively 42 times, with two refusals.

Staff members commented that it was nice to see him involved in something and enjoying it. They felt relieved about his improved state of well-being. They were shocked at the difference in his demeanor, "like he was another person."

John's wife had felt sad that her husband seemed so despondent. She expressed great relief that he appeared to gain solace from the tape if she could not visit.

## ☐ Evaluation of SimPres

### Beyond Case Studies

Formal evaluation has been an important component of the development of SimPres. Although case studies demonstrate that SimPres can be highly effective, they are limited in their generalizability. Without rigorous research designs, comparison with other interventions, and statistical analyses of specified outcomes, we can never be confident about how the technique in question will work with a variety of people or whether or not it is better than other (maybe less sophisticated) techniques.

The evaluation of SimPres has included four studies. Because the idea for SimPres was based on the experience with only a single individual, the first study was conducted to assess the feasibility of using this type of technology with other people who had Alzheimer's disease (Woods & Ashley, 1995). A second pilot study was conducted to assess the process of working with families to identify meaningful memories and used a SimPres staff member as the designated caller (Woods & Ashley, 1995). The third study was a much larger demonstration study, using a rigorous research design, and used primarily family members as the designated callers (Camberg et al., 1999). The fourth study examined the potential to improve family members' communication abilities, to improve their effectiveness as designated callers (McIntyre & Woods, 1998).

## Feasibility Study

The feasibility study ($N = 27$) showed that effects of a staff-made SimPres-type tape (with generic conversation) could be replicated on multiple individuals with dementia. Nursing-home staff reported improvement in 84.9% of the observations in which demented residents were viewed as socially isolated.

## Pilot Study

In the second study SimPres staff members acted as the designated callers but used personalized content for each of nine nursing-home residents with documented Alzheimer's disease. Nursing-home staff documented on behavior logs that problem behaviors, including agitation and withdrawal, improved with SimPres 91% of the time (425 observations). In 7% of their observations the behaviors either worsened or did not change. SimPres was refused only 2% of the time.

Of note, both of these early studies were conducted under tightly controlled conditions; that is, a few registered nurses responsible for implementing SimPres were highly trained in the use of the intervention, each resident was selectively screened for having a strong interactive capacity, and individual treatment plans were developed for each resident in the study so that the intervention was presented at times associated with specific predictable behaviors. Moreover, responses were assessed by the nurses who provided the intervention and therefore were not blinded.

## Demonstration Study: Evaluating the Impact of Family-Made SimPres Tapes

A demonstration study was implemented to more rigorously assess the observations made in the pilot studies. Its goals included assessing statistical confidence in observations by studying a larger sample, and assessing effects of SimPres compared with other interventions. This research was designed as a multisite study, based on a Latin-squares design; included a placebo treatment; and used observational measures that were collected by nonparticipant raters. Although the sample size was increased from previous pilot work ($N = 54$), screening criteria were loosened somewhat, allowing study subjects to be more cognitively impaired than previously. Cognitive tests indicated that subjects were severely cognitively impaired (mean Mini-Mental State Examination score 5.1 out of a maximum of 30 [Folstein, Folstein, & McHugh, 1975]), although all subjects could speak and were ambulatory. A common protocol for family-made SimPres audiotapes was implemented. Among nine study sites were 15 individual units (nine Alzheimer's disease special care units, four dementia units, and two mixed units).

Subject acceptance of the intervention was high. Twenty-three subjects (43%) accepted the intervention 100% of the time; only five subjects (9%) refused it more than 50% of the time. Several measures indicated that SimPres was superior to placebo and at least equal to usual care in improving behavioral manifestations of psychological well-being. For example, study subjects were observed with happy expressions at a statistically significant higher rate with SimPres than with placebo. In addition, staff reported that SimPres reduced agitation at a rate 14% greater than usual care and 46% greater than the placebo ($p < .001$). Withdrawn behavior was reduced with SimPres 25% more often than with usual care and at double the rate of the placebo ($p < .001$).

## Family-Training Evaluation

One of the weaknesses of the demonstration study described was the fact that the tape-making procedure, although standardized, did not account for differences in the skills of family callers and the need for more training and practice by some of them. Although a SimPres tape can be produced with input from families and SimPres staff making the call, the potential benefit of the intervention may be optimized if a family member is the designated caller.

Research was conducted to assess variation in caller skill levels and the potential to train family callers to present identified long-term memories in a warm and engaging manner. Trained tape raters, blinded to the type of tape, judged the caller's conversational skills for predetermined performance criteria. Case reports of family and trainer experiences were analyzed with qualitative methods. Finally, characteristics of callers were correlated with communication ability.

The study found that positive communication skills that are used for SimPres are generally not used by family members because they are not aware of these skills, and they believe that their loved one would not be responsive. This self-fulfilling prophecy was challenged by the experience of several family members in the training program study.

One example of this situation is a 78-year-old woman with Alzheimer's disease living in an assisted-living setting. Her cognitive level as measured by the Mini-Mental State Examination is quite low, with a score of 8 (maximum 30). When the designated caller, her daughter, first spoke with SimPres staff, she described her mother as being anxious, lost, worried, and confused. The daughter also was skeptical of her mother's ability to relate to SimPres. She commented,

> She can't carry on a conversation. She may say "yes" or "no" and "I love you." She knows me. We have the same conversation every time—talking about the weather and telling her I love her. You won't get much a response from her.

Once the daughter had completed her training and created her SimPres conversation, her comments reflected the cognitive dissonance she experienced based on her original assumptions and the results she observed:

> I am surprised she stayed on the phone for that long of a period. It is obvious that she is still enthralled with some of the memories. The memories can still connect her to some special times. I am amazed.

The family training study demonstrated the feasibility of training callers, with relatively little time, effort, and cost, to make successful SimPres audiotapes. Evaluation scores, on average, tripled after training. No specific demographic characteristics predicted callers' abilities to make a high-quality tape.

## ☐ Conclusion

The SimPres innovation is based on the premise that positive preserved memory and positive emotions are the most valuable assets of individuals with dementia, and their presentation by a beloved family member has the greatest therapeutic potential to enhance well-being and resolve problem behaviors. Because the individual with dementia is unable to connect with the usual environment, initiate meaningful activities, or hold onto new information, most interventions are unsuccessful or only momentarily successful. The SimPres innovation fills a void with positive personal memories and positive emotions that can be repeated over and over. Future directions for SimPres include applying the intervention in the at-home setting and studying the potential for SimPres to reduce the need for behavior-related medications.

# ☐ References

Beebe, L., & Giles, H. (1984). Speech-accommodation theories: A discussion in terms of second-language aquisition. *International Journal of the Sociology of Language, 46*, 5–32.

Bourgeois, M. S. (1990). Enhancing conversation skills in patients with Alzheimer's disease using a prosthetic memory aid. *Journal of Applied Behavioral Analysis, 23*, 29–42.

Bourgeois, M. S. (1992). Evaluating memory wallets in conversations with persons with dementia. *Journal of Speech and Hearing Research, 35*, 134–135.

Buckwalter, K. C., Gerdner, L. A., Hall, G. R., Stolley, J. M., Kudart, P., & Ridgeway, S. (1995). The humor and individuality of persons with Alzheimer's disease. *Journal of Gerontological Nursing, 20*, 11–15.

Burgener, S., & Chiverton, P. (1992). Conceptualizing psychological well-being in cognitively impaired older persons. *Image, 24*, 209–215.

Burgio, L., Scilley, J., Hardin, M., Hsu, C., & Yancey, J. (1996). Environmental "white noise": An intervention for verbally agitated nursing home residents. *Journal of Gerontology, 51B*, 364–373.

Butler, R. (1961). The life review: an interpretation of reminiscence in the aged. *Psychiatry, 26*, 65–76.

Camberg, L., Woods, P., Ooi ,W. L., Hurley, A., Volicer, L., Ashley, J., Odenheimer, G., & McIntyre K. (1999). Evaluation of Simulated Presence: A personalized approach to enhance well-being in persons with Alzheimer's disease. *Journal of the American Geriatric Society, 47*, 446–452.

Caroff, P., & Dobrof, R. (1974). Social work: Its institutional role. In B. Schoenberg (Ed.), *Anticipation of grief.* New York: Columbia University Press.

Ebersole, P. (1978). Establishing reminiscence groups. In I. Burnside (Ed.), *Working with the elderly: Group processes and techniques.* New York: Duxbury Press.

Folstein, M., Folstein, S., & McHugh, P. (1975). Mini-mental state a practical method for grading the cognitive state of patients for the clinician. *Journal of Psychiatric Research, 12*, 189–198.

Goldwasser, A., Auerbach, S., & Harkins, S. (1987) Cognitive, affective, and behavioral effects of reminiscence group therapy on demented elderly. *International Journal of Aging and Human Development, 25*, 209–222.

Hall, G., & Buchwalter, K. (1991). Progressively lowered stress threshold: A conceptual model for care of adults with Alzheimer's disease. *Archives of Psychiatric Nursing, 122*, 399–406.

Heine, C. A. (1986). Burnout among nursing home personnel. Journal of *Gerontological Nursing, 12*(3), 14–18.

Kemper, S., Anagnapoulos, C., Lyons, K., & Heberlein, W. (1994). Speech accomodations to dementia. *Journal of Gerontology, 49*, 223–229.

Linsk, N. L., Keigher, S. M. & Osterbusch, S. E. (1988). States' policies regarding paid family caregiving. *Gerontologist, 28*, 204–212.

Lund, D. A., Hill, R. D., Caserta, M. S., & Wright, S. D. (1995). Video respite: An innovative resource for family, professional caregivers, and persons with dementia. *The Gerontologist, 35,* 683–687.

McIntyre, K., & Woods, P. (1998). Linking technology and preserved memories for dementia: Phase I Final Report (NIA 1 R41 AG014292-DIAI).

Mintzer, J.E., Lewis, L., Pennypaker, L., Simpson, W., Bachman, D., Wohlreich, G., Meeks, A., Hunt, S., & Sampson, R (1993). Behavioral intensive care unit: A new concept in the management of acute agitated behavior in elderly demented patients. *The Gerontologist, 33,* 801–806.

Namazi, K., & Haynes, S. (1994). Sensory stimuli reminiscence for patients with Alzheimer's disease: Relevance and implications. *Clinical Gerontologist, 14,* 29–46.

Rentz, C. (1995). Reminiscence: A supportive intervention for the person with Alzheimer's disease. *Journal of Psychosocial Nursing & Mental Health Services, 33*(11), 15–20.

Ryden, M., & Feldt, K. S. (1992). Goal-directed care: Caring for aggressive nursing home residents with dementia. *Journal of Gerontological Nursing, 18,* 35–42.

Sandel, S. (1978). Reminiscence in movement therapy with the aged. *Art Psychotherapy, 5,* 217–221.

Smith, K., & Bengston, V. (1979). Positive consequences of instiutionalizations: Solidarity between elderly parents and their middle-aged children. *The Gerontologist, 4,* 438–447.

Smith, R. T. (1979). Rehabilitation of the disabled: The role of social networks in the recovery process. *International Rehabilitation Medicine, 1*(2), 63–72.

Tannen, D. (1986). *That's not what I meant!* New York: Ballantine Books.

Waters, G., Caplan, D., & Rochon, E. (1995). Processing capacity and sentence comprehension in patients with Alzheimer's disease. *Cognitive Neuropsychology, 12*(1), 1–30.

Wingfield, A., Lahar, C., & Stine, E. (1989) Age and decision strategies in running memory for speech: Effects of prosody and linguistic structure. *Journal of Gerontology, 44,* 106–113.

Woods, P., & Ashley J. (1995). Simulated presence therapy: Using selected memories to manage problem behaviors in Alzheimer's disease patients. *Geriatric Nursing, 16,* 9–14.

Wright, L. (1991). The impact of Alzheimer's disease on the marital relationship. *The Gerontologist, 31,* 224–237.

York, J., & Calsyn, R. (1977). Family involvement in nursing homes. *Gerontologist, 17,* 500–505.

CHAPTER

**9**

Suzanne B. Hanser

# Music Therapy with Individuals with Advanced Dementia

This chapter is dedicated to Johnny J, a gentleman who spent the last years of his life in the Alzheimer Unit of a Veterans hospital in California. Mr. J taught me about the importance of maintaining quality of life through late-stage dementia until the end of life. He showed me the inherent potential in every human being to express one's self in a unique and creative way if only we are given the means. Through him, I was inspired to learn more about the nature of human interaction and the need to communicate beyond words. He helped me see how music therapy facilitates experiencing life more fully just when that life appears empty and void on the surface. Mr. J gave me courage to expect more and explore more of who he was just when others were giving up on him.

The chapter follows the journey of Mr. J and others like him as they enhance their quality of life through music therapy. It examines the theories and functions of music therapy and presents a body of research supporting its use. It describes specific techniques that have been applied successfully with individuals who have advanced dementia. The chapter addresses both individual and group strategies as well as the inclusion of family caregivers in sessions. It provides case examples to illustrate different interventions, bringing a clearer sense of their impact. It attempts to introduce the reader to the potential of music to affect the lives of people with advanced dementia and their families.

> Mr. J had not spoken comprehensible words in many months. He became increasingly withdrawn on the unit and showed no interest in socializing

or participating in activities. As he isolated himself increasingly, he reacted to few stimuli, showing only apathy. When introduced to his first music-therapy session, he began vocalizing as the group started singing and waved his arms in rhythm to the music. Mr. J smiled and opened his eyes when asked to strum the autoharp. He laughed as he felt the vibrations and hummed in tune to the chords. When the therapist demonstrated other instruments, he reached out for them. He tapped his toes in rhythm and responded happily with every new song. When his wife discovered him in the music-therapy group on a visit one day, she started crying uncontrollably, saying that she had not seen him so alive in months.

Anecdotes like these are common in long-term care settings for individuals with dementia. In fact, there is considerable evidence that music therapy may affect behavior in many positive ways, and dramatically in people who respond to little else. Many individuals with advanced dementia who have closed themselves to the outside world appear to find a door to express themselves through music. Others who are agitated or anxious find a familiar, restful place when listening to music.

It may be said that music therapy for those in stages of advanced dementia involves the process of finding the "music within" the person. If a connection is made with someone like Mr. J who cannot communicate in a coherent manner, humming and toe tapping show that he is receiving environmental stimuli. Music sparks this connection and draws attention to the external world. When meaningful music cues associations and memories, it coaxes an apathetic or withdrawn individual to respond. For someone with impulsive tendencies, it may transform inappropriate behaviors into active, creative ones. The following is a case that illustrates this phenomenon.

Mrs. M was known to dash out of her room without warning or observable provocation. Nearly every day in the late afternoon, she would head directly for the exit, awaiting the next visitor to facilitate her escape. It was difficult for staff to direct her back to the day room where patients assembled because Mrs. M avoided others and often became belligerent when they approached her. She had resisted the invitation of the music therapist and other staff to attend activities.

One day, the music therapist came out with her flute and started playing in the corridor. As she walked down the hallway, beckoning others to follow (purely coincidental to the Pied Piper), the group made their way to the music room. When they arrived, Mrs. M had joined in and seated herself near the door. She remained for the entire session, participating actively throughout. The therapist made a habit of playing the flute, drum, or recorder outside the music room, and Mrs. M consistently was attracted to the sound. Later, staff used headphones with recorded flute music to calm Mrs. M in the late afternoon. Wearing the headphones, she would wander the halls but did not hover by the exit, nor did she elope if visitors came in.

Her disposition was quite pleasant while listening to the music, and she never showed signs of anger so common at this time of day.

For Mrs. M, her attraction to music seemed to evoke a change in mood and a distraction from the exit. The impulsiveness that she demonstrated when she bolted out of her room was channeled into more acceptable use of her energy during music therapy. Furthermore, the enticement of the therapist's flute generalized to the recording, evoking calm during the sundowning period of late afternoon. Not only did Mrs. M show interest in the music-therapy sessions, but her attention was focused on the appropriate tasks for the duration of the session. Certainly, the therapist had identified the type of music that was able to reach Mrs. M. and hold some meaning for her.

Finding the music that evokes positive responses is one of the first challenges in the therapy process. But music means many things. Music therapists use a variety of musical stimuli, which ranges from passive listening to sophisticated performance or analysis of music. They may use any performance medium, including traditional musical instruments and synthesized music via modern technology. Any genre may be appropriate, depending upon the taste, history, and preferences of the individual. A group of people may be engaged actively in making or creating music through such techniques as improvisation, accompanying, or ensemble playing. At the other extreme, individuals may relax and change their moods quickly just by passively listening. They may discuss memories evoked by the music, eliciting a sense of competence when reminiscing coherently about a meaningful time of life. Music therapists use composition techniques to help individuals with dementia or their families to express their ideas and feelings through songwriting. In all of these examples, however, people are involved in a nonverbal process that evokes a change in behavior or affect. Often, it focuses on the mastery of a skill or mode of expression. Fortunately, therapeutic music activities do not require complex cognitive functioning and demand only those behaviors that the individual is capable of performing successfully. In this way, musical expression or reception allows the person to explore new behaviors without risking failure.

Music therapy is the application of specific music techniques to meet physical, social, emotional, and psychological goals and objectives. Music therapists become qualified to practice in the United States if they have obtained a music-therapy degree from an approved college, completed an approved clinical internship, and passed a board certification examination. Because every person responds to some type of music, referral to music therapy may be considered for almost anyone. The music therapist, upon consultation with health professionals on the team, determines whether group therapy, individual work, or a bedside approach is most appropriate and what type of techniques will meet the person's needs. Although music therapy may be less effective in general for persons with hearing difficulties, many rhythmic improvisation and drumming activities still may be enjoyed and appreciated by people with the most severe hearing loss. As music is universal in its appeal, music therapy offers a viable methodology for individuals regardless of their functional abilities. An opportunity to sample music therapy may give the best indication of its potential effectiveness for a given individual.

Clearly, through music therapy, Mrs. M found a more appropriate way to relate to others and experience a sense of calm. Her ability to participate in a session without showing agitation or anger was testimony to the positive connection that she was able to make with music. Mr. J found a way to feel new feelings and demonstrate that he was more aware of his environment than others could tell. His toe tapping and vocalizing showed a degree of receptive language that could not be assessed otherwise. His emotional expressiveness, rarely seen in other situations, displayed the preserved abilities that Mr. J held that he had had neither reason nor opportunity to perform. The impact of this music-therapy session on Mrs. J was obvious in her commentary; the effect on her husband was evident to unit staff members when they, along with Mrs. J, witnessed an indication of the vitality that Mr. J was capable of feeling. Music made a difference in the way these people interacted with the world, and one could venture to say that it had positive impact on the quality of their lives.

## ☐ Music-Therapy Research

Music therapists work with people suffering from dementia caused by Alzheimer's disease, Parkinson's disease, AIDS, alcohol abuse, and other related disorders. Clinical outcomes are demonstrated in a growing research base, which documents the anecdotal evidence and provides empirical support for these observations. In a review of the literature on music and dementia, Brotons, Koger, and Pickett-Cooper (1997) discuss an impressive number of studies that demonstrate the wide applicability and efficacy of music therapy. The authors examined 69 studies that were published in the 10 years prior to their review. Kneafsey (1997) also presents recent clinical studies on the effect of music on older adults.

One of the unique features of music therapy is that it is used to build new skills as well as decrease undesirable behavior. Music therapy has been used to improve reality orientation (Riegler, 1980), socialization (Pollack & Namazi, 1992), face-name recognition (Carruth, 1997), and cognition (Smith, 1986). There are a number of studies that report increases in involvement in music activities (Christie, 1992; Clair & Bernstein, 1990a, b; Kovach & Henschel, 1996; Smith-Marchese, 1994). Overall quality of life is addressed in case studies by Lipe (1991).

Music-therapy strategies effectively have managed varied disruptive and inappropriate behaviors. If combined with behavioral techniques, they may be particularly efficient (Smith, 1990). According to Volicer, Hurley, and Mahoney (1998), the secondary symptoms of advanced progressive dementia are characterized by delusions and hallucinations, depression, functional impairment, anxiety, spatial disorientation, inability to initiate meaningful activities, dependence in activities of daily living, resistiveness or combativeness, agitation or apathy, and elopement and interference with other patients. Fortunately, music has been successful in managing many of these behaviors, including repetitive disruptive vocalizations (Casby & Holm, 1994), and reducing aggression during bathing (Thomas, Heitman, & Alexander, 1997). There are also music-therapy strategies to enhance sleep (Lindenmuth, Patel, & Chang, 1992), decrease overall agitation (Brotons & Pickett-Cooper, 1996; Clair & Bernstein, 1994; Gerdner & Swanson, 1993; Goddaer & Abraham, 1994; Tabloski, McKinnon-Howe, & Remington, 1995; Ward, Los Kamp, & Newman, 1996), and reduce wandering (Fitzgerald-Cloutier, 1992; Groene, 1993).

The aforementioned studies apply a variety of music-therapy techniques to meet specific objectives. Although there is considerable evidence of the efficacy of these strategies as a whole, it is not yet possible to provide a prescriptive paradigm that matches music-therapy strategies to individualized objectives. One reason for this is that the selection of techniques is based on assessment of the functional capacity and musical preference of every individual. Given the diversity of musical taste and ability, there is simply no piece of music that can be predicted to have a certain effect on an individual. Likewise, no particular musical activity will succeed in meeting a specific objective if the person cannot master the steps necessary to perform the task. Thus, the music therapist is engaged in an ongoing process of assessment and observation as new techniques are introduced and tested through the course of therapy.

## ☐ Background Music

Given the uniqueness and complexity of everyone's response to music, it is remarkable that several research studies have uncovered significant effects of prerecorded music on such behaviors as agitation and disruptiveness (Gaebler & Hemsley, 1991; Norberg, Melin, & Asplund, 1986; Sambandham & Schirm, 1995). Yet a study by Cohen-Mansfield and Werner (1997) points out the added efficacy of social interaction. They recommend interactive activities that provide more stimulation and meaning. This advice is consistent with the approach of music therapists who emphasize the importance of the therapeutic relationship and individual or group process in bringing music into the person's life.

Nevertheless, background music does have this ability to change the mood of the listening audience. It is, therefore, incumbent upon the person who decides to turn on the music to heed certain caveats. First of all, the music may be a noxious stimulus to anyone who does not like the particular selection that is playing. For people with dementia, this additional source of external sound easily may confuse or disturb. It is important to remember that music is affecting everyone who hears it. It is too easily imposed on persons who have no control over the selection or volume of music. Therefore, respecting a person's right to a pleasant environment as the person defines it is foremost in determining whether or not music is to be played. Conversely, "turning on the music" does not equate with "tuning into the music." Part of the music therapist's job is to help people focus and attend. Having music in the background teaches the opposite as people habituate to it, minimizing its effects.

Once it is determined that music is to be played, individual preference is one of the most critical factors in deciding what type of music to apply. The isoprinciple, established long ago for the use of music in hospitals (Taylor, 1981), states that the mood of the person should be matched with the music, and musical elements, such as tempo and dynamics, then may be changed to elicit a more stimulating or sedative effect in the listener. The principle purports that as the music itself changes, the psychological and physiological states of the person move in correspondence. Unfortunately, this idea may be overly simplistic. In one experiment, the author researched the function of the various musical elements, hypothesizing that music that was progressively slower, softer, and less complex in timbre would relax the listener more than music that moved faster and became louder and more complex in overtones (Hanser, 1997). She composed a simple melody and electronically varied the elements in three ways. The first recording started at a given tempo and doubled in speed over a 10-minute period. Dynamic level became gradually louder, and the timbre began with a pure tone and slowly added more overtones to the series. The second recording was of the same melody, but the dynamics and tempo started where the first recording ended, and the piece became slower and softer until it reached the levels at which the first recording began. Similarly, the timbre of the second recording started with a complex series of overtones and resolved over time into a pure tone. Galvanic skin response, heart rate, and blood pressure were measured in adult volunteers who listened to both recordings in a counterbalanced design to control for order effects. The physiological responses of the listeners of the two recordings were remarkably similar, showing no differential effects. However, when queried after the experiment, listeners who reported that they liked the music showed lower mean heart rate and blood pressure than those who did not like the music.

This result supports the conclusion that preference is far more important than structural elements of music. For that reason, determining the taste and preferences of the patient is an important part of the therapy process. It also means that it is impossible to prescribe a particular piece of music to achieve a desired outcome.

## ☐ Preserved Musical Abilities

There is another widely discussed phenomenon that has both anecdotal and clinical evidence to support its existence. That musical ability is preserved well into the course of progressive dementia has been observed in many cases. In one study, pianistic ability was attributed to an intact remote procedural memory (Crystal, Grober, & Masur, 1989). Other researchers pose theories to account for the ability to retain such complex functions after simpler tasks are lost. Neurological data support the theory that people with Alzheimer's disease may use different strategies to process musical stimuli (Swartz, Hantz, Crummer, Walton, & Frisina, 1989; Swartz, Walton, Crummer, Hantz, & Frisina, 1992; Walton , Frisina, Swartz, Hantz, & Crummer, 1988). Beatty and colleagues (Beatty et al., 1988, 1994; Beatty, Brumback, & Vansattel, 1997) suggest that there may be enhanced access to semantic memory or disproportionate impairment of right-hemispheric function in these patients.

For many with dementia, rhythmic abilities are maintained in the latest stages. It may be easier to process music because of the continuous, predictable rhythm that is a vital part of it. Individuals with severe dementia can play synchronously to the rhythm of a piece of music, especially if playing with others. This is known as the ability to entrain. With physical and verbal guidance, many individuals are able to maintain a steady drum beat after most other functional skills are lost (Clair, Bernstein, & Johnson, 1995).

The tendency for music to elicit emotional responses well into advanced dementia shows still another way that music continues to be processed. Meaningful music triggers functional activity and the display of emotions connected with early memories, spiritual experiences, and other associations (Clair & Bernstein, 1990b; Dietsche & Pollmann, 1982; Sacks & Tomaino, 1991).

## ☐  Music-Therapy Assessment

Referral to music therapy may be for the objectives mentioned previously, or it may be to enhance overall quality of life. When a referral is made, the care plan and patient expectations should articulate the role of music therapy. If a particular need is to be addressed, an assessment of the current behavior or level of functioning establishes a baseline for comparison with treatment conditions. Procedures for defining behaviors, setting objectives, and observing behaviors appear in other work by the author (Hanser, 1987). Previous musical experience is not required. In fact, Lipe (1995) discovered that musical background was unrelated to music-therapy task performance when she assessed persons with dementia.

To determine the appropriate music-therapy intervention, a thorough assessment of the individual's abilities and interests is essential to the process. York (1994) has provided a useful assessment through her Residual Music Skills Test, which is highly correlated with the Mini-Mental State Examination (Folstein, Folstein, & McHugh, 1975). The Residual Music Skills Test consists of items that test song recall, instrument identification, tonal memory, recall of instrument names, and musical language. These include such tasks as singing words to familiar songs, performing rhythmic patterns, and discriminating the sounds of different instruments. Responses on this test assist the music therapist in generating reasonable expectations about the kinds of musical tasks that can be mastered and performed successfully. Perhaps more importantly, skills that have been lost will not be demanded in therapy sessions.

A second source of significant background information is the musical taste and preference of the individual. In most cases, these data are best collected by family members or other informants who have known the person. Elements of an interview are as follows:

> Musical history and previous study
> Musical elements
> > Genre
> > Style
> Favorites
> > Artists
> > Performing groups
> > Radio stations
> > Instruments
> Meaningful music
> Cultural background

Through this process, the therapist seeks to identify the person's history and previous study based on such experiences as religious or community choir participation; concert attendance; ensemble, theater, or dance involvement; and instrumental or vocal music instruction (Hanser, 1996). Next, favorite musical genres, styles, artists, groups, radio stations, and instruments are elicited. The therapist attempts to find music that was played at important life events, such as weddings or religious services, and music that the person used to relax or enjoyed most. If the person or family members have played or sung, it is useful to identify the pieces. The therapist asks the informant to locate favorite recordings, if possible, and to bring them in for sessions. The therapist also takes into account the person's cultural, ethnic, and religious background and compiles a list of music to test. In the absence of an informant, music popular during the person's early adulthood may be advisable (Gibbons, 1977).

Via recording and live presentation if feasible, the music therapist plays several selections for the person, carefully watching for reactions. In most cases, observable behaviors are evident with music that carries the most personal significance. Immediate and spontaneous behaviors, such as vocalizing, humming, waving of arms, head swaying, drumming of the fingers, moving feet and legs, and raising eyebrows, give clues that this music will prompt new responses and may change mood. This last step in the assessment is all important, as previously appreciated music may not always evoke the same responses. For Mr. P, this was the case.

> The music therapist on an Alzheimer's disease unit was delighted to hear that Mr. P had been a trumpet player who enjoyed performing at local nightclubs. Mr. P could not name the pieces he once played but reminisced about meeting famous jazz players and the exciting nightlife surrounding his many "gigs." After considerable searching, the therapist found a recording of Dixieland jazz that she thought Mr. P would like. She played it for the group, expecting that Mr. P would feel great pride. His reaction was quite the reverse. He started crying hysterically and stormed out of the room. It took the staff several minutes to calm him.

This example shows the immense power that music can have. This music had tremendous impact on Mr. P, but the outcome was an upsetting one. Although it is always difficult to predict behavior, had the music therapist played this music for Mr. P alone during an assessment, she might have learned that the music could have such an effect. The music might have triggered a great loss for Mr. P, or it could have been associated with negative feelings about his career. The therapist could have helped him process his response in a safe, protected manner, allowing him the opportunity to express his feelings while she supported his sadness or grief, empathizing along the way.

This case raises another issue regarding referral to music therapy. It is not always the musician who benefits most from music therapy, for music may arouse unresolved questions or inadequacies in one whose identity is associated strongly with music. In this situation, styles of music that are different from those that were performed may provide a better expressive outlet. For the amateur musician or audience member, music is usually more benign and brings thoughts and feelings that are outside of the realm of one's professional life.

This is another rationale for a thorough assessment that takes into account the person's history with music as well as taste and preference. Not only is it helpful in preparing the kind of music to include in a session, but it also assists in selecting tasks that can be mastered successfully and experiences that evoke positive associations.

## ☐  Music-Therapy Techniques

Presenting overviews of some of the music-therapy techniques that have been implemented with people with advanced dementia, this section focuses on guidelines for group sessions using singing, movement, performance on melodic or rhythmic instruments, improvisation, songwriting, and stress-reduction techniques. Readers who wish to learn specific activities are referred to the bibliography at the end of this chapter. Most of these sources detail procedures and accompanying music for program planning.

This section also outlines the use of music therapy for behavior management of individuals and discusses how family caregivers may be included in the therapy. Finally, the role of music therapy at the end of life is presented.

### Group Music Therapy

After completing the assessment, the music therapist is ready to place the person in group or individual therapy. Group therapy holds certain advantages in addition to efficiency, particularly in the areas of socialization and stimulation. Persons with differing levels of functioning may participate at their own levels in groups. But the number of individuals with disruptive behaviors must be taken into account, so that all group members may benefit from the session. Fortunately, if persons are engaged in purposeful, successful experiences, disruptive behavior is minimized; however, behavior-management strategies may be necessary to keep the group on task and involved.

Each group session should be structured in a regular, predictable fashion. This section of the chapter starts with a recommended format and provides examples of activities that incorporate singing, movement, performance on melodic and rhythmic instruments, improvisation, songwriting, and stress reduction.

## Recommended Format

The following is a simple order of activities, following a traditional "sonata form." This includes an introduction, exposition or theme, development, recapitulation, and coda or closing. Other examples of session formats appear in Hanser and Clair (1995).

**Part I: Introduction.**   Participants are welcomed with a song or chant that incorporates their names. Group members participate in singing along as they are able. The greeting may be sung to a familiar tune such as "Good-night, Ladies" or chanted. A "rondo" form (ABACA) is useful for this initial activity, in which a theme chant (A) is introduced. An example is: "Tell us your name and we'll all have a good time" (A). The therapist shakes hands with the first person and chants, "Here's Mr. [name], and we'll all have a good time" (B). The chant is repeated by the entire group (A). The next participant is greeted in the same way (C). The chant is spoken again (A), and the rondo continues around the circle until everyone is greeted.

This rondo form creates opportunities to repeat a simple phrase in a predictable rhythmic pattern. It allows participants to participate with few demands placed on them. They may chant along, greet others, or simply listen as the others chant. They may shake hands or merely look at the therapist if they are capable of providing eye contact.

**Part II: Exposition.**   The theme of the session is introduced. Group goals and objectives are based on the needs of the individuals as stated in their care plans. Activities are provided to offer opportunities for successful expression of targeted responses. Any musical medium may be used. Singing offers an expressive outlet; movement provides stimulation and exercise to improve balance, coordination, and body awareness; dancing allows for appropriate social interaction; rhythmic activities aim to increase attention and focus; improvisation promotes nonverbal communication; performing on musical instruments may support self-esteem; writing songs helps to communicate unspoken ideas and feelings; and music listening may affect a positive mood change.

**Part III: Development.**   This activity takes the theme one step further and develops it. Often, a passive activity is followed by an active one, or vice versa. If the previous activity involved singing a popular song, this activity may ask the group to provide rhythmic accompaniment. If the theme activity included whole-body movement, this one might try to help the participants cool down slowly by listening and waving the arms only.

**Part IV: Recapitulation.**  This part of the session is designed to ensure mastery. Having observed exactly what behaviors were competently performed by group members in the early part of the session, the therapist is now aware of these competencies. During this part, the therapist provides opportunities for each group member to repeat that performance. This may be a chance to solo on part of a song, provide the same rhythmic accompaniment previously practiced, move to the music in a certain way, or do whatever was modeled earlier.

**Part V: Coda.**  This activity provides closure for the end of the session. It is recommended that the same song or activity be performed each time at this point so that there is a better chance that it will become familiar and predictable. Popular activities include the word "good-bye" or some clear cue for ending. Sometimes this is best performed as a transitional activity for the next program. Marching (or wheeling) out of the room may be done with musical or singing accompaniment to facilitate the movement of the group into another room or prepare them for the next activity of the day.

## Singing

> Ms. L had stopped speaking and spent her time in bed unless the staff of the nursing home wheeled her out into the living-room area. There, she stared off, unresponsive to the presence or conversation of staff or visiting family members. Neither books, photographs, nor television interested her, and she completely ignored attempts to attract her attention with something new. When Ms. L was referred to music therapy for sensory stimulation, the therapist learned that she had grown up in an Orthodox Jewish section of Brooklyn, New York, and later became active in her local reform temple.
>
> She was wheeled into her first music-therapy session the week before Passover. Appropriate for this time of year, the therapist began singing a traditional melody, "Dayeinu." When she came to the chorus, Ms. L began to mouth the words and then opened her eyes wide and started singing, louder and louder, "Day, day-ei-nu, day day-ei-nu, day day-ei-nu, day-ei-nu day-ei-nu!" Applause broke out from the group and the nursing staff members exclaimed that there was a sparkle in Ms. L's eyes that they had not seen before.

Singing sometimes brings out the best in a person. Remembrance of a special or familiar song may not be as dramatic as in the example of Ms. L, but it typically elicits a sense of joy or at least a smile. Prickett and Moore (1991) documented that sung material was recalled more effectively than spoken material in their experiment with patients diagnosed with probable Alzheimer's disease. Familiar songs were recalled more accurately than new songs, but surprisingly, several patients were able to learn new material as well. Millard and Smith (1989) demonstrated that patients with Alzheimer's disease participated more vocally and verbally and remained in their seats if singing in a group as opposed to being engaged in a similar nonmusic activity. Clair (1996) reports that singing evoked eye contact, vocalization, body movements, and changing facial expression in people with advanced dementia.

Moore, Staum, and Brotons (1992) offer important guidelines for singing activities. Their research shows that the most comfortable singing range for older men is from the second G-sharp below middle C to the D above middle C. Women's vocal range spans from F below middle C to one octave above middle C. Older adults prefer patriotic songs, hymns, and popular music with a slow tempo, and choose live or recorded chordal accompaniment over recorded melodic line or electronic keyboard accompaniments.

Table 9.1 displays sample vocal tasks in a hierarchy of successively more demanding skills. This chart shows the many acceptable responses that each member of a group may give during a singing activity. The responses range from listening to a familiar song to singing a solo and illustrate the many competencies that are demonstrated while singing. Beyond these skills are such activities as discussing the song and the memories it evokes, accompanying music with rhythm instruments, applying hand movements, acting out parts of the song, conducting the group, and pointing to the words on a large poster. But the key to a successful activity is simplicity and mastery, and so these enhancements may be superfluous.

Several songbooks are listed in the bibliography, including *So Much More than a Sing-a-long* (Wenrick, 1996). Many of these references include creative ways to sing, accompany, and fully experience the songs.

## Movement

Mrs. G had not danced with her husband in many years. Now in a long-term care facility, Mr. G had trouble walking and no longer recognized his wife. They had enjoyed dancing when they first married, but now Mr. G was clumsy and awkward and showed no interest towards his wife when she visited. The music therapist had set up refreshments and was playing some music by the big bands. Immediately, Mr. G swooped up his wife, and they danced cheek to cheek for the next hour. His ease and grace was dis-

**TABLE 9.1. Hierarchy of progressively demanding vocal tasks**

→

| | Requiring Hearing Ability | Requiring Ability to Make Vocal Sounds | Requiring Ability to Imitate One Word of Chant | Requiring Ability to Verbalize | | | | | | |
|---|---|---|---|---|---|---|---|---|---|---|
| Music task | Listen to familiar song | Vocalize or hum song | Imitate sounds of chant | Imitate one word of song | Sing one word of song with verbal prompt | Sing one word of song spontaneously | Sing part of phrase with leader or group | Sing part of song with leader or group | Sing phrase solo | Sing song solo |
| Desired outcome | Show any observable response | Show receptive language | Show receptive and expressive language | Show receptive and expressive language | Show imitative ability in song | Perform unaided responses | Show ability to sequence words on cue | | Master independent response and develop self-confidence | Demonstrate self-esteem |

tinctly different from his typical shuffling gait. A stunned Mrs. G remarked that she had not felt that intimacy with her husband since well before he started showing signs of dementia.

This intervention shows the potential for dance not only to facilitate balance and flexibility but also to unite a couple in a natural, intimate way. There is a profession devoted to movement and dance therapy, but dance is so inextricably linked to music that it must be mentioned here in abridged form. People with dementia often display a rigidity in posture, and if they are depressed or apathetic they tend not to move their bodies in functional ways. Dance and movement activities have the ability to free the body in people who are losing their sensory awareness and their relationships to people. It is a medium to improve posture and coordination while exercising the body to promote circulation and health. In advanced stages of dementia in which mobility is limited, wheelchair dancing is sometimes feasible, and exercise, to the extent that it is possible, is indicated. Music adds structure, familiarity, and creativity to movement activities (Watson, 1996; Weisberg & Wilder, 1985). In addition, Shively and Henkin (1986) reveal how agitation and restlessness diminish in groups of people with Alzheimer's disease through creative movement and music.

In a fascinating study, McIntosh, Brown, Rice, and Thaut (1997) used rhythmic auditory stimulation in patients with Parkinson's disease to improve gait speed, cadence, and stride length. This technique was extremely effective, demonstrating that individuals who have basal ganglia dysfunction still may be capable of rhythmic entrainment. Staum (1983) used music successfully in a similar intervention with people who had other gait disorders.

For those in the latest stages of dementia, moving to music may incorporate massage and sensory stimulation with accouterments such as skin creams, cotton, and silk scarves. Stimulating the senses with familiar smells also may promote alertness and responsiveness. It is significant that Hanson, Gfellar, Woodworth, Swanson, and Garand (1996) found that more purposeful responses were observed during movement activities than if group members were singing. But if rhythmic and singing activities placed few demands on participants, these elicited the greatest involvement.

## Performance on Melodic and Rhythmic Instruments

Mrs. H often was seen in her recliner weeping. If anyone tried to console her, she spoke incoherently and was unable to make her needs known. She appeared to be in good physical health but was in an advanced stage of dementia. She was referred to music therapy to lift her mood and provide a positive distraction. Mrs. H did not participate actively in her first music-therapy sessions, but in a subsequent group the music therapist introduced a large tom-tom drum. Mrs. H reached for a mallet and spontaneously started drumming. The therapist drummed along and assisted other group members on their own drums. The therapist introduced new rhythms while Mrs. H kept drumming. Her eyes were focused on the drum, and she played independently in the center of the drum head and with great force. After a few minutes, the therapist cued each participant to stop, physically guiding some of them, and landed a strong down beat in front of Mrs. H to signal the finale. Mrs. H followed with a loud thrash on the drum, raised her hand high, and started giggling, seemingly proud of her new skill.

Mrs. H was engaged in "vibrotactile" drumming, a rhythmic task that involved both touching and feeling the vibrations of the drum. Percussion activities of this sort, especially with large, vibrating drum heads, require few skills on the part of the player and can be mastered with minimal range of motion, gross motor coordination, or muscle strength. A sense of rhythm is a preserved ability in most people with dementia, and the musical outcome of a well-managed percussion group can be very pleasing aesthetically. One approach to leading a successful percussion ensemble is to start with a strong, slow, steady beat; add one instrument at a time; provide obvious cues for starting and stopping; and maintain simple rhythmic patterns.

There appears to be an inherent appeal to these sorts of activities. Clair and Bernstein (1990a, 1993) found that vibrotactile instrument playing evoked more participation than singing in severely regressed persons with dementia. In another study, individuals with Alzheimer's disease were able to participate longer in instrument-playing, dance and movement, and game-playing activities than in composition or improvisation (Brotons & Pickett-Cooper, 1994). Percussion also may be used to accompany group singing or other instruments. Specific group percussion strategies are detailed by Reuer and Crowe (1995).

Thanks to new technology, instrumental performance is much easier. With the Musical Instrument Digital Interface, the music therapist may program music into a synthesizer and create sounds and melodies that may be performed by depressing one or a few keys. The "Anyone Can Play" option on the new Kurzweil synthesizer enables the keyboard player to press any key and only sound keys that are part of a major chord above the depressed bass note, thus sounding harmonious (Kurzweil Music Systems, 1996). Jon Adams's (1996) Switch-Ensemble is computer software that allows any touch to signal the notes of a selected melody.

Traditional performance is also possible for many who have had musical training and maintain this skill. Performing for others and hearing applause can generate a tremendous sense of self-worth and self-esteem. For those who have not had previous training, accompanying a group on an instrument may offer an alternative source of pride. Instruments such as the autoharp are easy to play. It requires depressing a bar and strumming the strings in rhythm. Even a guitar can be tuned to a single chord, and the player can provide an appropriate accompaniment on cue. Using prompts, physical guidance, and verbal cues as required, unsophisticated players may produce a beautiful musical sound.

## Improvisation

Mr. B frequently would lash out physically at others, both staff members and patients, without provocation. He often appeared frightened and would call out, "No!" His apparent hallucinations did not respond to medication, and Mr. B became very difficult to manage. Referred to group music therapy to develop a more acceptable means of social interaction, Mr. B attended weekly sessions. During the assessment, the music therapist learned that he had no living relatives and he was not capable of communicating his musical history or interests. She brought out several songbooks and instruments and experimented with Mr. B. She had tuned a xylophone to the pentatonic (five-note whole-tone) scale. When she placed it before him, Mr. B immediately grasped the mallet and started playing spontaneously. The therapist faced him and played another similarly tuned xylophone with him. Mr. B continued for several minutes, playing some interesting patterns and improvising comfortably. When he slowed and stopped, he looked directly at the therapist and said, "Ya!"

In group music-therapy sessions, Mr. B expressed different musical ideas, at times playing slowly and pensively, and then loud and staccato. He improvised playing opposite other group members without incident. In fact, he would look up during the playing as if to ask, "And what is that you are playing with me?" The music therapist directed the players to shake hands after each improvisation, and Mr. B did so congenially and happily. One staff member commented, "He seems to be seeing others differently now."

This approach to improvisation was developed by Carl Orff and later adapted for music-therapy purposes (Orff, 1980). His method of creating music through basic and familiar ideas such as the descending minor third found in children's early games, the rondo form, rhythmic ostinati (rhythmic patterns that are repeated over and over throughout a piece of music), and use of the pentatonic scales produces a success-oriented formula for creative group expression.

Bruscia (1987) has identified no fewer than 25 methods of improvisation used by music therapists. Many entail the music therapist taking the lead from the client, intuiting the mood, letting the person choose an instrument, and attempting to communicate nonverbally. This type of clinical improvisation has evolved into a sophisticated methodology and has been applied extensively by Lee (1996).

## Songwriting

Mrs. W was near the end of life. The friends and members of her family who gathered at the bedside were either uneasy or distraught. "Are we just waiting here to see her die?" yelled her daughter. As the music therapist entered, he asked if anyone would like to tell him about Mrs. W. Although uncomfortable at first, the daughter volunteered a story about her mother, a fond memory of her baking in the kitchen. That reminded Mrs. W's brother about another time when Mrs. W cooked a magnificent Thanksgiving feast. Soon, the ambiance changed as family members were chatting and laughing.

The therapist said, "Would you help me write a song about this?" He hummed a simple melody and accompanied on guitar. He started, "My mother . . . " The daughter filled in, "was a fabulous cook."

    Therapist: "She always . . . "
    Sister-in-law: "baked"
    Friend: "never by the book."
    Therapist: "The smells in her kitchen were"
    Daughter: "something grand."
    Friend: "And everything was tasty that touched her hand."

The group sang the newly composed song together as the daughter copied the words. Soon, they returned to her bedside and began stroking Mrs. W's, smiling, and talking with her in an animated manner.

On the next day, the daughter pinned a copy of their song to the wall above her mother's bed. She sang it tenderly to her mother.

A song is an aesthetic creation designed to express feelings, thoughts, and experiences. An original song is a lasting memento for communicating something personal, an essence or identity, or a glimpse into a relationship. A skillful therapist helps people find a melody to fit that feeling and the words to capture the significance of a moment.

In an account of their songwriting experience with a patient with Alzheimer's disease, Silber and Hes (1995) describe helping this person communicate and feel pleasure. They conclude that writing songs is a significant way in which to improve the quality of life of an individual with dementia. For nonverbal individuals, music therapists may take familiar tunes and substitute the person's name and descriptions of the person for the existing words. In many instances, unresponsive persons will show signs of recognition and interest when they hear the song.

## Stress Reduction

In the course of 1 month, four patients were referred to music therapy to help manage combativeness, anxiety, agitation, and insomnia, respectively. It was time to establish a stress-reduction group. After assessing each person's musical preferences and history, several recordings were collected. The therapist played excerpts for the group in an attempt to determine which music would be best suited to reduce stress. Although each of the four had distinct taste in terms of musical style (two classical, one country-western, one jazz), several recordings evoked calm responses in the entire group.

The therapist began with gentle movements to the music, stretching and circling motions as the music played. A gentle facial massage came next, and then progressive muscle relaxation, in which the therapist physically assisted each participant in making a fist and flexing the fingers, and then shaking them out and relaxing the muscles of the extremities. The therapist modeled taking deep breaths to the tempo of slow music and moving in an easy, flowing manner to long musical themes.

These techniques have been applied by the author in long-term care settings (Hanser, 1996) and with depressed and anxious older adults in the community (Hanser, 1990). An experiment by Hanser and Thompson (1994) found that depression, distress, and anxiety were reduced significantly through this protocol compared with a no-contact control group. The complete protocol (Hanser, 1996) includes:

- Gentle exercise to familiar music
- Facial massage to familiar music
- Progressive muscle relaxation to music that suggests tension and relaxation
- Guided imagery to programmatic music that transports the listener to a favorite place (recommended for caregivers; contraindicated for those with dementia)
- Individualized special imagery to clear the mind and begin problem solving (recommended for caregivers; contraindicated for those with dementia)
- Music to sleep by—guidelines for identifying music to induce sleep
- Waking up to music—guidelines for identifying music to boost energy
- Making music a part of the day—guidelines for enhancing life through music

Guided imagery and individualized imagery are not feasible with severely cognitively impaired older adults, but the other programs have been quite effective in helping persons with dementia to relax. Guidelines are offered in the protocol for identifying music that produces the desired effects.

## Individual Music Therapy

Six months after his first music-therapy session, Mr. J became immobile and unable to attend the group. The music therapist was able to arrange to come to his bedside. There, she sang some of his favorite songs, placing the autoharp on his lap so that he could feel the vibrations. Singing the next song without accompaniment, she took his arms and gently swayed in rhythm. Mr. J seemed alert and calm. He tapped his fingers to the music. When the therapist left, he fell asleep quickly and slept soundly throughout the night.

For people such as Mr. J who can no longer participate in groups, brief individual sessions are indicated. Here the therapist applies live or recorded music that is familiar and enjoyable to the individual. Any of the techniques described in this chapter may be implemented on an individual basis.

Individual therapy also is called for to manage specific problems or catastrophic behavior. Persons who are difficult to control during activities of daily living may benefit from the distraction of music that captures the attention. Playing music and singing directly to the person while bathing or dressing often distracts from an anxiety-provoking stimulus. Singing along, clapping hands, or moving to music engages the person actively in a positive, functional behavior that is incompatible with inappropriate behavior.

## Music Therapy with Families

Mrs. V had found it difficult to visit her husband. She still felt guilty about placing him in the nursing home. She felt strangely distant towards him, afraid to touch him. She knew he would not recognize her. She wondered why she bothered to visit every day. Of course, she still loved him, but the visits took a toll on her. Her hypertension was exacerbated; she returned home with a headache. She did not know how long she could continue.

The nursing staff suggested that she talk with the music therapist. The therapist interviewed Mrs. V and found out that they had enjoyed musical theater. Mrs. V brought in some of their favorite show recordings and the couple listened to them together. The therapist urged Mrs. V to establish physical contact with her husband by massaging his back and shoulders while they listened together. When she talked with him, Mr. V relaxed and reached out for her hand. Mrs. V was able to feel far more relaxed as well, sensing that she reclaimed a part of the Mr. V who was tender and loving toward her.

The stress and burden of caring for a person with advanced dementia is tremendous. Whether a family member is providing physical care in the home or emotional concern at a distance, the loss of the relationship to a person who cannot communicate is overwhelming. Although there is no way to retrieve the many losses, music therapy attempts to rekindle a connection, however briefly, with loved ones.

Whenever feasible, family members and friends may be invited to partake in music therapy. Because music activities so carefully structure positive interactions, everyone has a chance to create, succeed, and interact through music. Clair, Tebb, and Bernstein (1993) found that family caregivers learned and enjoyed ways to spend time with their loved ones through music therapy.

Family and friends may engage in activities such as any of those discussed in this chapter. In addition, the focus for music therapy may be on restoring shared positive experiences and interacting nonverbally. Any permanent product of music therapy, such as a recording of the music performed in sessions or copies of original songs composed through music therapy, acts as a legacy for significant others.

Intergenerational programs are another way that the youngest and oldest and the most and least capable are able to interact in community. Self-concept and self-esteem have been enhanced through such structured music programs (Newman & Ward, 1993; Ward et al., 1996).

## Music Therapy at the End of Life

Mr. J contracted pneumonia in the winter, and Mrs. J spent much time with him. Mrs. J recalled the way her husband had benefited from music therapy and brought music cassettes from home for the two of them to enjoy together. The music reminded her of stories about friends and family members, holidays and good times. She would talk with her husband about those times, and when she tired, she practiced some of the stress-reduction programs she had learned from the music therapist. When she could sit no longer, she stood up and exercised to the music, and when she felt sad, she sat closer to her husband and massaged his temples.

When the music therapist came in, they sang softly to Mr. J. Mrs. J often would play an accompaniment on the autoharp. In their last session together, Mrs. J composed a song for Mr. J with the help of the music therapist. It was about a bird who came to her window:

Little bird, little bird
You are so bright and blue
I find you in the sunlight
And then I turn to you

But, my dearest husband
You are not here now
You are sleeping soundly
As deep sleep will allow

I miss you, my dearest
Now when the bird is near
I shall always think of you
As though you are right here

It may be said that the greatest benefits of music therapy are experienced without words, and for some in a new or spiritual realm. The meaning of this experience can be understood only by Mrs. J herself.

Several books describe music-therapy techniques for hospice and palliative care (Lane, 1994; Martin, 1991; Munro, 1984). The role of music therapy at the end of life has been addressed by many (Aldridge, 1995; Burns, 1993; Gilbert, 1977; Mandel, 1993; Salmon, 1993; Yamamoto, 1993). The proceedings of the International Conference: Music Therapy in Palliative Care (Lee, 1995) cite cases and theories to support the importance of this work. Remarkably, even comatose patients respond to music (Boyle & Greer, 1983). If familiar recorded music is played contingent upon movement, these motions of the body continue.

Music-therapy methodologies draw upon any medium that can be applied successfully. It is challenging to articulate how music affects a person at the end of life, but there is clear evidence that it can be heard and received, if not acknowledged, in people with advanced dementia.

For a dying person, the music therapist must make choices for the person based on all they know about that person. It is up to the therapist to determine how active the music-making or listening experience should be, what music should be played, and at what volume. The versatile therapist is alert to small cues that reveal that a favorite song is being appreciated or that an improvisation is truly matching the mood of the moment.

Thus, music therapy is a rather intuitive process that attempts to support the person and enhance the overall quality of life. At this point in the lifecycle, it is a nonverbal process that has been likened to the midwife's place at the beginning of life (West, 1994). Family members who participate in music therapy along with their loved ones say that they have difficulty describing the impact of what they experience.

## ☐ Conclusion

As anecdotal evidence of the effects of music therapy builds through stories like the ones presented in this chapter, there is a scientific basis for the application of music therapy to persons with advanced dementia. Yet it is the uniqueness of each person's experience that makes it so meaningful. Indescribable events and peak experiences are challenging to verify scientifically. But, when they occur, they are most certainly related to quality of life.

This chapter attempts to provide an overview of the theory and practice of music therapy and include the state of the research in this area. If it succeeds, it will have encouraged the reader to learn more about the impact of music on behavior and explore the meaning of music in the lives of those with advanced dementia.

# ☐ References

Adams, J. (1996). Switch-ensemble [Computer software]. Boston: Switch-in-Time.

Aldridge, D. (1995). Spirituality, hope and music therapy in palliative care. *Arts in Psychotherapy, 22,* 103–109.

Beatty, W. W., Brumback, R. A., & Vonsattel, J. P. (1997). Autopsy-proven Alzheimer disease in a patient with dementia who retained musical skill in life. *Archives of Neurology, 54,* 1448.

Beatty, W., Winn, P., Adams, R., Allen, E., Wilson, D., Prince, J., Olson, K., Dean, K., & Littleford, D. (1994). Preserved cognitive skills in dementia of the Alzheimer type. *Archives of Neurology, 10,* 158–164.

Beatty, W., Zavadil, K., Bailly, R., Rixen, G., Zavadil, L., Farnham, N., & Fisher, L. (1988). Preserved musical skill in a severely demented patient. *International Journal of Clinical Neuropsychology, 10,* 158–164.

Boyle, M. E., & Greer, R. D. (1983). Operant procedures and the comatose patient. *Journal of Applied Behavior Analysis, 16,* 3–12.

Brotons, M., Koger, S. M., & Pickett-Cooper, P. (1997). Music and the dementias: A review of literature. *Journal of Music Therapy, 34,* 204–245.

Brotons, M., & Pickett-Cooper, P. (1994). Preferences of Alzheimer's disease patients for music activities: Singing, instruments, dance/movement, games, and composition/improvisation. *Journal of Music Therapy, 31,* 220–233.

Brotons, M., & Pickett-Cooper, P. (1996). The effects of music therapy intervention on agitation behaviors of Alzheimer's disease patients. *Journal of Music Therapy, 33,* 2–18.

Bruscia, K. (1987). *Improvisational models of music therapy.* Springfield, IL: Charles Thomas.

Burns, S. (1993). In hospice work, music is our great ally. *Pastoral Music, 17,* 11–13.

Carruth, E. K. (1997). The effects of singing and the spaced retrieval technique on improving face-name recognition in nursing home residents. *Journal of Music Therapy, 34,* 165–186.

Casby, J. A., & Holm, M. B. (1994). The effect of music on repetitive disruptive vocalizations of persons with dementia. *American Journal of Occupational Therapy, 48 ,* 883–889.

Christie, M. E. (1992). Music therapy applications in a skilled and intermediate care nursing home facility: A clinical study. *Activities, Adaptation and Aging, 16,* 69–87.

Clair, A. A. (1996). The effect of singing on alert responses in persons with late stage dementia. *Journal of Music Therapy, 33,* 234–247.

Clair, A. A., & Bernstein, B. (1990a). A comparison of singing, vibrotactile and nonvibrotactile instrumental playing responses in severely regressed persons with dementia of the Alzheimer's type. *Journal of Music Therapy, 27,* 119–125.

Clair, A. A., & Bernstein, B. (1990b). A preliminary study of music therapy programming for severely regressed persons with Alzheimer's type dementia. *Journal of Applied Gerontology, 9,* 299–311.

Clair, A. A., & Bernstein, B. (1993). The preference for vibrotactile versus auditory stimuli in severely regressed persons with dementia of the Alzheimer's type compared to those with dementia due to alcohol abuse. *Music Therapy Perspectives, 11,* 24–27.

Clair, A. A., & Bernstein, B. (1994). The effect of no music, stimulative background music and sedative background music on agitation behaviors in persons with severe dementia. *Activities, Adaptation and Aging, 19 ,* 61–70.

Clair, A. A., Bernstein, B., & Johnson, G. (1995). Rhythm playing characteristics in persons with severe dementia including those with probable Alzheimer's type. *Journal of Music Therapy, 32,* 113–131.

Clair, A. A., Tebb, S., & Bernstein, B. (1993). The effects of socialization and music therapy intervention on self-esteem and loneliness in spouse caregivers of those diagnosed with dementia of the Alzheimer's type: A pilot study. *American Journal of Alzheimer's Disease and Related Disorders and Research, 1,* 24–32.

Mansfield, J., & Werner, P. (1997). Management of verbally disruptive behaviors in nursing home residents. *Journal of Gerontology, 52,* M369–M377.

Crystal, H. A., Grober, E., & Masur, D. (1989). Preservation of musical memory in Alzheimer's disease. *Journal of Neurology, Neurosurgery, and Psychiatry, 52,* 1415–1416.

Dietsche, L. M., & Pollmann, J. N. (1982). Alzheimer's disease: Advances in clinical nursing. *Journal of Gerontological Nursing, 8,* 97–100.

Fitzgerald-Cloutier, M. L. (1992). The use of music therapy to decrease wandering: An alternative to restraints. *Music Therapy Perspectives, 11,* 32–36.

Folstein, M. F., Folstein, S. E., & McHugh, P. R. (1975). Minimental state: A practical method for grading the cognitive state of patients for the clinician. *Journal of Psychiatric Research, 12,* 189–198.

Gaebler, H., & Hemsley, D. (1991). The assessment and short-term manipulation of affect in the severely demented. *Behavioural Psychotherapy, 19,* 145–156.

Gerdner, L. A., & Swanson, E. A. (1993). Effects of individualized music on confused and agitated elderly patients. *Archives of Psychiatric Nursing, 7,* 284–291.

Gibbons, A. C. (1977). Popular music references of elderly people. *Journal of Music Therapy, 30,* 138–157.

Gilbert, J. (1977). Music therapy perspectives on death and dying. *Journal of Music Therapy, 14,* 165–171.

Goddaer, J., & Abraham, I. (1994). Effects of relaxing music on agitation during meals among nursing home residents with severe cognitive impairment. *Archives of Psychiatric Nursing, 8,* 150–158.

Groene, R. W. II. (1993). Effectiveness of music therapy: 1:1 intervention with individuals having senile dementia of the Alzheimer's type. *Journal of Music Therapy, 30,* 138–157.

Hanser, S. B. (1987). *Music therapists handbook.* St. Louis: Warren Green.

Hanser, S. B. (1990). A music therapy strategy for depressed older adults in the community. *Journal of Applied Gerontology, 9,* 283–298.

Hanser, S. B. (1996). Music therapy to reduce anxiety, agitation, and depression. *Nursing Home Medicine, 4,* 20–22.

Hanser, S. B. (1997). *Music therapy for Alzheimer's patients and families. Proceedings of the 1997 Annual Meeting of the American Psychiatric Association.* San Diego, CA: APA.

Hanser, S. B., & Clair, A. A. (1995). Retrieving the losses of Alzheimer's disease for patients and caregivers with the aid of music. In T. Wigram, B. Saperston, & R. West (Eds.), *The art and science of music therapy: A handbook* (pp. 342–360). Chur, Switzerland: Harwood Academic Publishers.

Hanser, S. B., & Thompson, L. W. (1994). Effects of a music therapy strategy on depressed older adults. *Journal of Gerontology, 49,* 265–269.

Hanson, N., Gfeller, K., Woodworth, G., Swanson, E., & Garand, L. (1996). A comparison of the effectiveness of differing types and difficulty of music activities in programming for older adults with Alzheimer's disease and related disorders. *Journal of Music Therapy, 33,* 93–123.

Kneafsey, R. (1997). The therapeutic use of music in a care of the elderly setting: A literature review. *Journal of Clinical Nursing, 6,* 341–346.

Kovach, C., & Henschel, H. (1996). Behavior and participation during therapeutic activities on special care units. *Activities, Adaptation and Aging, 20,* 35–45.

Kurzweil Music Systems. (1996). *Introduction to the Kurzweil Mark 152/12 Ensemble Grand.* Seoul, Korea: Hal Leonard.

Lane, D. (1994). *Music as medicine.* Cleveland, OH: Zondervan Publishing.

Lee, C. A. (Ed.). (1995). *Lonely waters.* Oxford: Sobell Publications.

Lee, C. A. (1996). *Music at the edge: The music therapy experiences of a musician with AIDS.* London: Routledge.

Lindenmuth, G. F., Patel, M., & Chang, P. K. (1992). Effects of music on sleep in healthy elderly and subjects with senile dementia of the Alzheimer type. *American Journal of Alzheimer's Disease and Related Disorders and Research, 2,* 13–20.

Lipe, A. (1991). Using music therapy to enhance the quality of life in a client with Alzheimer's dementia: A case study. *Music Therapy Perspectives, 9,* 102–105.

Lipe, A. (1995). The use on music performance tasks in the assessment of cognitive functioning among older adults with dementia. *Journal of Music Therapy, 32,* 137–151.

Mandel, S. E. (1993). The role of the music therapist on the hospice/palliative care team. *Journal of Palliative Care, 9,* 37–39.

Martin, J. A. (Ed.). (1991). *The next step forward: Music therapy with the terminally ill.* Bronx, NY: Calvary Hospital.

McIntosh, G. C., Brown, S. H., Rice R. R., & Thaut, M. H. (1997). Rhythmic auditory-motor facilitation of gait patterns in patients with Parkinson's disease. *Journal of Neurology, Neurosurgery & Psychiatry, 62,* 22–26.

Millard, K. A. O., & Smith, J. M. (1989). The influence of group singing therapy on the behavior of Alzheimer's disease patients. *Journal of Music Therapy, 26,* 58–70.

Moore, R. S., Staum, M. J., & Brotons, M. (1992). Music preferences of the elderly: Repertoire, vocal ranges, tempos, and accompaniments for singing. *Journal of Music Therapy, 29,* 236–252.

Munro, S. (1984). *Music therapy in palliative/hospice care.* St. Louis, MO: MMB.

Newman, S., & Ward, C. (1993). An observational study of intergenerational activities and behavior change in dementing elders at adult day care centers. *International Journal of Aging and Human Development, 36,* 321–333.

Norberg, A., Melin, E., & Asplund, K. (1986). Reactions to music, touch, and object presentation in the final stage of dementia: An exploratory study. *International Journal of Nursing Studies, 23,* 315–323.

Orff, G. (1980). *The Orff music therapy: Active furthering of the development of the child.* London: Schott & Co.

Pollack, N. J., & Namazi, K. H. (1992). The effect of music participation on the social behavior of Alzheimer's disease patients. *Journal of Music Therapy, 29,* 54–67.

Prickett, C. A., & Moore, R. S. (1991). The use of music to aid memory of Alzheimer's patients. *Journal of Music Therapy, 28,* 101–110.

Reuer, B., & Crowe, B. (1995). *Best practice in music therapy: Utilizing group percussion strategies for promoting volunteerism in the well older adult.* St. Louis, MO: MMB.

Riegler, J. (1980). Comparison of a reality orientation program for geriatric patients with and without music. *Journal of Music Therapy, 17,* 26–33.

Sacks, O., & Tomaino, C. (1991). Music and neurological disorder. *International Journal of Arts Medicine, 1,* 10–12.

Salmon, D. (1993). Music and emotion in palliative care. *Journal of Palliative Care, 9,* 48–52.

Sambandham, M., & Schirm, V. (1995). Music as a nursing intervention for residents with Alzheimer's disease in long-term care. *Geriatric Nursing, 16,* 79–83.

Shively, C., & Henkin, L. (1986). Music and movement therapy with Alzheimer's victims. *Music Therapy Perspectives, 3,* 56–58.

Silber, F., & Hes, J. (1995). The use of songwriting with patients diagnosed with Alzheimer's disease. *Music Therapy Perspectives, 13,* 31–34.

Smith, D. S. (1990). Therapeutic treatment effectiveness as documented in the gerontology literature: Implications for music therapy. *Music Therapy Perspectives, 8,* 36–40.

Smith, G. (1986). A comparison of the effects of three treatment interventions on cognitive functioning of Alzheimer patients. *Music Therapy, 6A,* 41–56.

Smith-Marchese, K. (1994). The effects of participatory music on the reality orientation and sociability of Alzheimer's residents in a long-term care setting. *Activities, Adaptation and Aging. 18,* 41–55.

Staum, M. (1983). Music and rhythmic stimuli in the rehabilitation of gait disorders. *Journal of Music Therapy, 29*, 69–87.

Swartz, K. P., Hantz, E. C., Crummer, G. C., Walton, J. P., & Frisina, R. D. (1989). Does the melody linger on? Music cognition in Alzheimer's disease. *Seminar in Neurology, 9*, 152–158.

Swartz, K. P., Walton, J., Crummer, G., Hantz, E., & Frisina, R. (1992). P3 event-related potentials and performance of healthy older adults and AD subjects for music perception tasks. *Psychomusicology, 11*, 96–118.

Tabloski, P., McKinnon-Howe, L., & Remington, R. (1995). Effects of calming music on the level of agitation in cognitively impaired nursing home residents. *The American Journal of Alzheimer's Care and Related Disorders and Research, 10*, 10–15.

Taylor, D. B. (1981). Music in general hospital treatment from 1900 to 1950. *Journal of Music Therapy, 18*, 62–73.

Thomas, D. W., Heitman, R. J., & Alexander, T. (1997). The effects of music on bathing cooperation for residents with dementia. *Journal of Music Therapy, 34*, 246–259.

Volicer, L., Hurley, A. C., & Mahoney, E. (1998). Behavioral symptoms of dementia. In L. Volicer & A. Hurley (Eds.), *Hospice care for patients with advanced progressive dementia*. New York: Springer.

Walton, J., Frisina, R, Swartz, K., Hantz, E., & Crummer, G. (1988). Neural basis for music cognition: Future directions and biomedical implications. *Psychomusicology, 7*, 127-138.

Ward, C. R., Los Kamp, L., & Newman, S. (1996). The effects of participation in an intergenerational program on the behavior of residents with dementia. *Activities, Adaptation and Aging, 20*, 61-76.

Watson, B. (1996). *Music, movement, mind and body*. Forest Knolls, CA: Elder Books.

Weisberg, N., & Wilder, R. (Eds.). (1985). *Creative arts with older adults: A sourcebook*. New York: Human Sciences Press.

Wenrick, N.A. (1996). *So much more than-a-sing-along*. Forest Knolls, CA: Elder Books.

West, T. M. (1994). Psychological issues in hospice music therapy. *Music Therapy Perspectives. 12*, 117-124.

Yamamoto, K. (1993). Terminal care and music therapy. *Japanese Journal of Psychosomatic Medicine, 22*, 25-28.

York, E. (1994). The development of a quantitative music skills test for patients with Alzheimer's disease. *Journal of Music Therapy, 31*, 280-296.

## ☐ Bibliography: Further Readings on Music Therapy

Andsell, G. (1995). *Music for life*. London: Jessica Kingsley.

Bright, R. (1981). *Practical planning in music therapy for the aged*. Melbourne: Alfred Publishing.

Bright, R. (1988). *Music therapy and the dementias: Improving the quality of life*. St. Louis, MO: MMB.

Bright, R. (1991). *Music in geriatric care: A second look*. Melbourne, Australia: Music Therapy Enterprises.

Bruscia, K. (1987). *Improvisational models of music therapy*. Springfield, IL: Charles C Thomas.

Chavin. M. (1991). *The lost chord: Reaching the person with dementia through the power of music*. Mount Airy, MD: Eldersong Publications.

Clair, A. A. (1996). *Therapeutic uses of music with older adults*. Baltimore, MD: Health Professions Press.

Cordrey, C. (1995). *Hidden treasures: Music and memory activities for people with Alzheimers*. Mount Airy, MD: G & H Printing.

Cornish, P. M. (1975). *Activities for the frail aged.* Buffalo, NY: Potentials Development of Health & Aging Services.

Douglass, D. (1981). *Accent on rhythm: Music activities for the frail aged.* St. Louis, MO: MMB.

Gfeller, K., & Hanson, N. (Eds.). (1995). *Music therapy programming for individuals with Alzheimer's disease and related disorders.* Iowa City, IA: The University of Iowa College of Liberal Arts and College of Nursing.

Gibbons, A. C. (1977). Popular music preferences of elderly people. *Journal of Music Therapy, 14,* 180–189.

Grant, R. E. (1973). *Sing along senior citizens.* Springfield, IL: Charles C Thomas.

Hanser, S. B. (1987). *Music therapists handbook.* St. Louis, MO: Warren Green.

Hanser, S. B., & Clair, A. A. (1995). Retrieving the losses of Alzheimer's disease for patients and caregivers with the aid of music. In T. Wigram, B. Saperston, & R. West (Eds.), *The art and science of music therapy: A handbook* (pp. 342–360). Chur, Switzerland: Harwood Academic Publishers.

Kluft, E. S. (Ed.). (1993). *Expressive and functional therapies in the treatment of multiple personality disorder.* Springfield, IL: Charles C Thomas.

Lane, D. (1994). *Music as medicine.* Cleveland, OH: Zondervan Publishing.

Lee, C. A. (Ed.). (1995). *Lonely waters.* Oxford: Sobell Publications.

Munro, S. (1984). *Music therapy in palliative/hospice care.* St. Louis, MO: MMB.

Orff, G. (1980). *The Orff music therapy: Active furthering of the development of the child.* London: Schott & Co.

Reuer, B., & Crowe, B. (1995). *Best practice in music therapy: Utilizing group percussion strategies for promoting volunteerism in the well older adult.* St. Louis, MO: MMB.

Rykov, M. (1994). *Last songs: AIDS and the music therapist.* St. Louis, MO: MMB.

Shaw, J. (1993). *The joy of music in maturity.* St. Louis, MO: MMB.

Shaw, J., & Manthey, C. (1996). *Musical bridges: Intergenerational music programs.* St. Louis, MO: MMB.

Smith, B. B., & Knudson, L. A. (1995). *A song to set me free.* Logan, UT: Sunshine Terrace Adult Day Care Center.

Unkefer, E. F. (1990). *Music therapy in the treatment of adults with mental disorders: Theoretical bases and clinical interventions.* St. Louis, MO: MMB.

Watson, B. (1996). *Music, movement, mind and body.* Forest Knolls, CA: Elder Books.

Weisberg, N., & Wilder, R. (Eds.). (1985). *Creative arts with older adults: A sourcebook.* New York: Human Sciences Press.

Wenrick, N. A. (1996). *So much more than a sing-along.* Forest Knolls, CA: Elder Books.

## CHAPTER 10

Elizabeth J. Brown

# SNOEZELEN®[1]

A primary challenge in caring for individuals with advanced dementia is finding appropriate leisure activities. The world for these people is often confusing, threatening, and one that they find difficult to control, engage in, or understand. They generally are controlled by others, coaxed into activities by others, or left in environments that do not provide any stimulation for personal involvement (Cunningham, Hutchinson, & Kewin, 1991; Haggar & Hutchinson, 1991).

Use of sensory experiences to reduce tension and produce pleasure is not a new concept; however, it may be difficult for staff to accept the value involved in very basic sensory experiences when traditionally its role has been to act as director helping people make things, develop domestic skills, or improve effectiveness of self care.

> We frequently stand away from our residents, touching them for direct purposes only. While there are exceptions—the fact remains that many residents of institutions receive very little positive contact with others. They may have to draw attention to themselves by developing threatening or demanding behavior. Those who are less mobile and present little threat may spend long periods of time facing the same spot in a room or looking at the ceiling because they are unable to move themselves or change their position. (Kewin, 1991)

SNOEZELEN is a multisensory experience designed to gently stimulate the primary senses. It springs from the belief that all persons need stimulation and recreation—even those with special needs (Haggar & Hutchinson, 1991). The term *snoezelen* is a contraction of two Dutch words that loosely translated mean "to sniff" and "to doze." The word was coined in an attempt to describe the comfortable, lazy feeling the environment fosters. SNOEZELEN uses a combination of soft lighting effects, gentle music, tactile surfaces, and essential oils to stimulate the senses in a comfortable, safe environment. A specific room may be set up with furnishings with which people can interact (fiberoptic light sprays, bubble tubes, sound-activated light kiosks, and so forth), or selected pieces of equipment such as a tape player and projector wheel may be transported to the individual if needed. It has been used with a wide variety of age groups, for those with severe learning or emotional handicaps, for pain control, and for stress management. SNOEZELEN provides a wide range of sensory experiences that improve the quality of life for the individual. Its greatest asset lies in its ability to provide meaningful activity without intellectual reasoning or verbal responses. This enables participants to engage at whatever level is appropriate for them, the result being a release of stress and frustration.

This chapter reviews SNOEZELEN, its definition, its origin, and its evolution as described in available literature and research. Information on designing and equipping a SNOEZELEN room is offered. Additionally, existing large programs in the United Kingdom, Europe, and the United States are described.

For those who have experienced SNOEZELEN, describing the environment in a simple sentence often is quite difficult. SNOEZELEN is a concept—a means of stimulating the primary senses of sight, touch, hearing, and smell. For example, sight may be stimulated through the use of fiberoptic light sprays, bubble tubes, or color wheels projected onto a wall or ceiling. Touch can be stimulated by anything with tactile interest—again fiberoptic light sprays, textured wall panels, or crinkly paper. Hearing may be stimulated through music, voice-activated lights, or animal or nature tapes. Stimulation of smell can happen through aromatherapy or objects with familiar smells such as warm cookies, mulled cider, fresh flowers, and so forth. How the senses are stimulated, what equipment is used, and how the room is designed truly have an infinite number of variations. Perhaps what makes SNOEZELEN so successful is that ability to be adaptable to each individual's unique needs, from a large formal SNOEZELEN room or suite of rooms to a carefully chosen piece of equipment to be used in the individual's home.

The aims of SNOEZELEN as stated by Pinkney and Barker (1994) are as follows:

- To provide a stimulating environment to heighten awareness
- To provide an interesting atmosphere to encourage participants to explore their environment

- To provide an environment offering security, allowing participants mental and physical relaxation
- To provide an unrestrained atmosphere in which participants feel able to enjoy themselves

Others direct the vast majority of activities designed to stimulate those with severe learning disabilities or dementia. In essence, someone is choosing the extent of interaction for the patient, which may or may not coincide with the patient's wishes. With SNOEZELEN, the individual is free to decide how much or how little he or she is actually comfortable with; the staff member's role becomes that of a facilitator rather than director. For the person with senile dementia, SNOEZELEN offers a sense of control, a means of enjoying the immediate experience with few if any intellectual demands or accompanying stresses of these demands. Communication and understanding between patient and staff often are improved as the pressure to achieve is removed (Baker, Dowling, Wareing, Dawson, & Assey, 1997; Kewin, 1991).

The Dutch Society for the Study of Mental Retardation first introduced a SNOEZELEN room at a conference on play in the late 1970s. Further developments were made at subsequent summer fairs offered as respites from usual routines for severely learning-disabled children. These fairs included activities such as pony rides, bike trips, brass bands, a circus, and a large tent for refreshments and games. It was here that SNOEZELEN was offered as a specific activity. It now can be found in use across Europe, Japan, India, the United States, and Canada for a broad spectrum of ages and abilities (Hulsegge & Verheul, 1987).

Use of SNOEZELEN with the elderly is relatively new, having been introduced as recently as the early 1990s. Elders suffering from dementia lose their ability to assimilate information from their environment, and therefore their interpretations may be seen as disoriented and inappropriate. As with severely learning-disabled children, the elderly with dementia were identified as needing appropriate leisure activities that were not dependent upon intellectual reasoning or verbal responses. Adaptations to the approach and environment of SNOEZELEN were made, holding to principles of the original concept (Pinkney & Barker, 1994). Caring for elders with a dementing illness requires far more than the impersonal clinical technology of the diagnosis and drug treatment of traditional medical interventions. Dementia-care providers are called upon to provide a feeling of warmth and stimulation that encourages feelings of identity, security, and safety and addresses the psychological needs of the individual. Because staff and family members are participating as facilitators in SNOEZELEN along with the client, they are able to experience the emotions and sensations, thereby fostering a relationship of trust (Morrissey & Biela, 1997).

# ☐ Relevant Research[2]

Britain's Limington House in Basingstoke, a center for students with profound learning disabilities and serious physical handicaps, was one of the first schools to design and use a room specifically for SNOEZELEN (Bunsen, 1994). The money to build the specially designed building that holds the SNOEZELEN room came solely from charitable contributions.

The justification for the "relaxation" room is well founded, and true to its flexible characteristics, it offers activities for a diverse population. Extremely violent students are calmed; children with cerebral palsy are aided in developing fine-motor skills by touching and pushing switches that control lights and music. Children confined to wheelchairs can experience a soft breeze by operating a fan that gently blows cool air. Hearing- and speech-impaired children benefit from light screens that are sensitive to sound. Pictures on the screen change if music volume changes or the child makes a sound. Additionally, the room offers a place to just let off steam, to be free of their wheelchairs and helmets and just have fun. For parents it allows a rare chance for them to see their children relaxed and enjoying themselves. SNOEZELEN use now has expanded beyond the pupils at Limington House to those outside in the community who also have sensory disabilities.

Whittington Hall Hospital in Chesterfield was the first large-scale SNOEZELEN Center in the United Kingdon. Whittington Hall designed its center specifically for people with profound and multiple handicaps (Cunningham et al., 1991). Their rationale for developing this type of facility stemmed from the recognition that "recreational activities enable people to recuperate, recuperation being defined as 'not merely resting, but the feeling of restoration and refreshment which one attains from engaging in stimulating activities which are free from pressure and enjoyed for their own sake' " (Cunningham et al., 1991; Haggar & Hutchinson, 1991). As stated by Haggar and Hutchinson (1991), "People with profound handicaps, like all human beings, have a primary need for stimulation but their disabilities often prevent them from expressing and fulfilling this need in an appropriate way. . . . Whilst the concept of normalization stresses that people's life style should allow access to a range of high quality leisure facilities, no such facilities have been available for this group."

The Whittington Hall project was interesting in its deliberate goal to train staff. The staff members involved all were committed to working with people with profound and severe handicaps. Many already had been involved with activities similar to SNOEZELEN. As such, team members were able to identify specific needs of individuals and developed strategies to enable patients to gain the greatest benefit from the sensory, relaxation, and play sessions. All staff members received extensive training in sensory techniques, stimulation, and improving communication. Speech therapists, physiotherapists, occupational therapists, and psychologists from within the hospital staff led experiential workshops. The aim of these training sessions was to equip the team with a "range of skills to employ in a creative and imaginative way, to enable users to gain maximum enjoyment from the SNOEZELEN environment" (Haggar & Hutchinson, 1991).

An enabling approach was felt to be critical to the success of the program. Haggar and Hutchinson (1991) defined enabling as "a sensitive, caring, non-directive approach in which an atmosphere of safety and security is created and free choice encouraged." It is expected that enablers will share a common positive emotional experience with users while involved in the activity with them. The nine-member SNOEZELEN team coordinated all activities at the center and met on a regular basis to evaluate and make any necessary changes to the program. As with Limington House, Whittington Hall was used by a variety of groups and individuals as the need warranted. The Whittington Hall center was a wonderful example of a large-scale SNOEZELEN facility.

Kings Park Community Hospital in Bournemouth, United Kingdom, provided the first real effort at utilizing SNOEZELEN specifically for elders with dementia (Pinkney & Barker, 1994). As such it has been instrumental in identifying appropriate development of equipment and the approach that is best adapted for the elderly.

Because very little information was available on using SNOEZELEN with elders, a pilot study was completed prior to a research project. The pilot study, along with observations from staff and caregivers, provided necessary data to design a multibaseline research format that would evaluate the effects of the SNOEZELEN environment on mood and behavior. Two groups were studied, six day-hospital patients and six continuing-care patients. Prior to the research the SNOEZELEN room was used to develop an approach felt to be suitable for the elderly. Caregivers from the day hospital were sent questionnaires to explore mood and stress levels on a single-blind basis.

As would be expected, some participants were much more responsive than others, but all patients were allowed to set their own pace. Having staff members that are familiar with patients is important not only to be able to explore a new activity but also to be able to pick up on cues that the patient desires to end the session. For most patients 30 minutes seemed to be the best length of time per session.

Bringing patients in and out of the SNOEZELEN environment requires careful attention. Gradually dimming the lights after patients have entered the room allows them to become acclimated to the environment more gently. Similarly, gradually returning the lights to their full brightness allows them to remain more relaxed when the session is completed. Staff also noted that patients were much more aware of their environment and would respond more appropriately to stimuli when leaving. Staff and caregivers also reported feeling relaxed and expressed enjoyment at being in the SNOEZELEN environment. Additionally, they recommended limiting attendance in the room to two patients and two staff members or caregivers to allow for spontaneous conversation and interaction with staff. Patients are able to totally dictate the pace and structure of the session.

The staff required somewhat of a role adjustment in that the patient became the controller of the activity. It was helpful to allow staff and caregivers time to experience the room and determine their own reactions to SNOEZELEN, positive or negative. Those involved felt strongly that team members needed to be sure of their commitment to the approach if the program was to be successful. Ultimately, the staff members and caregivers felt positively about their experiences.

Baker et al. (1997) conducted a randomized clinical trial at Kings Park to investigate the long and short-term effects of SNOEZELEN as it relates to the behavior, mood, and cognition of elderly patients with dementia. Eight standardized SNOEZELEN sessions were compared with eight standardized activity sessions that were designed to be as similar as possible. Assessments of long- and short-term effects of SNOEZELEN were carried out in the home and at the hospital. No real differences in short-term benefits were found between the SNOEZELEN and activity groups. An improvement in behavior and mood for both groups indicated that quality one-on-one interaction with a key caregiver offers a positive result. The long-term benefits showed a greater change in behaviors at home. The SNOEZELEN group showed a significant decrease in socially disturbed behavior. The results of this study imply that SNOEZELEN may be a beneficial intervention for reducing or improving socially disturbed behavior in dementia patients.

Long and Haig (1992) conducted another exploratory study at the Botleys Park Resource Center, where a sensory SNOEZELEN environment was built. The hypothesis for this study stated that "a designed change in care, in this case the sensory SNOEZELEN environment, will give rise to an observable change in behavior of the recipients of that care" (Long & Haig 1992). The study attempted to compare the leisure time of four individuals at both their places of residence and the sensory SNOEZELEN environment. The environment consisted of a quiet room with a "cocoon-like atmosphere." Because of limitations in the study design, it was difficult to prove the hypothesis; however, positive observable changes in behavior for three of the four clients indicated that this hypothesis indeed could withstand an experimental study design. A lack of negative behaviors also was felt to be significant in the potential benefits possible with the general SNOEZELEN environment.

## ☐ Specific Description and Technique

SNOEZELEN is a concept of leisure and recreation and as such has no fixed rules for its design. The makeup of any given SNOEZELEN room is determined by space, resources, and individual preferences, with a broad array of equipment choices available. There are, however, a few components that are found in most SNOEZELEN environments. Detailed in the next few paragraphs are examples of existing facilities and equipment recommendations, followed by a general summary of the process involved in using these rooms.[3]

The Whittington Hall Center is an example of a large-scale formal SNOEZELEN environment (Cunningham et al., 1991), composed of six individual rooms, each with its own purpose, to collectively provide a full range of stimulation activities. The room designs are as follows:

*Adventure room*: Designed for "adventurous and robust activity," this is a large, colorful, and soft room with a variety of spaces and shapes. A large ball pool is present here as well, allowing either play or relaxation. The ball pool is a container filled with small round plastic balls, generally large enough to stretch out in or sit. The effect in this pool is quite similar to floating in water as the balls support the weight of the user's body.

*Jacuzzi room*: A large Jacuzzi pool provides soothing and massaging water effects.

*Sitting room*: This is an open area for snacks, waiting, or relaxing.

*Sound and light room*: Specially adapted switches operate sound and light equipment that can be controlled by even the most severely disabled. The user experiences wonderful sights and sounds; additionally, a vibrating floor provides tactile stimulation.

*Touch corridor*: Differing shaped objects and textures cover hallway walls, inviting exploration.

*White room*: Primarily white walls, ceiling, floor, and furnishings enhance gentle patterns of light and soft music providing a sense of relaxation, calm enjoyment, and security.

Activity boards and facilities to stimulate taste and smell also are scattered throughout the center.

Kings Park Community Hospital, as noted previously, offers a smaller-scale environment with a main SNOEZELEN room and a sitting room

that allows a relaxed transition in and out of the SNOEZELEN environment (Pinkney & Barker, 1994). Within the SNOEZELEN room, the walls
are painted white to highlight visual stimuli and a heavy cream-colored
curtain blocks light from the only window. The floor is partially covered
with deep-pile cream carpeting and soft floor covering to allow maximum tactile stimulation and a choice of positioning in the room. A ball
pool also offers tactile stimulation, as well as color and size recognition. A
panoramic rotator projects images onto the main wall. Abstract projection wheels are more popular; they are less apt to monopolize attention
and conversation. In addition to the projector, a mirrored ball and spotlight provide colorfully patterned, slowly moving spots of light that tend
to soften the edges of the room. The revolving spots generally have a
hypnotic relaxing effect, although there have been a few reports of nau-
sea and dizziness. A side-glow fiberoptic light spray is positioned to be
accessible both from a chair and floor cushions. The colors in the spray
change, encouraging most patients to focus their attention. A few patients also try to touch and manipulate it. This piece of equipment also
seems to relax patients as they become more focused on it; unfortunately,
it cannot be reached easily by all patients.

Music was chosen initially for its reminiscent, recognizable qualities,
but this proved too distracting. Meditative peaceful music ultimately
proved more beneficial. A bubble bank was used initially but was found
to be too noisy, and the solution left the floor slippery. Handheld bubble
blowers were better at providing sensory stimulation and movement. Other
pieces of equipment used include the following:

- Bird mobile
- Vibrating cushion activated by hugging, which worked particularly well
  with severely disoriented patients
- Aroma diffuser—lavender and peppermint were chosen for their familiar olfactory appeal.
- Large bubble unit placed in a corner in front of two mirrored wall panels, with the intention of giving the illusion of multiple units—this was
  distracting and confusing to patients. Some felt another room was
  present within the mirrors, while others felt uncomfortable with reflections of themselves that they tended to mistake for strangers. A cushioned
  platform was used as a base for support as well as for seating.
- Seating—patients preferred a variety of seating arrangements. Some
  liked upright chairs; some found large beanbags comfortable and easy
  to reposition; others preferred using soft floor cushions with chunky
  pillows.

Risbridge Hospital in Suffolk, United Kingdom (Doble, Goldie, & Kewell,
1992) uses two rooms as well. In an effort to control costs, this facility's

approach was to take advantage of existing pieces of equipment that were available from other departments within the hospital (a vibraboard from the physiotherapy department and an optikinetic solar projector from the recreation department).

One room was designed as a "sensory activities" room. Options available for participants in this room vary from a "feely" wall with different textured materials, floor mats, and objects that encourage participation and relaxation to sessions tailored around music, smell, and touch. Touch sessions may use water play, finger painting with shaving cream or liquid soap, and "feely" trays with sand. Furniture in this room is minimal, allowing for a flexible layout.

The second room is a white room with a black ceiling and floor padding. Equipment used in this room consists of a pin spotlight, mirror ball, bubble machine, and assorted projector wheels.

At Botleys Park Resource Center in Surrey, a single "quiet" room is used (Long & Haig, 1992). This room follows the general "white room" design, with walls painted white and external light from the window blocked by a shade. Some of the equipment found in this room is a vibrating bed and spotlights that change color in response to sudden sounds and music.

Entry into the SNOEZELEN environment, particularly the white room, is best done slowly by gradually dimming the lights after entering the room so as not to frighten the individual. Sessions typically last anywhere from 30 to 60 minutes. The recommended staff ratio is two or three staff members for a group of three or four participants. The role of the staff members is not to direct involvement but merely to act as facilitators to encourage involvement and share the experience. The level of interaction within the room depends on the participant. For some, simply sitting and actively gazing at the sights and movement within the room is a tremendous accomplishment; for others there may be fairly active movement and exploration of tactile and interactive pieces of equipment. In either case, it is best left to the participant to determine the extent of involvement that is appropriate. SNOEZELEN also may be used in a more portable manner, bringing selected pieces of equipment to individuals who may be physically unable to relocate to a formal SNOEZELEN room.

The Veterans Administration Medical Center in Bedford, Massachusetts, has a large SNOEZELEN room with numerous pieces of equipment. The room layout encourages exploration of the various pieces of equipment. Again a white-room approach is the basis for the design, with external light blocked from the window. A swing chair hangs from the ceiling in one corner with a colorful wall mural of flowers and much artificial greenery surrounding it. Several bubble tubes that change color and speed in response to sound are positioned about the room, as are light kiosks and fiberoptic light sprays. Mobiles of fish, a mirrored ball, and solar projector also are found here. There are rocking chairs and "easy" chairs to encourage relaxation. Music is provided, and aromatherapy diffusers provide the fragrance in the room. An African rain stick and small brightly colored wands are other examples of equipment available for individuals to handle and explore.

Staff and patients have access to the room during the morning, and the staff/patient ratio is usually one-to-one during these sessions. Afternoons are made available to families. These briefing sessions for families enable them to become familiar with the room and its equipment. This enables families to use the room without waiting for staff to be available. The SNOEZELEN room offers a positive means of interacting and socializing with their family member with dementia in a nonclinical setting.

There are several excellent resources provided by ROMPA®, the SNOEZELEN parent company in the United Kingdom, and Flaghouse, which is the U.S. headquarters for SNOEZELEN. Both companies are quite helpful in providing information and answering any questions about SNOEZELEN. By design, SNOEZELEN is infinitely adaptable, limited only by the imagination, space, and individual needs. It can be as simple as one or two pieces of equipment or as elaborate as a specially designated room. There are some common elements to SNOEZELEN. Flaghouse has put together a guide to allow users to benefit from the experience of others who have set up SNOEZELEN rooms.[4]

## Measuring

To best design and make decisions regarding a SNOEZELEN room, it is important to be sure that measurements are accurate, including all angles and interruptions in wall surfaces. Flaghouse offers a free guide to measuring for a SNOEZELEN room, which is available upon request by calling Flaghouse at 1-800-793-7900.

## Planning

The actual combination of equipment in a SNOEZELEN facility fluctuates with the needs of the user group and budget and space considerations. It is nonetheless a good idea to begin by making a complete plan. This overall vision provides some structure to purchasing and design work and can be helpful to fund raisers and donors.

## Walls

If a solar projector, mirrored ball, or other projected light effects are being used in the SNOEZELEN room, walls may be painted white or a light pastel to provide a good reflective surface on which to project. For a "white room," walls do not need to be padded. The walls of a soft playroom may be padded for safety, or for a very small space to create a soft "cocoon"-like atmosphere. This improves the atmosphere of the room by eliminating as much of the "visual clutter" as possible from wall surfaces (removable lockers, storage cabinets, etc.). Fixed wall structures such as chalkboards or bulletin boards can be "covered" by projection screens. Screens as large as 9 × 9 ft can be ordered from Flaghouse. Radiators, sinks, and other built-in fixtures can be boxed over with plywood painted to match walls.

If only part of a room is to be used for a SNOEZELEN environment, it may be helpful to consider curtaining off the rest of the room. Again, Flaghouse is a willing resource for help with curtains and tracking.

## Floors and Seating Surfaces

The needs and abilities of the population that will be using the SNOEZELEN facility is the best source of direction as to floor covering. If the population is mostly ambulatory, the floor surface may be better with minimal matting. Mats are somewhat tricky for most people to maneuver; for someone whose balance skills are not great they can be a real problem. Bare floor with some small, easily moveable mats and beanbags for seating by each piece of equipment may be the best choice. Wall-to-wall carpeting offers another option with a little more warmth. Both of these surfaces provide good accessibility for wheelchairs and gurneys. If the user population is mostly nonambulatory, one should consider including several areas of built-up matting or covered benches, or even floor mats on lifts to accommodate patient-lift devices. The greater height of these areas makes transfer from wheelchairs easier for staff members.

The choice of seating surfaces is dictated by the needs of the population. Mats provide good relaxation surfaces for younger walkers and nonwalkers alike; soft chairs and benches with backrests are better for geriatric users. For nonambulatory individuals in particular, a variety of surfaces, such as mats, water beds, or billowing cushions, greatly enhances enjoyment and stimulation from the SNOEZELEN experience.

## Light Control

Light control is an important factor in obtaining the best results from the light effects equipment. If possible, the best choice for a SNOEZELEN facility is a room with no windows. This is not always feasible, however.

Light from existing windows can be dimmed or eliminated in various ways. White vinyl room-darkening shades or heavy curtains can be used. Windows can be painted over or "tiled" with mirrored tiles cut to fit.

Not everyone is ready to explore in a darkened room. For this reason, it is a good idea to install a dimmer switch to work the room lighting. This allows lights to be adjusted to the comfort level of each individual, which is especially helpful as the individual is introduced to this brand new "world" of experiences.

## Choosing Equipment

The choice of equipment is one of the major ways in which to tailor the SNOEZELEN environment to meet the needs of the individuals who will be using the room. The choices are determined by the uses foreseen for SNOEZELEN, and by what is hoped to be accomplished there. Certainly, personal preference also is a factor.

## Avoiding Problems

Because of the special nature of the populations most frequently using SNOEZELEN, the question of seizures often arises. SNOEZELEN lighting effects are designed particularly with these people in mind. Lighting effects build slowly over a period of several seconds to avoid sudden flashes. Some wheels allow for client control of speed, with a governor knob on the side to allow the therapist or enabler to put a "ceiling" on the speed of movement that can be attained. This should allow the professional to effectively screen out those speeds that he or she feels are too intense for any individual user.

There have been some reports of individuals being bothered by the reflected light of the color-wheel spotlight flashing from tile to tile on the mirrored ball as it turns. Those who suffer from motion sickness also may tolerate poorly this piece of equipment. A good way to avoid these problems is to have the turning of the mirrored ball controlled by a wall switch. This allows the facilitator to stop the spinning ball if someone who would find the effects problematic is using the room. The familiar "dots" still appear, and they continue to change color, but there is no movement, and therefore no spinning or flashing. Another alternative is to cover the mirrored ball when these people are using the room.

Finally, although most people using SNOEZELEN tend to find mirrors great fun and very interesting, experience has shown that individuals with advanced dementia sometimes find them confusing and troubling. It may be best to avoid using mirrors if designing a facility to be used by this population.

## Using Present Resources

Other materials can be incorporated effectively to enhance the SNOEZELEN environment with minimal additional cost. Many of these items already may be available within the facility to which SNOEZELEN is being added. This is a wonderful opportunity to exercise one's professional (and artistic) creativity. The main criterion for determining what is appropriate for use in the SNOEZELEN environment is that the activity or material be something that users find interesting and enjoyable.

# ☐ Outcome Evaluation

The Geriatric Research Education and Clinical Center (GRECC) at the Edith Nourse Rogers Memorial Veteran's Medical Center in Bedford, Massachusetts (VA Bedford) has conducted an ongoing longitudinal study of dementia since 1978. The inpatient Alzheimer GRECC Dementia Study Unit provides care for approximately 100 patients.

In the early to mid-1990s the recreational therapists assigned to the patients with Alzheimer's disease were feeling frustrated at the lack of appropriate activities for relaxation for nonambulatory patients. Traditional therapies were found to be inadequate for reducing anxious behaviors, as patients were unable to effectively follow through or interact with staff members who were trying to provide activities. The staff also was interested in finding relaxation activities that ultimately could reduce the numbers of antianxiety medications used by the patients.

Two initial pieces of equipment were purchased: a projector that uses colored light wheels that rotate slowly, providing gently changing colors and designs, and a stereo system for music. Response was positive, with a significantly reduced level of agitation and restlessness noted. At about this time a participant in the vocational rehabilitation program through VA Bedford expressed an interest in working in the recreation-therapy service. He became interested in the SNOEZELEN program and, drawing on his musical background, offered to develop a cassette tape of relaxation music specifically for SNOEZELEN. This tape of music and the projector remain integral pieces of SNOEZELEN at VA Bedford.

The anecdotal evidence of apparent patient benefit resulting from SNOEZELEN was the impetus for a research project developed at VA

Bedford (Brown, Crowther, Jones, & Volicer, 1999) to formally test its benefit as a behavioral intervention. Previous research available for SNOEZELEN focused almost exclusively on its benefit as a leisure activity rather than its effectiveness as a behavioral intervention. A study was designed to evaluate the ability of SNOEZELEN to effectively reduce anxious and resistive behaviors in patients with Alzheimer' disease as they received routine dental-hygiene care.

The study design was a randomized cross-over clinical trial. Thirty-six patients with Alzheimer's disease identified by nursing and dental staff as having a history of resistive behaviors during regular daily care (bathing, dressing, feeding, and so forth) were enrolled in the study. Twenty-nine subjects completed the study and were included in the final data analysis. The patients were randomly assigned to one of three treatment groups of nine patients each. Three treatment modalities were provided, with each group receiving the treatments in a different sequence. The three treatment modalities were as follows:

1. *Control session*: dental-hygiene treatment only (toothbrush scrub, scaling, and a 2% neutral sodium fluoride application)
2. *Combined session*: 20 minutes of SNOEZELEN alone (soft music and gentle lighting display using the projector with a blue gel wheel), then dental-hygiene treatment provided during remaining 40 minutes of SNOEZELEN as noted for the control visit
3. *Separate session*: 60 minutes of SNOEZELEN alone followed by dental-hygiene treatment upon completion of SNOEZELEN

To compensate for the inability to control for blindness (a means of maintaining unbiased objectivity) in this study, heart rate and body temperatures were monitored at 5-minute intervals for the initial 20 minutes of each session to provide objective physiologic measures. At the completion of each session, patients were assessed using a resistive behavior score that was developed at VA Bedford (Medford et al., 1999). Sessions were approximately 3 months apart. Additionally, each patient was characterized by the number of teeth present and the Community Periodontal Index of Treatment Needs, a scale that estimates periodontal therapy needs. Patients enrolled in the study were 55 to 84 years old and had middle- to late-stage Alzheimer's disease.

The music and projector were chosen for use in the study based on their ease of portability. It was important to be able to bring SNOEZELEN to the patient in this case, as many of the study subjects were not ambulatory. Additionally, many of the ambulatory patients become easily confused and anxious if taken out of their familiar environments, potentially increasing resistiveness.

Although slightly short of achieving statistical significance ($p = .08$), trends were evident in the analysis of heart rates and resistive behaviors. It is interesting to note that the control session actually had the lowest overall heart rates, followed by the separate session (60 minutes of SNOEZELEN alone), and the highest heart rates were seen in the combined session (SNOEZELEN concurrent with dental-hygiene care). Body temperatures were virtually unchanged.

Resistiveness showed a somewhat different picture. The overall resistiveness was lowest during separate sessions, greatest during the combined session. It appears that trying to provide dental-hygiene care as the SNOEZELEN was in progress, for this particular group, was perhaps too much stimulation.

As a result of this study, SNOEZELEN will be available for use as an intervention when providing dental care to patients with Alzheimer's disease at VA Bedford. SNOEZELEN also has been used at VA Bedford for those with other types of psychiatric problems. Nursing staff members traditionally found morning care particularly difficult to provide because the patients often would become loud, agitated, and resistive to care. Almost as a last resort, SNOEZELEN was tried, again on the ward rather than bringing the patients to a SNOEZELEN room. All patients who were able were brought into the day room, and the same two pieces of equipment, music and the projector, were set up and started. After approximately 20 to 30 minutes the nursing staff started bringing out two patients at a time to provide morning care and returning them to the day room when finished. Within a few days the patients began to anticipate the SNOEZELEN environment and would quiet more easily and remain relatively calm during care.

VA Bedford now uses SNOEZELEN both on the ward and in the formal SNOEZELEN room that is found in the recreation-therapy department. Geriatric, psychiatric, and counseling groups all take advantage of SNOEZELEN, with positive results.

## ☐ Effectiveness of Technique

The Whittington Hall project established the importance of training staff members to be facilitators in the SNOEZELEN environment. There it was recognized that in order for this concept to be effective the staff and family members who are participating need to feel comfortable with the whole process. Staff members received extensive training through experiential workshops in sensory integration techniques, stimulation, and improving communication. Speech therapists, physiotherapists, occupational therapists, and psychology staff members all led the sessions. The aim of these sessions was to "equip the SNOEZELEN team with a range of skills to employ in a creative and imaginative way, to enable users to gain the maximum enjoyment from the SNOEZELEN environment" (Haggar & Hutchinson, 1991). A role-playing format was used, with participants temporarily sensorily disabled to help sensitize them to limitations experienced by people with severe disabilities.

Groups and individuals now use the Whittington Hall facility. The individual sessions allow for the staff to meet individual needs and preferences in a more sensitive manner than possible with a group. Family members and other care providers also are encouraged to come and participate in the sessions. This facility is also available to the public. One morning each week the room is made available to paramedics and local community mental-health teams. The facility is open weekends, with Sunday afternoons being set aside for children with profound handicaps and their parents. The level of interest in this facility both from the community and the hospital continues to grow.

Initial observations drawn from the Kings Park study (Pinkney & Barker, 1994) found that morning sessions were much more enjoyable, with greater levels of concentration noted than in the afternoon. Participants needed more persuasion to attend the afternoon sessions than the morning. Because of the difficulty in recreating the atmosphere once begun, patients' toilet needs were attended to before the session. Less reluctance was observed if patients were allowed to enter the room with normal lighting before gradually dimming the lights. Seating preferences varied once in the room, depending on the level of disorientation.

Three patients were observed in the pilot study at Kings Park. Each was observed at 5-minute intervals, and the observations were translated into percentages of the 30-minute sessions. The greatest percentage of interaction was found in overall alertness during the session. The first gentleman was found to be alert but not focusing on anything in particular for 52% of the thirty-minute session. This was a proportionally long time for this gentleman, as he typically would stay focused for only 5 minutes at a time. The second gentleman was found to be alert 82% of the session, again without any real focus on a particular stimulus but apparently engaged by the collective environment. The third gentleman was alert for 50% of the session, again a marked improvement over his usual 5-minute span of focus. For each of these gentlemen, positive responses to visual, auditory, and tactile stimuli were also recorded.

Risbridge Hospital offers 1-hour sessions four times a day (Doble et al., 1992). The two morning sessions are group activities, with two to three staff members available; the afternoon sessions are one-to-one with clients, with the possibility for a second staff member to participate if needed. Risbridge offers a multidisciplinary approach that involves 6-month evaluation of progress for each client. A chart is kept for each participant in order to record which interventions best benefit the client. This chart then is used as a basis for discussions at client review meetings attended by staff. Anecdotal observations have included notations of a reduction in agitated, noisy behaviors during the SNOEZELEN sessions, with patients completing their time with behaviors noticeably soothed and calmed. The success of this format has since led to expansion of the SNOEZELEN program and the planning of added rooms.

The Botleys Park pilot study evaluated the response of four individuals in a SNOEZELEN room and compared those responses with behaviors at their homes. Of note from this study was that the SNOEZELEN environment "does not invite the participants to be highly physically active but to be receptors for interesting stimuli, both visually and musically" (Long & Haig, 1992).

The VA Bedford study was unique in that it evaluated the SNOEZELEN environment from a portable perspective. As noted previously, this study used only two components, based upon their portability. This study also indicated that use of SNOEZELEN as a behavioral intervention before routines that tend to elicit resistiveness (bathing, daily mouth care, and so forth) has potential benefit and warrants further study.

## ☐ Conclusion

Providing care both to and for elders with dementia poses unique stresses and demands on the individual and the caregiver. The issues are far greater than simply addressing the clinical and medical needs of the individual. SNOEZELEN offers a nonpharmacological approach to dealing with the inherent behavioral issues without the use of behavior medications.

As a recreational activity, SNOEZELEN provides the opportunity for independence and control for the individual who in most aspects of life may have lost control. There is no longer any stress to perform, to accomplish a task, to make another happy because one has followed directions correctly. There is only the freedom to explore and enjoy the activity in a safe and uninhibited manner.

As a behavioral intervention, SNOEZELEN becomes a nonpharmacological management tool. Often the conflicts that result with demented patients come from an inability to understand the motivation behind the task. Patients become resistant, unwilling to cooperate. SNOEZELEN provides a means of enabling patients to relax and more willingly accept the care needed from staff members.

# ☐ Notes

[1] SNOEZELEN is a registered Trade Mark of Robinson & Sons Ltd. of Chesterfield, England.

[2] Research information from Limington House, Whittington Hall, and Kings Park Community Hospital is provided with permission from ROMPA. ROMPA is a registered Trade Mark of Robinson & Sons Ltd. of Chesterfield, England.

[3] Information concerning techniques at Whittington Hall and Kings Park Community Hospital is provided with permission from ROMPA.

[4] Information from "Planning Your Snoezelen Environment" provided with permission from Flaghouse, Inc.

# ☐ References

Baker, R., Dowling, Z., Wareing, A., Dawson, J., & Assey, J. (1997). Snoezelen: Its long-term and short-term effects on older people with dementia. *British Journal of Occupational Therapy, 60,* 213–218.

Brown, E., J., Crowther, J., Jones, J. A., & Volicer, L. (1999). Snoezelen therapy as a means of reducing resistive behavior in Alzheimer's patients. Unpublished manuscript.

Bunsen, A. (1994). A study in the use and implication of the resources at Limington House School. In R. Hutchinson & J. Kewin (Eds.), *Sensations and disability* (pp. 138–146). Chesterfield, UK: ROMPA®.

Cunningham, C. C., Hutchinson, R., & Kewin, J. (1991). Recreation for people with profound and severe learning difficulties: The Whittington Hall Snoezelen Project, In R. Hutchinson (Ed.), *The Whittington Hall Snoezelen Project: A report from inception to the end of the first twelve months.* Chesterfield, UK: North Derbyshire Health Authority.

Doble, D., Goldie, C., & Kewell, C. (1992). The white approach. *Nursing Times, 88,* 36–37.

Haggar, L. E., & Hutchinson, R. B. (1991). Snoezelen: An approach to the provision of a leisure resource for people with profound and multiple handicaps. *Mental Handicap, 19,* 51–55.

Hulsegge, J., & Verheul, A. (1987). *Snoezelen® another world.* Chesterfield, UK: ROMPA®.

Kewin, J. (1991). Snoezelen: Pulling the strands together. In R. Hutchinson (Ed.), *The Whittington Hall Snoezelen Project: A report from inception to the end of the first twelve months.* Chesterfield, UK: North Derbyshire Health Authority.

Long, A., & Haig, L. (1992). How do clients benefit from Snoezelen? An exploratory study. *British Journal of Occupational Therapy, 55,* 103–106.

Mahoney, E. K., Hurley, A. C., Volicer, L., Bell, M., Gianotis, P., Hartshorn, M., Lane, P., Lesperance, R., MacDonald, S., Novakoff, L., Rheaume, Y., Timms, R., & Warden, V. (1999). Development and testing of the resistiveness to care scale. *Research in Nursing & Health, 22,* 27–38.

Morrissey, M., & Biela, C. (1997). Snoezelen: Benefits for nursing older clients. *Nursing Standard, 12,* 38-40.

Pinkney, L., & Barker, P. (1994). Snoezelen: An evaluation of an environment used by people who are elderly and confused. In R. Hutchinson & J. Kewin (Eds.), *Sensations and disability* (pp. 172–183). Chesterfield, UK: ROMPA®.

David G. Harper
Yvette Rheaume
Barbara C. Manning
Ladislav Volicer

# Light Therapy in Alzheimer's Disease

Cognitive impairment is the central, defining symptom of Alzheimer's disease. This deficit, particularly in the ability to retain and recall new information, is generally the first symptom observable to patients, their employers, or their families (Albert, 1996). The illness, and the dementia that accompanies it, interferes with occupational and other necessary activities of daily living. Eventually, the gradual worsening of the cognitive impairment leaves the patient defenseless and entirely dependent upon caregivers for survival.

There is a large cluster of noncognitive and psychopathological symptoms that can develop over the course of the illness. The noncognitive disturbances most often identified with Alzheimer's disease are depression, psychomotor agitation or wandering, physical or verbal aggression, sleep disturbance or reversal, and delusions or hallucinations (Aarsland, Cummings, Yenner, & Miller, 1996; Hope, Keene, Fairburn, McShane, & Jacoby, 1997; van Someren, Mirmiran, & Swaab, 1993). Only 8% of patients remain free from all noncognitive disturbances through the course of the illness (Devanand et al., 1997).

These psychopathological symptoms develop independently, last for varying periods of time (Devanand et al., 1997), and add to the difficulty of caring for patients with Alzheimer's disease. Caregivers report that their decisions to institutionalize their loved ones result more from exhaustion caused by managing these disruptive behaviors than any other reason (Cohen-Mansfield, 1995; Steele, Rovner, Chase, & Folstein, 1990; Vitiello, Bliwise, & Prinz, 1992). The most effective intervention to postpone the institutionalization of patients is treatment aimed at alleviating these noncognitive symptoms.

Sleep disturbance is especially disruptive to the life of those around patients with Alzheimer's disease and is a major contributor to caregiver exhaustion. Sleep disturbance may cause fatigue, which increases the agitation of patients (Cohen-Mansfield, Werner, & Freedman, 1995), making them more difficult to manage. Insomnia usually is characterized by four distinct temporal patterns: initial insomnia, in which patients have difficulty falling asleep; sleep-maintenance insomnia, in which patients awaken in the middle of the sleep period for an extended period of time before returning to sleep; early morning awakening, in which patients awaken before their desired wake-up time and cannot return to sleep; and sleep reversal, in which the sleep period occurs during the normal waking time. The sleep of individuals suffering from Alzheimer's disease is fragmented (Prinz et al., 1982), reflecting initial and sleep maintenance insomnia and less time in stages of deep sleep (Loewenstein et al., 1982; Prinz et al., 1982). Sleep with rapid eye movement also is inhibited by Alzheimer's disease (Prinz et al., 1982). Given the converging evidence associating such sleep and memory formation (Maquet et al., 1996), it is possible that inhibition of this sleep is associated with the cognitive aspects of the illness. Finally, sleep reversal is a significant problem with Alzheimer's disease as well (Okawa et al., 1991), leading to caregiver exhaustion.

Many noncognitive or psychopathological symptoms show circadian variation either directly (i.e., sleep disturbance, depression) or indirectly (agitation) in a syndrome known as sundowning (Evans, 1987; Little, Satlin, Sunderland, & Volicer, 1995). Sleep disturbance has been observed to be related to disturbances in circadian physiology (Campbell, Dawson, & Anderson, 1993; Dorsey et al., 1996; van Someren et al., 1993), with reduced amplitude of the rhythm often cited as a cause of sleep-maintenance insomnia. This type of insomnia is very similar to the type of sleep disturbance seen in Alzheimer's disease. Depression often is noted to have a chronobiological component (Souetre et al., 1989; Teicher et al., 1993), with seasonal affective disorder (SAD) being strongly linked to the type of circadian disturbances seen in Alzheimer's disease (Rosenthal et al., 1984; Teicher et al., 1997), in which circadian frequency can become quite variable (Satlin, Volicer, Stopa, & Harper, 1995).

In sundowning, however, the actual temporal distribution of the disruptive behavior is a matter of some debate. Most commentators speak of disruptive behavior in the late afternoon and evening (Cohen-Mansfield, Marx, Werner, & Freedman, 1992; Cohen-Mansfield, Werner, & Marx, 1990; Evans, 1987; Little et al., 1995), but some speak of nocturnal disruptive behavior (Bliwise et al., 1995) and others report disruptive behavior occurring in some patients more commonly in the morning (Cohen-Mansfield et al., 1992). Examples of these temporally dependent and disruptive behaviors include increased vocalizations, agitation, wandering, and resistiveness to care during the sundowning period. Patients exhibiting the "sundown syndrome" are noted to induce higher levels of caregiver stress (Gallagher-Thompson, Brooks, Bliwise, Leader, & Yesavage, 1992) because of the disruptive and temporally isolated symptomatology that characterizes this disorder.

There may be some association between these disturbances and the breakdown of the central circadian timing system that is occurring as a result of the disease. The central time-keeping mechanism is located in the suprachiasmatic nuclei (SCN) of the brain (Moore, 1995). The cells in the SCN maintain an endogenous rhythm that cycles close to (*circa*, hence circadian) 24 hours (see Figure 11.1). The rhythm that these cells maintain is translated to the body via various pathways and keeps the disparate physiological functions requiring circadian regulation in optimal balance. The SCN receive information from the environment via two pathways. The first is the retinohypothalamic tract, which runs from the retina to the SCN. This pathway carries light information from the retina to the central clock, allowing it to adjust to the external light schedule (Card & Moore, 1991) and thus keeping the organism entrained to the environment. The second pathway is the geniculohypothalamic tract, which leads from the intergeniculate leaflet to the SCN (Moore, 1995). This pathway is involved in feeding information on physical activity and possibly other events (such as eating) to the SCN.

Circadian rhythms in physiological activity often are described by reference to their sinusoidal shape and characterized mathematically by mapping them to a cosine function. Qualitative changes in circadian rhythms then are described by the relevant components of a cosine function that delineate its shape including the mesor, amplitude, frequency, and phase (see Figure 11.1). The mesor is the mean of the function; amplitude is the absolute difference between the mesor and the peak of the function; and the phase is the time of the peak of the function. Several techniques have been developed to assess these relevant features including cosinor analysis, spectral analysis, and many others.

In Alzheimer's disease, the control of circadian rhythms breaks down, measurably changing the shape of circadian rhythms, as the disease progresses. In mild cases, the circadian rhythm of temperature is not different from that of normal aging (Prinz, Moe, Vitiello, Marks, & Larsen, 1992); however, the amplitude of the activity rhythm is significantly blunted (Pollack & Stokes, 1997). In moderate to severe cases of Alzheimer's disease, the amplitude of the rhythms of temperature and activity (Satlin et al., 1995; van Someren et al., 1996) are reduced (Figure

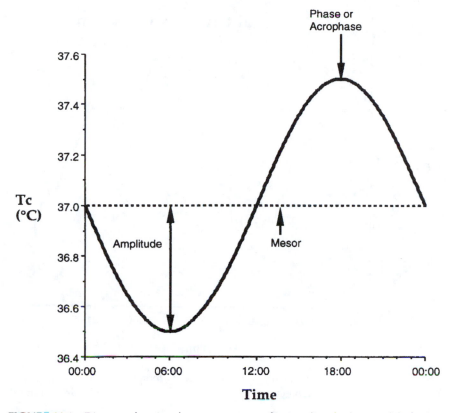

**FIGURE 11.1.** Diagram showing the components of a circadian rhythm modeled using cosinor analysis. Mesor is the mean of the model around which the circadian rhythm oscillates. Amplitude is the absolute difference between the mesor and the extreme high or low of the model. Phase or acrophase is the time at which the model hits its peak. Tc = core body temperature.

11.2) and the phases of temperature and activity rhythms become delayed relative to the environment (Ancoli-Israel et al., 1997; Satlin, Volicer, Ross, Herz, & Campbell, 1992; Satlin et al., 1995). The phase delay of temperature and activity rhythms observed in patients with Alzheimer's disease is distinct from changes seen in normal aging in which the acrophase of the temperature and activity rhythms occurs earlier. Although insomnia is a problem in both normal aging and dementia and amplitude reductions are seen in both groups, the phase disturbances are opposite.

In addition to phase delay, the coordination between different circadian systems in Alzheimer's disease can become chaotic (Satlin et al., 1995; van Someren et al., 1996). This lack of coordination between dif-

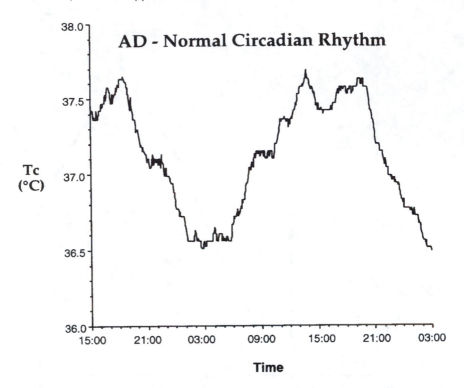

**FIGURE 11.2A.** The human circadian rhythm of body temperature in a subject with Alzheimer's disease. This subject maintains a rhythm with high amplitude and good environmental coordination.

ferent systems may be particularly important for development of some of the noncognitive disturbances in Alzheimer's disease, because enforced desynchrony between circadian rhythms of temperature and sleep-wake or rest-activity cycles affects mood, producing dysphoria in the desynchronized state (Boivin et al., 1997). There are several possible reasons for breakdown of circadian coordination, and they may involve one or more components of the circadian system. The first possibility is that the environment in which the patient lives, particularly the institutional environment, has insufficient cuing to entrain the circadian system appropriately (Ancoli-Israel et al., 1997). For example, as patients begin to lose mobility, they spend more time during the day inside where artificial light levels are low. Meanwhile, during the night, hall lights are on, and light levels are higher than in the home environment. These factors would tend to reduce the environmental cues (motor activity and variations in light) that adjust a circadian rhythm. Even patients with mild Alzheimer's disease living at home are exposed to less diurnal light than their age-

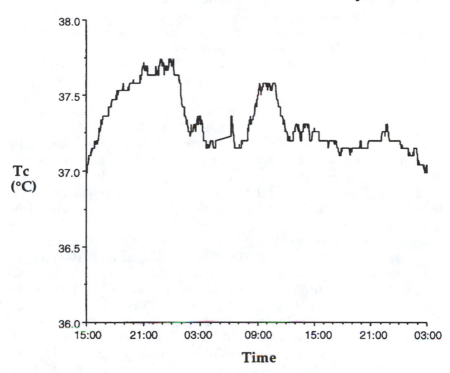

**AD - Abnormal Circadian Rhythm**

**FIGURE 11.2B.** Body temperature recorded over 36 hours in an Alzheimer's disease patient with a markedly abnormal circadian rhythm. The amplitude is low and there is not good association with the environment.

matched healthy counterparts (Campbell, Kripke, Gillin, & Hrubovcak, 1988).

The second area in which the breakdown could occur is in the system involved in bringing light information to the SCN. Optic-nerve degeneration (Blanks, Hinton, Sadun, & Miller, 1989) or loss of conductivity of the retinohypothalamic or geniculohypothalamic tract would leave the SCN without environmental information. There are reports of optic-nerve degeneration in Alzheimer's disease (Hedges et al., 1996; Sadun & Bassi, 1990); however, some investigators did not find these optic-nerve abnormalities (Davies, McCoubrie, McDonald, & Jobst, 1995). A recent report shows that the retinohypothalamic tract in Alzheimer's disease is unaffected by the illness and makes good synaptic connections with SCN peptidergic neurons (Dai, Swaab, & Buijs, 1998; Dai, Van der Vliet, Swaab, & Buijs, 1998).

The third area in which this breakdown could emerge is in the degeneration of the cells in the SCN itself. Neuropathological examination of the SCN of patients with Alzheimer's disease reveals significant generalized cell loss and specific decreases in vasopressin, vasoactive intestinal peptide, and neurotensin neurons (Stopa et al., 1999; Swaab, Fliers, & Partiman, 1985; Zhou, Hofman, & Swaab, 1995). This cell loss likely would lead to impairment in the ability of patients to maintain a strong circadian rhythm.

Last, the many different pathways and structures receiving innervation from the SCN could be differentially affected by the disease process. The circadian regulation of cortisol and growth hormone is affected by the presence of Alzheimer's disease (Hartmann, Veldhuis, Deuschle, Standhardt, & Heuser, 1997; Heuser et al., 1992). These hormones affect ubiquitous physiological functions, and variations in their temporal regulation could lead to significant disruption of optimal homeostasis (Axelrod & Reisine, 1984).

Most likely, some combination involving more than one of these factors is involved in the circadian disturbances of Alzheimer's disease. The most clear evidence exists for environmental influences and SCN degeneration. It is also quite possible that each patient has a different combination of disturbances creating several possible profiles.

Ultimately, the cause of noncognitive symptoms of dementia remains unclear, making treatment choices difficult (Aarsland et al., 1996). Furthermore, the progressive dementia also inhibits the range of therapeutic options for the psychopathological symptoms. Often, pharmacological therapies increase the patient's confusion, leading to decreased functional capacity and further raising stress on the caregiver (Satlin et al., 1992; Pfeiffer et al., 1997). Nonpharmacological therapies are limited by the inability of the patients to cooperate with treatment. These two facts, combined with the lack of knowledge of what is causing the disturbances, have created a conundrum in which treatment choices become difficult to make. One treatment that could be efficacious in restoring rhythmical balance and addressing several of the noncognitive symptoms of Alzheimer's disease is light therapy. Light therapy is nonpharmacological and therefore less likely to make cognitive symptoms worse.

# ☐ Effects of Light Therapy

Light therapy has been demonstrated to be efficacious in a wide spectrum of disorders. The first (Rosenthal et al., 1984), and the most common, usage for light therapy is for SAD. SAD is a disorder characterized by disturbances of mood and the circadian rhythms of temperature (Avery et al., 1997) and activity (Teicher et al., 1997). Sleep disturbances (Rosenthal et al., 1984), similar to those seen in patients with Alzheimer's disease, are seen in SAD as well. Light therapy also has been shown to be efficacious in several other disorders besides SAD. Age-related sleep disturbance, jet lag, and shift-work adjustments also are treated effectively with light therapy (Campbell et al., 1993; Cooke, Kreydatus, Atherton, & Thoman, 1998). With the similarity of several of these disorders to noncognitive disturbances in Alzheimer's disease, light therapy would seem to be a candidate for the treatment of noncognitive symptoms in Alzheimer's disease.

Light therapy has a well-defined ability to shift circadian rhythms. The degree and direction of the shift depend on the time of day at which therapy is administered (Minors, Waterhouse, & Wirz-Justice, 1991), the duration of the administration session, and the intensity of light used (Boivin, Duffy, Kronauer, & Czeisler, 1996). The relationship between the time of administration of light therapy and the temperature minimum determines whether the phototherapy causes a phase advance or delay. Phototherapy given prior to the temperature nadir causes a delay in the rhythm, whereas treatment given following the nadir advances the rhythm, causing the acrophase to become earlier. There are three factors that determine the amount of phase shift induced by any given light-treatment protocol. The first factor is light intensity (Boivin et al., 1996): the more intense the light the greater the phase shift. The second factor is the duration of the treatment (Minors et al., 1991): the longer the duration, the greater the shift. The third factor is the proximity of the treatment to the time of the temperature nadir (Minors et al.): the closer to the nadir the therapy is given, the greater the phase shift (Figure 11.3).

However, light therapy also may have several other effects that could be beneficial for those suffering from Alzheimer's disease. It can increase the amplitude of the circadian rhythm of temperature in sleep-disturbed (Campbell et al., 1993) as well as normal subjects. Light therapy increases the overall organization of activity rhythms (van Someren, Kessler, Mirmiran, & Swaab, 1997) and possibly the interaction of these rhythms with temperature rhythms. Although shifting the phase of the circadian rhythm so that it is more synchronized to the external light cycle appears important for treating sleep disturbance (Campbell et al., 1993; Cooke et al., 1998), the timing of the light exposure may not be critical in treating seasonal depression (Lee, Blashko, Janzen, Paterson, & Chan, 1997; Wirz-Justice et al., 1993) as long as the time of administration is consistent.

Light treatment is used to treat sleep disturbance in elderly populations in which circadian phase is not in optimal phase relationship to the environment (Campbell et al., 1993; Cooke et al., 1998). Normal elderly often develop a circadian phase advance, with the nadir of body tempera-

## Phase Response Curve

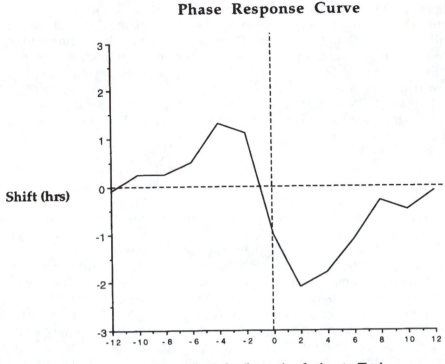

**Shift (hrs)**

**Time of Light (hours) relative to Tmin**

**FIGURE 11.3.** The graph of the human phase response curve to light (from Minors et al., 1991). In this graph the ordinate (x-axis) is time of day relative to the measured temperature minimum. The abscissa (y-axis) is the amount of shift following a single light pulse.

ture getting progressively earlier, which results in fragmented sleep. Evening bright light delays the phase, resulting in improved sleep as measured by sleep electroencephalography (Campbell et al., 1993) and subjective quality of sleep (Cooke et al., 1998). Patients with Alzheimer's disease appear to develop the opposite problem: The phase of body temperature becomes delayed (Satlin et al., 1995). This abnormality again results in fragmented sleep. Phototherapy, however, is an effective treatment for rest-activity and sleep disturbance in Alzheimer's disease, as described subsequenly here (Mishima et al., 1994; Satlin et al., 1992; van Someren et al., 1997).

Light therapy is important in the treatment of SAD, a form of depression that manifests during the winter months. SAD is linked to deficits in circadian physiology (Teicher et al., 1997), and it is uniquely sensitive among the affective illnesses to treatment with light therapy. It is possible that some of the depressive symptomatology seen in Alzheimer's disease could be similar to that in SAD (Satlin et al., 1995; Teicher et al., 1997). This hypothesis stands unsupported by any known published data, and further research on light treatment and vegetative signs of depression and mood in this population is warranted. In SAD, the importance of light treatment may be to stabilize the circadian rhythm rather than shift it in one direction or the other (Lee, Blashko, et al., 1997; Wirz-Justice et al., 1993), and this treatment approach also may have benefit in patients with Alzheimer's disease.

# ☐ Methods

There are currently several methods for delivering light therapy. Each has fairly distinct advantages and disadvantages. The main index by which these treatment modalities should be assessed is their ability to actually deliver light to the retina. Because each patient is different and there are many considerations in choosing a delivery method for light therapy, there is no one best treatment for all individuals.

## Light Box

The most common method is the light box, generally a box (approx 60 × 60 × 15 cm) and weighing approximately 10 to 20 lb. There are several suppliers including Northern Light Technologies (St. Laurent, Quebec), and SunBox Designs (London, UK) that offer light-box products. Light boxes have varying intensities from 2000 lux to 10,000 lux. To use a light box, the patient sits in front of the box and looks into it or performs activities while looking in its general direction. Although this is a fairly straightforward task for an unimpaired person, it can be challenging for someone with dementia, particularly if he or she is agitated. Even with the partial restraint of a recliner, the dosage of light received still can be affected by the patient turning his or her head or otherwise avoiding looking at the light.

Light boxes have been used effectively in a number of studies of patients with Alzheimer's disease. In one study, 1500 to 2000 lux of light was given for 2 hours in the evening (7:00–9:00 PM) via a light box to an identified group of sundowners who experienced agitation in the afternoon and sleep fragmentation (Satlin et al., 1992). Patients were improved in clinical ratings of sleep and wakefulness and circadian rhythms of motor activity during the week the light treatment was being given. Improvement in sleep persisted during the week following discontinuation of the light therapy; activity measurements did not remain improved during this time. Nursing staff members did not notice improvement of agitation or other behavioral disturbances, and use of medication given as needed did not decrease during the course of the study.

A second study measured the effects of morning bright light on a group of patients with Alzheimer's disease (Mishima et al., 1994). This group previously had reported that the use of morning light was superior to the use of evening light in this patient population (van Someren et al., 1993). Patients were given 2 hours (9:00–11:00 AM) of light therapy (3000–5000 lux) daily for 4 weeks. During the 4 weeks of light therapy, the patients' behavioral disturbance as rated by nurses was reduced, nocturnal sleep was increased, and diurnal sleep was reduced. All of these changes were statistically significant. In addition, the nocturnal sleep was significantly increased after the cessation of light therapy. There also was a significant association between the degree of baseline insomnia and the amount of additional nocturnal sleep achieved. As an added benefit, patients who were hypersomnic at baseline experienced modest sleep reductions.

## Light Visor

A second method for administering light therapy is by use of a light visor. A light visor is a device that is worn on the forehead (like a golfer's visor) and delivers diffuse light to the eye. There are currently two vendors, BioBrite (Baltimore, MD) and Light Sciences (Wellesley, MA). The intensities achieved usually vary between 1500 lux and 3000 lux depending on the method of light generation used. The visor has the advantage of being essentially an article of clothing and not requiring the patient to sit still. This advantage is useful in delivering light therapy to a patient who is agitated. However, patients can remove the visor or simply fiddle with it, rendering it inoperative.

A recent study assessed the efficacy of light therapy using a BioBrite light visor to deliver 2000 lux for 2 hours in the morning (Colenda, Cohen, McCall, & Rosenquist, 1997). This study found no changes in the circadian rhythms of rest-activity data. There are several possible interpretations for these results in comparison with light-treatment studies conducted with light boxes. The most important consideration is that the light treatment is not reaching the retina with appropriate intensity. This light visor has not been found to provide more benefit than a placebo visor in patients suffering from SAD (Rosenthal et al., 1993).

We recently tested a new 3000-lux light visor (Light Sciences) and found that it has clear efficacy in shifting the circadian temperature rhythms of healthy, young adult males; a placebo visor (less than 50 lux) did not. We also observed amplitude increases in core body temperature in the subjects using the light visor. It is possible that this visor may be efficacious in delivering light therapy to patients with Alzheimer's disease, in which intensity of light is of paramount importance. Further research may help to clarify the answer to this question.

## Light Room

The third method for light treatment, and the one currently used at the Veterans Medical Center in Bedford, Massachusetts, is a light room with high-intensity phototherapy lights (Shift Work Systems, Cambridge, MA) installed in the ceiling. The phototherapy room has 10,000-lux lights; however, that intensity is only delivered if a patient looks directly at the lights. The light delivered in the horizontal plane, in which patients generally direct their gaze, is between 2000 and 3000 lux. The advantages of a light-therapy room are numerous in terms of effectiveness of delivery of the treatment. The patient can remain ambulatory throughout the treatment and does not have to be monitored closely. The treatment can be given without interrupting any of the patient's normal activities or routines, and dosage becomes more certain because of the pervasiveness of the light. The clear disadvantage is cost, and this method is probably only within the reach of institutions or day-care facilities.

In a recent study (van Someren et al., 1997), patients with Alzheimer's disease were given the opportunity to spend time during the diurnal period in a light-treatment living area with high-intensity lights installed. Patients received $1136 \pm 89$ lux based on a continuous light-meter recording. Patients received this light during the diurnal period; however, patients could position themselves to receive more or less light at will. Patients showed significant improvement in the circadian rhythm of their rest-activity cycle. This improvement did not occur in the patients included in the study who were blind.

Two patients who benefited from exposure to the light treatment room at the Bedford VA are reported on here.

## Case 1

Mr. B was a 64-year-old male with a 6-year history of Alzheimer's disease. He suffered from insomnia at home and after admission to a dementia specific unit. Initially, he would follow night staff during bedside rounds and watch them go about their work. After rounds, he would sit in the staff room, enjoying snacks and sometimes watching television for a few hours before allowing staff to put him to bed. Eventually, he would fall asleep for a couple of hours. He would wake again and wander into patients' bedrooms, disrupting their sleep. He also would rummage in closets and cover and uncover bed sheets. As his dementia progressed, efforts to redirect him, such as engaging him with food or conversation, were met with increasing resistance. Treatment with trazadone and chloral hydrate proved ineffective, and an increased dose of chloral hydrate caused lethargy in the morning, which interfered with his ability to eat.

Because drug therapy was ineffective in this case, light treatment was initiated. The light-treatment regimen involved placing the patient in the light room in a reclining chair from 10:00 PM to midnight. After initial fidgeting, Mr. B settled down and relaxed but never slept or closed his eyes while in the room. After the light exposure, he was moved to a dark, quiet area to relax for 30 to 60 minutes before being put to bed, where he slept without incident until he awoke late the following morning. Additionally, with the initiation of light therapy, the dose of chloral hydrate was reduced, and Mr. B required no other medications except an occasional low dose of lorazepam.

## Case 2

Mr. C, aged 75 years, on the unit for 1 year, had an 8-year history of Alzheimer's disease before admission. Pacing (psychomotor agitation) and occasional insomnia were the major reasons for his institutionalization. Prior to admission, trazadone was given to him nightly with little effect. Because of his inability to fall asleep and stay asleep, he was placed into his bed late (around 11:00 PM). He was agitated and would attempt to get out of bed many times, disrupting the staff's ability to provide care for other patients. When the trazadone dose was increased and given later in the evening, Mr. C would be difficult to wake for breakfast and not fully awake and able to eat until 10 AM. The trazadone adjustments that enabled him to sleep left him drowsy, more confused, and incoherent. These changes were followed by a new disruptive behavior, his incessant talking for an hour or more when placed into bed. This behavior also affected other patients. He was moved to a semiprivate room to minimize vocalization effects on sleeping patients.

A staff decision was made to initiate light treatment for 2 hours late in the evening. During the treatment, Mr. C was able to read or at least appeared focused on reading material left on a table by his chair. Light treatment resulted in peaceful sleep without frequent awakenings, although the patient still experienced some difficulties falling asleep.

# ☐  **Evaluation of Technique**

Light therapy shows great promise in reducing the noncognitive symptoms of Alzheimer's disease. Unlike other available treatments for these conditions, light therapy does not increase confusion or cause other unwanted side effects. Light boxes appear to be an effective way to deliver light therapy to patients with moderate to severe dementia, as shown in the two studies detailed previously (Mishima et al., 1994; Satlin et al., 1992). The limitations of using a light box in this population are illustrated by the by the need for table bar restraint in one study (Satlin et al., 1992) and the need for constant nursing supervision and aid in directing the patient to the light in the other (Mishima et al., 1994). It is possible that morning light is superior to evening light in aiding patients with Alzheimer's disease; however, evening light was effective as well. Timing issues are very important because of the phase-response curve of the circadian timing system to light, and more research is needed to evaluate the effects of different timing regimens on the overall efficacy of light therapy. The behavioral improvement noted in the Mishima study may have been caused by the timing of the light therapy (morning versus evening) or the longer duration of treatment (4 weeks as opposed to 1 week).

The difficulties with compliance and need for nursing supervision or mild restraint may be reduced by the light-visor method. However, efficacy of these devices still remains to be demonstrated in this patient population. Light therapy with a visor at home may be an alternative for therapy given in an institution if efficacy can be demonstrated. Although even relatively low levels of light can be efficacious in causing phase shifts in healthy young adults (Boivin et al., 1996), the same is probably not true in patients with Alzheimer's disease, and further work needs to be done to demonstrate the efficacy of this potentially useful device.

The use of a light room in delivering light therapy has great promise as a nonintrusive method for delivering light (van Someren et al., 1997). Indeed, in the study by van Someren et al., they demonstrate that the problem of timing the light therapy can be eliminated by simply giving the therapy during the diurnal period. This increasing of diurnal light in the institutional environment effectively removes the question of morning versus evening light therapy. Light is present at both times and is only efficacious during the sensitive portion of the phase-esponse curve of the individual. What this means is that patients who have a phase delay are phase-advanced to a more normal schedule. For patients who are phase-advanced, the opposite is true. Temperature amplitude should increase for both groups, leading to more stable sleep patterns.

If administering light over the entire diurnal period is impractical, as it is with a light box or a visor, it may be possible to customize the timing of the therapy to the patient by measuring the nadir of the patient's temperature rhythm and calculating the appropriate time of intervention via the phase-response curve. Temperature often can be measured accurately and unobtrusively with a tympanic-membrane thermometer during the night and morning. This eliminates the danger of making a patient more desynchronized to the environment by giving, for example, light in the morning but before the actual temperature nadir has been reached rather than after the temperature nadir. This error would yield further phase delays, as opposed to the desired phase advance. More research would help to determine if this technique would improve on a "one size fits all" approach of simply giving patients light therapy at a uniform time.

It appears from the two case reports that both patients probably were suffering from a circadian phase-delay disorder. Both experienced difficulty initiating sleep and wandered at night. They also experienced difficulty with sleep maintenance. Medications were of little benefit and, indeed, considerable detriment, as dosages had to be pushed to extreme ranges for limited efficacy. It is possible that morning light would have been more effective in these cases; however, even evening light provided improved sleep maintenance. However, as could be predicted, the patients' initial insomnia was not treated by evening light.

## ☐ Potential for Deleterious Effects

Some of the potential problems, side effects, and pitfalls of light therapy should be mentioned here as well. The most important danger is the ability of light under certain conditions to cause lesions in the ocular structures. There are two distinct types of damage that can occur with light therapy: acute lesions and chronic cumulative damage (Reme, Rol, Grothmann, Kaase, & Terman, 1996). Chronic cumulative damage is of more concern over, perhaps, decades of light therapy. Consequently, this damage is not a great risk in this geriatric population suffering from a terminal disease. However, acute damage occurring in the cornea and conjunctiva is a concern.

The first approach to preventing ocular damage is to remove the damaging parts of the spectrum. Ultraviolet light is the most damaging area of the spectrum and is not necessary for the efficacy of the light treatment, so it should be filtered out (Lam, Buchanan, Mador, Corral, & Remick, 1992; Lee, Chan, Paterson, Janzen, & Blashko, 1997). Most manufacturers of light-therapy equipment already have reduced the ultraviolet emissions of their products. However, both visible and ultraviolet light can damage the eye, so it is important not to use drugs that might sensitize the eye to light in the visible spectrum. Several factors ultimately determine the phototoxicity of a compound including the absorption spectrum, ability to pass the blood-ocular interface, binding to ocular tissues, and rate of clearance from the eye (Roberts & Dillon, 1990). Various pharmaceutical compounds meet these criteria, thereby making the eye more vulnerable to the damaging effects of visible light.

In this discussion, one drug imperatively deserving of mention is exogenous melatonin, which causes strong absorption of light in the visible range and has characteristics that indicate that it could cause ocular damage (Leino, Aho, Kari, Gynther, & Markkanen, 1984). Because exogenous melatonin often is given for circadian disturbances, the potential for hazardous interaction with light therapy is great. Therefore, it is best to use one treatment method only for circadian disturbances. If it is necessary to use both melatonin and light therapy, then it is important not to give light treatment before any exogenous melatonin has been fully metabolized. This precondition should be relatively easy to accomplish, because the phase-response curves of the activities of the two treatments are almost opposite (Reme et al., 1996). Therefore melatonin and light therapy exert opposite effects if given at approximately the same time.

There are several other drugs that can cause problems, including tricyclic or heterocyclic compounds (Reme et al., 1996). Other medications also have been tested. Chlorpromazine, propranolol, and iprindole bind to lens proteins and have absorption spectra that are active in the eye and have been found to damage lens proteins in vitro. Fluoxetine and imipramine are only mildly phototoxic but still cause minor damage to lens proteins in vitro. It is important to check for these possible interactions before beginning light therapy.

Several commentators also have described the need for ophthalmological examination to ensure that there is no preexisting retinal or other ocular pathology before initiating light treatment. Pathological conditions such as age-related maculopathy and other retinal degenerative diseases (Roberts & Dillon, 1990) could be exacerbated by light treatment, and the inability of the patients to self-report visual difficulties further reinforces this need. There is some controversy on this point, because there is no evidence that prior light-induced photoreceptor damage can be detected in this way (Waxler et al., 1992). Nevertheless, in this patient population, which may be impaired in reporting preexisting visual difficulties, it would seem prudent to exercise caution.

Some side effects also have been noted in patients using light therapy for SAD (Labbate, Lafer, Thibault, & Sachs, 1994). Hypomania is an uncommon but serious side effect. It may be less prevalent in Alzheimer's disease, but no studies have looked for adverse effects of light treatment in Alzheimer's disease. Agitation, which could be a precursor of hypomania because it is one of the symptoms, was reported more frequently than hypomania. Agitation even not leading to full hypomania could be a significant problem for patients with Alzheimer's disease, because it is one of the noncognitive behavioral disturbances found in Alzheimer's disease.

# ☐ Conclusion

Light therapy is an important new treatment for the noncognitive symptoms of Alzheimer's disease. The fact that it is a nonpharmacological treatment decreases the likelihood of side effects that increase confusion or otherwise make the cognitive symptoms worse. Further research needs to be performed to find the optimal treatment conditions for patient populations with Alzheimer's disease; however, it seems clear that patients suffering from Alzheimer's disease can derive considerable benefit from light therapy.

# ☐ References

Aarsland, D., Cummings, J. L., Yenner, G., & Miller, B. (1996). Relationship of aggressive behavior to other neuropsychiatric symptoms in patients with Alzheimer's disease. *American Journal of Psychiatry, 153*, 243–247.

Albert, M. S. (1996). Cognitive and neurobiologic markers of early Alzheimer disease. *Proceedings of the National Academy of Sciences of the United States of America, 93*, 13547–13551.

Ancoli-Israel, S., Klauber, M. R., Jones, D. W., Kripke, D. F., Martin, J., Mason, W., Pat-Horenczyk, R., & Fell, R. (1997). Variations in circadian rhythms of activity, sleep, and light exposure related to dementia in nursing-home patients. *Sleep, 20*(1), 18–23.

Avery, D. H., Dahl, K., Savage, M. V., Brengelmann, G. L., Larsen, L. H., Kenny, M. A., Eder, D. N., Vitiello, M. V., & Prinz, P. N. (1997). Circadian temperature and cortisol rhythms during a constant routine are phase-delayed in hypersomnic winter depression [published erratum appears in *Biological Psychiatry, 42*, 636, 1997]. *Biological Psychiatry, 41*, 1109–1123.

Axelrod, J., & Reisine, T. D. (1984). Stress hormones: their interaction and regulation. *Science, 224*, 452–459.

Blanks, J. C., Hinton, D. R., Sadun, A. A., & Miller, C. A. (1989). Retinal ganglion cell degeneration in Alzheimer's disease. *Brain Research, 501*, 364–372.

Bliwise, D. L., Watts, R. L., Watts, N., Rye, D. B., Irbe, D., & Hughes, M. (1995). Disruptive nocturnal behavior in Parkinson's disease and Alzheimer's disease [see comments]. *Journal of Geriatric Psychiatry and Neurology, 8*, 107–110.

Boivin, D. B., Czeisler, C. A., Dijk, D. J., Duffy, J. F., Folkard, S., Minors, D. S., Totterdell, P., & Waterhouse, J. M. (1997). Complex interaction of the sleep-wake cycle and circadian phase modulates mood in healthy subjects. *Archives of General Psychiatry, 54*, 145–152.

Boivin, D. B., Duffy, J. F., Kronauer, R. E., & Czeisler, C. A. (1996). Dose-response relationships for resetting of human circadian clock by light. *Nature, 379*, 540–542.

Campbell, S. S., Dawson, D., & Anderson, M. W. (1993). Alleviation of sleep maintenance insomnia with timed exposure to bright light. *Journal of the American Geriatrics Society, 41*, 829–836.

Campbell, S. S., Kripke, D. F., Gillin, J. C., & Hrubovcak, J. C. (1988). Exposure to light in healthy elderly subjects and Alzheimer's patients. *Physiology and Behavior, 42,* 141–144.

Card, J. P., & Moore, R. Y. (1991). The organization of visual circuits influencing the circadian activity of the suprachiasmatic nucleus. In D. C. Klein, R. Y. Moore, & S. M. Reppert (Eds.), *Suprachiasmatic nucleus: The mind's clock* (pp. 51–76). New York: Oxford University Press.

Cohen-Mansfield, J. (1995). Assessment of disruptive behavior/agitation in the elderly: function, methods, and difficulties. *Journal of Geriatric Psychiatry and Neurology, 8*(1), 52–60.

Cohen-Mansfield, J., Marx, M. S., Werner, P., & Freedman, L. (1992). Temporal patterns of agitated nursing home residents. *International Psychogeriatrics, 4,* 197–206.

Cohen-Mansfield, J., Werner, P., & Freedman, L. (1995). Sleep and agitation in agitated nursing home residents: an observational study. *Sleep, 18,* 674–680.

Cohen-Mansfield, J., Werner, P., & Marx, M. S. (1990). Screaming in nursing home residents. *Journal of the American Geriatricx Society, 38,* 785–792.

Colenda, C. C., Cohen, W., McCall, W. V., & Rosenquist, P. B. (1997). Phototherapy for patients with Alzheimer disease with disturbed sleep patterns: Results of a community-based pilot study. *Alzheimer Disease and Associated Disorders, 11*(3), 175–178.

Cooke, K. M., Kreydatus, M. A., Atherton, A., & Thoman, E. B. (1998). The effect of evening light exposure on the sleep of elderly woman expressing sleep complaints. *Journal of Behavioral Medicine, 21*(1), 103–114.

Dai, J., Swaab, D. F., & Buijs, R. M. (1998a). Retinohypothalamic projections in Alzheimer's disease. *Neurobiology of Aging, 19*(Suppl. 4), 242.

Dai, J., Van der Vliet, J., Swaab, D. F., & Buijs, R. M. (1998b). Human retinohypothalamic tract as revealed by in vitro postmortem tracing. *Journal of Comparative Neurology, 397,* 357–370.

Davies, D. C., McCoubrie, P., McDonald, B., & Jobst, K. A. (1995). Myelinated axon number in the optic nerve is unaffected by Alzheimer's disease. *British Journal of Ophthalmology, 79,* 596–600.

Devanand, D. P., Jacobs, D. M., Tang, M. X., Del Castillo-Castaneda, C., Sano, M., Marder, K., Bell, K., Bylsma, F. W., Brandt, J., Albert, M., & Stern, Y. (1997). The course of psychopathologic features in mild to moderate Alzheimer disease. *Archives of General Psychiatry, 54,* 257–263.

Dorsey, C., Lukas, S., Teicher, M., Harper, D., Winkleman, J., Cunningham, S., & Satlin, A. (1996). Effects of passive body heating on the sleep of older female insomniacs. *Journal of Geriatric Psychiatry and Neurology, 9,* 83–90.

Evans, L. K. (1987). Sundown syndrome in institutionalized elderly. *Journal of the American Geriatric Society, 35*(2), 101–108.

Gallagher-Thompson, D., Brooks, J. O. d., Bliwise, D., Leader, J., & Yesavage, J. A. (1992). The relations among caregiver stress, "sundowning" symptoms, and cognitive decline in Alzheimer's disease. *Journal of the American Geriatric Society, 40,* 807–810.

Hartmann, A., Veldhuis, J. D., Deuschle, M., Standhardt, H., & Heuser, I. (1997). Twenty-four hour cortisol release profiles in patients with Alzheimer's and Parkinson's disease compared to normal controls: ultradian secretory pulsatility and diurnal variation. *Neurobiology of Aging, 18,* 285–289.

Hedges, T. R. R., Perez Galves, R., Speigelman, D., Barbas, N. R., Peli, E., & Yardley, C. J. (1996). Retinal nerve fiber layer abnormalities in Alzheimer's disease. *Acta Ophthalmologica Scandinavica, 74,* 271–275.

Heuser, I. J., Baronti, F., Marin, C. A., Ma, N., Merriam, G. R., Chase, T. N., & Mouradian, M. M. (1992). Growth hormone secretion in Alzheimer's disease: 24-hour profile of basal levels and response to stimulation and suppression studies. *Neurobiology of Aging, 13,* 255–260.

Hope, T., Keene, J., Fairburn, C., McShane, R., & Jacoby, R. (1997). Behaviour changes in dementia. 2: Are there behavioural syndromes? *International Journal of Geriatric Psychiatry, 12,* 1074–1078.

Labbate, L. A., Lafer, B., Thibault, A., & Sachs, G. S. (1994). Side effects induced by bright light treatment for seasonal affective disorder. *Journal of Clinical Psychiatry, 55*(5), 189–191.

Lam, R. W., Buchanan, A., Mador, J. A., Corral, M. R., & Remick, R. A. (1992). The effects of ultraviolet-A wavelengths in light therapy for seasonal depression. *Journal of Affective Disorders, 24,* 237–243.

Lee, T. M., Blashko, C. A., Janzen, H. L., Paterson, J. G., & Chan, C. C. (1997a). Pathophysiological mechanism of seasonal affective disorder. *Journal of Affective Disorders, 46,* 25–38.

Lee, T. M., Chan, C. C., Paterson, J. G., Janzen, H. L., & Blashko, C. A. (1997). Spectral properties of phototherapy for seasonal affective disorder: A meta-analysis. *Acta Psychiatrica Scandinavica, 96,* 117–121.

Leino, M., Aho, I. M., Kari, E., Gynther, J., & Markkanen, S. (1984). Effects of melatonin and 6-methoxy-tetrahydro-beta-carboline in light induced retinal damage: A computerized morphometric method. *Life Sciences, 35,* 1997–2001.

Little, J. T., Satlin, A., Sunderland, T., & Volicer, L. (1995). Sundown syndrome in severely demented patients with probable Alzheimer's disease. *Journal of Geriatric Psychiatry and Neurology, 8*(2), 103–106.

Loewenstein, R. J., Weingartner, H., Gillin, J. C., Kaye, W., Ebert, M., & Mendelson, W. B. (1982). Disturbances of sleep and cognitive functioning in patients with dementia. *Neurobiology of Aging, 3,* 371–377.

Maquet, P., Peters, J., Aerts, J., Delfiore, G., Degueldre, C., Luxen, A., & Franck, G. (1996). Functional neuroanatomy of human rapid-eye-movement sleep and dreaming. *Nature, 383,* 163–166.

Minors, D. S., Waterhouse, J. M., & Wirz-Justice, A. (1991). A human phase-response curve to light. *Neuroscience Letters, 133*(1), 36–40.

Mishima, K., Okawa, M., Hishikawa, Y., Hozumi, S., Hori, H., & Takahashi, K. (1994). Morning bright light therapy for sleep and behavior disorders in elderly patients with dementia. *Acta Psychiatrica Scandinavica, 89*(1), 1–7.

Moore, M. R. (1995). Organization of the mammalian circadian system. In D. J. Chadwick & K. Ackrill (Eds.), *Circadian clocks and their adjustment* (pp. 88–99). New York: John Wiley and Sons.

Okawa, M., Mishima, K., Hishikawa, Y., Hozumi, S., Hori, H., & Takahashi, K. (1991). Circadian rhythm disorders in sleep-waking and body temperature in elderly patients with dementia and their treatment [see comments]. *Sleep, 14,* 478–485.

Pfeiffer, E., Baxter, D., Candelora, E., Haag, S., Nadiminti, L., & Leaverton, P. (1997). Finding and treating depression in Alzheimer's patients: A study of the effects on patients and caregivers. *Psychopharmacology Bulletin, 33,* 721–729.

Pollack, C. P., & Stokes, P. E. (1997). Circadian rest-activity rhythms in demented and nondemented older community residents and their caregivers. *Journal of the American Geriatrics Society, 45,* 446–452.

Prinz, P. N., Moe, K. E., Vitiello, M. V., Marks, A. L., & Larsen, L. H. (1992). Entrained body temperature rhythms are similar in mild Alzheimer's disease, geriatric onset depression, and normal aging. *Journal of Geriatric Psychiatry and Neurology, 5*(2), 65–71.

Prinz, P. N., Vitaliano, P. P., Vitiello, M. V., Bókan, J., Raskind, M., Peskind, E., & Gerber, C. (1982). Sleep, EEG and mental function changes in senile dementia of the Alzheimer's type. *Neurobiology of Aging, 3,* 361–370.

Reme, C. E., Rol, P., Grothmann, K., Kaase, H., & Terman, M. (1996). Bright light therapy in focus: Lamp emission spectra and ocular safety. *Technology and Health Care, 4,* 403–413.

Roberts, J. E., & Dillon, J. (1990). Screening for potential in vivo phototoxicity in the lens/retina. *Lens and Eye Toxicity Research, 7,* 655–666.

Rosenthal, N. E., Moul, D. E., Hellekson, C. J., Oren, D. A., Frank, A., Brainard, G. C., Murray, M. G., & Wehr, T. A. (1993). A multicenter study of the light visor for seasonal affective disorder: No difference in efficacy found between two different intensities. *Neuropsychopharmacology, 8,* 151–160.

Rosenthal, N. E., Sack, D. A., Gillin, J. C., Lewy, A. J., Goodwin, F. K., Davenport, Y., Mueller, P. S., Newsome, D. A., & Wehr, T. A. (1984). Seasonal affective disorder: A description of the syndrome and preliminary findings with light therapy. *Archives of General Psychiatry, 41*(1), 72–80.

Sadun, A. A., & Bassi, C. J. (1990). Optic nerve damage in Alzheimer's disease [see comments]. *Ophthalmology, 97,* 9–17.

Satlin, A., Volicer, L., Ross, V., Herz, L., & Campbell, S. (1992). Bright light treatment of behavioral and sleep disturbances in patients with Alzheimer's disease. *American Journal of Psychiatry, 149,* 1028–1032.

Satlin, A., Volicer, L., Stopa, E. G., & Harper, D. (1995). Circadian locomotor activity and core-body temperature rhythms in Alzheimer's disease. *Neurobiology of Aging, 16,* 765–771.

Souetre, E., Salvati, E., Belugou, J. L., Pringuey, D., Candito, M., Krebs, B., Ardisson, J. L., & Darcourt, G. (1989). Circadian rhythms in depression and recovery: Evidence for blunted amplitude as the main chronobiological abnormality. *Psychiatry Research, 28,* 263–278.

Steele, C., Rovner, B., Chase, G. A., & Folstein, M. (1990). Psychiatric symptoms and nursing home placement of patients with Alzheimer's disease. *American Journal of Psychiatry, 147,* 1049–1051.

Stopa, E. G., Volicer, L., Kuo-Leblanc, V., Harper, D., Lathi, D., Tate, B., & Satlin, A. (1999). Pathologic evaluation of the human suprachiasmatic nucleus in severe dementia. *Journal of Neuropathology and Experimental Neurology, 58*(1), 29–39.

Swaab, D. F., Fliers, E., & Partiman, T. S. (1985). The suprachiasmatic nucleus of the human brain in relation to sex, age and senile dementia. *Brain Research, 342*(1), 37–44.

Teicher, M. H., Glod, C. A., Harper, D., Magnus, E., Brasher, C., Wren, F., & Pahlavan, K. (1993). Locomotor activity in depressed children and adolescents: I. Circadian dysregulation. *Journal of the American Academy of Child and Adolescent Psychiatry, 32,* 760–769.

Teicher, M. H., Glod, C. A., Magnus, E., Harper, D., Benson, G., Krueger, K., & McGreenery, C. E. (1997). Circadian rest-activity disturbances in seasonal affective disorder. *Archives of General Psychiatry, 54,* 124–130.

van Someren, E. J., Hagebeuk, E. E., Lijzenga, C., Scheltens, P., de Rooij, S. E., Jonker, C., Pot, A. M., Mirmiran, M., & Swaab, D. F. (1996). Circadian rest-activity rhythm disturbances in Alzheimer's disease. *Biololgical Psychiatry, 40,* 259–270.

van Someren, E. J., Kessler, A., Mirmiran, M., & Swaab, D. F. (1997). Indirect bright light improves circadian rest-activity rhythm disturbances in demented patients. *Biological Psychiatry, 41,* 955–963.

van Someren, E. J., Mirmiran, M., & Swaab, D. F. (1993). Non-pharmacological treatment of sleep and wake disturbances in aging and Alzheimer's disease: Chronobiological perspectives. *Behavioural Brain Researcg, 57,* 235–253.

Vitiello, M. V., Bliwise, D. L., & Prinz, P. N. (1992). Sleep in Alzheimer's disease and the sundown syndrome. *Neurology, 42*(7 suppl. 6), 83–93; discussion 93–84.

Waxler, M., James, R. H., Brainard, G. C., Moul, D. E., Oren, D. A., & Rosenthal, N. E. (1992). Retinopathy and bright light therapy [letter]. *American Journal of Psychiatry, 149,* 1610–1611.

Wirz-Justice, A., Graw, P., Krauchi, K., Gisin, B., Jochum, A., Arendt, J., Fisch, H. U., Buddeberg, C., & Poldinger, W. (1993). Light therapy in seasonal affective disorder is independent of time of day or circadian phase. *Archives of General Psychiatry, 50,* 929–937.

Zhou, J. N., Hofman, M. A., & Swaab, D. F. (1995). VIP neurons in the human SCN in relation to sex, age, and Alzheimer's disease. *Neurobiology of Aging, 16,* 571–576.

**12**
CHAPTER

John Zeisel
Joan Hyde
Linda Shi

# Environmental Design as a Treatment for Alzheimer's Disease

A new holistic approach towards Alzheimer's disease is taking hold of the imaginations of caregivers, clinicians, designers, and others concerned with people living with dementia. This approach centers on systematically co-ordinated nonpharmacological treatments and emphasizes the concept that although Alzheimer's disease is presently incurable, this does not mean it is untreatable. This treatment approach includes the use of environment, lifestyle management, continuous monitoring, ongoing support, and modified communication to systematically ameliorate the symptoms of the disease (Raia & Koenig-Coste, 1996).

This chapter describes the contributions that environmental design can make to the treatment of people with Alzheimer's and related dementias. Specifically, the chapter focuses on research findings and applied design experience that demonstrate the effects of eight critical environmental-design features on patients and their care.

Designing residences for people with Alzheimer's disease and related dementias provides designers with special challenges and opportunities to explore the question of "healing" environments. These diseases are not mental illnesses, they are diseases of the brain—brain matter is lost over time. It is difficult for persons with these diseases to lay down new memories, such as remembering a message just taken over the phone or the name of a person just met, but it is easy for them to draw on "deep" memories of the past, of their long life. It is difficult for persons with these diseases to carry out complex tasks, such as organizing a multicourse meal or balancing a checkbook, but they can understand environments that are presented clearly and legibly.

Environments that heal—healing environments—for people with Alzheimer's disease clearly have to represent and reflect deep memories. What are these deep memories? They may be memories of workplaces, of traditional houses, of streets they have lived on. Or they may be even more profound environmental memories.

What are profound memories? *Fire* represents warmth, safety, and food. In traditional house settings the "inglenook"—that small corner of the covered hearth with a built-in bench—evokes such profound feelings. The *kitchen*, related to fire, evokes food, family and friendly communication. *Personal objects*, such as a familiar photograph or an old housecoat, bring back memories of friendship and caring to demented residents. *Music* evokes great joy and profound sadness among residents with Alzheimer's disease, letting them know that they are still alive. And *just outside the front door*—like in the clearing in front of a cave—one knows one can feel the elements but one is still close enough to home to be safe.

Design that touches people's deep and profound understanding of their surroundings is equally powerful for those without dementia as for those with such a disease. Healing design principles for people with Alzheimer's disease can be translated into archtypical deep-healing design principles:

- Feeling safe, secure, and free
- Understanding what is expected in the community
- Being able to get away by oneself and unwind
- Knowing where one is going and having fun getting there
- Enjoying the outdoors and the changes of seasons and weather
- Knowing that anything one does is OK, because where one is is safe and familiar
- Celebrating what one can do, not dwelling on one's failures
- Not having to struggle to understand one's surroundings

Environments for living, work, and play that provide their users with these profound opportunities are likely to be healing environments.

## ☐ Relevant and Current Research

Numerous publications in the past decade discuss the therapeutic advantages of environmental design features for people with Alzheimer's disease (Calkins, 1988; Cohen & Weisman, 1991; Coons, 1991; Hiatt, 1992; Hyde, 1989; Weisman, Cohen, Ray, & Day, 1991). However, there is little systematic research indicating that special features commonly found in special care units (SCUs) are, in fact, effective in reducing symptoms and enhancing the quality of life or care for residents with dementia (Mathew, Sloane, Kirby, & Flood, 1988; Ohta & Ohta, 1988; Office of Technology Assessment, 1992).

Zeisel et al. (1999) carried out a National Institute on Aging study to overcome this deficit in our knowledge. Methods for the study were drawn from health service delivery research, particularly the common core research tools employed in the National Institute on Aging (NIA) Collaborative Studies of Special Care Units for Alzheimer's Disease (Ory, 1994). Methods also were drawn from environmental psychology postoccupancy evaluation research that captures environment-behavior interactions in buildings in use. The research was conducted in three phases over 6 years starting in 1992.

In phase I of research, the team developed an environment-behavior (E-B) model of environment and outcomes interactions. The E-B model, developed by investigators to describe and organize influences that the physical environment of SCUs has on residents and caregivers, comprises eight primary environmental concepts and 16 secondary dimensions.

A literature review first was carried out to develop a comprehensive list of research-based design characteristics for therapeutic SCUs, and to elaborate a set of testable environment-behavior hypotheses describing potential effects of these characteristics on health and behavior outcomes (Zeisel, Hyde, & Levkoff, 1994). A panel of experts[1] then was employed to test and refine the model and its related outcome measures (Lawton, 1995; Zeisel, Epp, & Demos, 1978; Zeisel, Welch, Epp, & Demos, 1983). After the panel reviewed and ranked the E-B model on a 7-point scale, the model was modified and a final model adopted defining eight environment-behavior concepts that contribute to the quality of life and treatment of people with Alzheimer's disease.

Two critical dimensions for each E-B model concept were identified, measurable characteristics of the environment in use that serve as empirical indicators of the degree to which the concept describes a particular setting. For example, the unmeasurable E-B concept *common space structure* comprises the two dimensions *quantity* and *variability*, both of which are measurable.

The final eight E-B model concepts discussed in the next section include one boundary condition (exits), four spatial categories (private, shared, and outdoor spaces, and pathways), and three ambient qualities (residentiality, autonomy support, and comprehensibility). These eight factors reflect the most current knowledge in design for residential assisted-living units for the care of people with Alzheimer's disease, and in the design, plan review, and evaluation of SCUs.

Phase II of the study tested and finalized the Hearthstone Environment Rating Scale (HERS), a coding system derived from the E-B model, in 30 SCUs throughout New England. Before finalizing the HERS, comparative analysis was performed with the Therapeutic Environment Screening Scale (TESS-2+) employed in the NIA collaborative studies of SCUs (Sloane & Matthew, 1990) to be certain the HERS was exhaustive of the E-B model categories.

In phase III, a purposive subsample of 15 SCUs was selected to test in depth the impact of the eight environmental criteria on health outcomes. Independent design variables first were measured using the HERS. Data on potentially intervening quality-of-care variables then were gathered through questionnaires distributed to administrators and SCU directors, as well as from qualitative analysis of facility documentation.

The Administrator Questionnaire (NIA, 1993) includes items on ownership, certification, bed utilization, discharges, reimbursement sources and rates, and hours and types of services. The Special Care Unit Director Questionnaire (NIA, 1993) measures facility history, bed utilization, size, discharges, reimbursement sources and rates, administrative and direct-care hours, staffing and care assignments, length of employment, training and care planning, criteria for admission and discharge, resident possessions, family participation, and structured group activity (recreation, music, art, range of motion, bladder, and bowel therapies, exercise, family-support groups), care practices (restraint policy, targeted activities, use of volunteers, isolation rooms, unit dining rooms), and resident needs.

Data also were collected on the health and functional capacities of all 436 patients in the 15 SCUs. Health-outcome scales, captured in the Resident Profile (NIA, 1993), represent health symptoms likely to be influenced by some aspect of the physical care environment as well as symptoms associated in early drug trial research with delayed institutionalization. Resident profiles were completed by a nurse informant familiar with each patient employing personal judgment and medical records. These profiles captured data on aggressive and agitated behavior (Cohen-Mansfield, Marx, & Rosenthal, 1989), misidentification and paranoid delusions (Reisberg et al., 1987), and depression and social withdrawal (Helmes, Csapo, & Short, 1987).

Analysis of data required addressing what Teresi (1994) describes as the problematic nature of "studies of intervention effects when institutional units [SCUs] are assigned to experimental or control conditions, but the individual is the unit of analysis." She points out that because the resulting mixed units of analysis (unit and individual resident) can result in attenuated standard errors for the estimates of effects, "special modeling techniques may be needed in these situations" (Teresi, 1994). Therefore, hierarchical linear modeling (Bryk & Raudenbush, 1992, Bryk,

Raudenbush, Seltzer, & Congdon, 1988) approaches were employed to avoid false positive results. Hierarchical linear modeling analysis uses both the 15 SCU sites and the 436 patients as the unit of analysis simultaneously to determine the effects of the environmental-design characteristics of SCUs (unit variables) on outcome measures of patients (individual variables) and control for intervening quality-of-care variables.

The results demonstrate that design interventions have clear and positive health effects on reducing aggression, agitation, depression, social withdrawal, misidentification, and paranoid delusions in people with Alzheimer's disease. This research is the first to test common beliefs about SCU design based on empirical data. The research design developed for this project is important in that it establishes a replicable model for determining health outcomes affected by environmental design and other nonpharmacological approaches in actual diverse care settings.

## ☐ Outcomes

The ultimate success of a treatment approach can be seen in improved quality of life, delayed institutionalization, slowed rate of progression of disease symptoms as measured by preserved function and motor skills, reduced need for medication, reduced behavioral symptoms and psychiatric distress, and improved mood and social reaction.

## ☐ Description of the Technique

The principles embodied in the E-B model are incorporated easily into any Alzheimer's disease care setting. Table 12.1 describes the eight concepts and 16 dimensions that can be used to provide a higher quality of life for those with Alzheimer's disease. These criteria reflect the physical design elements of the deep healing design principles described previously. They organize E-B design research information and concepts in terms of therapeutic and quality-of-life outcomes critical to residents' lives.

### Exit Control

The brains of patients with Alzheimer's disease cannot hold cognitive maps, and they frequently forget how to return home. Therefore, people with dementia should only leave their homes accompanied by someone else. Doorways from a residence that open to the larger public community therefore need to be controlled. Residents who spend so much time indoors become agitated by doors with mixed messages: On the one hand windows and hardware on doors attract residents and seem to invite them

---

**TABLE 12.1. Environment-behavior criteria for design**

| Eight Concepts | Definition/Examples | Dimensions |
|---|---|---|
| **Boundary control** | | |
| 1. Exit control | Boundary conditions of each special care unit; surrounding walls, fences, doors and how they are locked or otherwise limit and allow people to come and go | A. Immediacy of control<br>B. Unobtrusiveness |
| **Spatial characteristics** | | |
| 2. Walking paths | Circulation space residents use for wandering and moving around | A. Continuousness<br>B. Wayfinding |
| 3. Personal places | Spaces—primarily bedrooms—used mostly by and sometimes assigned to individuals or a limited number of residents | A. Privacy<br>B. Personalization |
| 4. Common space | Sizes, relationships, and qualities of spaces used by all residents | A. Quantity<br>B. Variability |
| 5. Healing gardens | Residents' access to common areas out of doors and the way these places support residents' needs | A. Availability<br>B. Supportiveness (includes safety) |
| **Ambient conditions** | | |
| 6. Residentiality | Degree to which the size of the care setting reflects a small "community" and degree to which the setting uses residential furnishings, design features, and personal objects | A. Size<br>B. Familiarity |
| 7. Independence | Ways in which the facility encourages and supports residents to use their remaining faculties to carry out basic tasks and activities independently and with dignity | A. Safety<br>B. Prosthetics |
| 8. Sensory comprehensibility | Quality of the sensory environment—acoustic, visual, thermal, odor, and kinesthetic environment in all spaces—and degree to which these conditions may confuse residents | A. Management<br>B. Meaningfulness |

*Note.* For a fuller discussion of these criteria see Zeisel, Hyde, & Levkoff (1994).

to go out; on the other hand locks and keypads prevent their use. Exit doors that are less visible—more unobtrusive—with no attracting hardware reduce agitation. Increasing the visibility and making more inviting any "safe" door to a secure healing garden further diverts attention from doors that exit to dangerous areas.

If exit doors need signals that indicate to the staff that they have been opened without supervision, such signals can be chosen so that they do not disturb the ambiance of the residential setting, such as chimes rather than alarms. The less obvious the door, the signal, the hardware, and the other side of the door, the greater the independence the residents have in their safe environment.

## Walking Paths

One of the symptoms of Alzheimer's disease for certain people is the desire to walk, perhaps looking for something without knowing precisely what. Although aimless wandering can be a problem for the staff in a facility that has no place for this activity, a well-designed pathway can transform wandering into walking. A pathway can achieve this goal if it is interesting and not a dead end. Such a pathway need not be a specially designed circular track but rather can be the thoughtful connection of corridors that pass through common areas and connect up again to corridors going in another direction. Interest along the path is important so that those walking always have some goal in sight—the next interesting picture, view, or plant. Also, interest at the end of the path, a social space or a fireplace, provides a place to walk to, a destination that gives purpose to the trips.

## Personal Places

Because residents spend so much time together, they also need places to be alone, to avoid the pressures of social interaction. Just because someone is demented does not mean that he or she can stand being together with others 24 hours a day. Individual spaces residents can use to get away by themselves can include private bedrooms or small out-of-the-way corner sitting areas in a living room or garden. Residents who need to sit together quietly with visiting family members also can use places like this. Private areas are also places residents and their families use to decorate and furnish personally, thus creating a soothing mood that triggers positive memories.

## Common Space

Residents in Alzheimer's disease assisted-living facilities spend almost all their time in the facility and together. To satisfy their need for diversity and reduce boredom and agitation it is essential to have at least two if not three different common spaces—dining room, kitchen, living room, foyer.

The more the settings of these rooms are different and interesting, the easier it is for staff to manage smaller family-like activities there and for residents to feel stimulated by the differences in ambiance they can sense.

## Healing Gardens

Not every residence is able to provide its residents a safe and secure outdoor area immediately adjacent to the residential area. But this ideal gives residents a sense of nature, weather, and plants. If nothing else, patients with Alzheimer's disease enjoy being outdoors and are relaxed by being able to get out of the confinement they feel inside. Yet a healing garden is even more than a place to get out—it is a sanctuary in which the basic drive to have contact with normal forces can be met.

If such an amenity is not easily provided, for example if the residential area is on an upper floor of an urban building, designers and operators need to arrange alternatives. One possibility is to have an outdoor area nearby that residents can use regularly, accompanied by staff members. If such an arrangement is to be made, the path there and back must be thought through carefully to avoid creating anxiety and a breakdown in safety.

## Residentiality

The fireplace, front porch, and garden are residential environmental design elements that create positive moods in residents by touching deep-seated memories. The familiarity of residential furniture, spaces, decorations, and lighting fixtures relaxes everyone in Alzheimer's facilities—residents, their families, and staff members. Managing the size of features to be residential—a scale people can relate to and grasp easily—itself can be soothing. A refrigerator, a window, a small room, and a small group gathering all are familiar, understandable, and manageable elements for demented residents and everyone with whom they interact.

## Independence

Details in the environment such as handrails and floors that prevent slips and falls contribute to the independence and autonomy of residents, because they support each person's ability to do things on her or his own. It may seem obvious that a toilet so low that it prevents an older person from standing up alone limits independence, but it does. Any nonprosthetic or unsafe design element has this effect. The safer the environment, the more likely the staff is to permit residents to move about by themselves and make independent choices.

## Sensory Comprehensibility

Patients with Alzheimer's disease are not confused by everything around them. If the sounds, sights, and smells they experience are familiar, they can cope with them and enjoy them. A common myth and mistake in design for dementia care is the belief that if everything is sedate and bland, residents will be soothed. This is not the case. Soothing can be anxiety-producing if taken to an extreme. What is needed is to create enough activity to keep residents interested, and to make sure that the activity provided is understandable to them. Colors are fine, and traditional patterns for wallpaper are better than abstract patterns. A television is fine; recorded films that have fewer rapid changes for advertisements are more satisfying than random violence and loud noises from the television. Comprehensibility comes from sensible, common-sense management.

## ☐  Case Examples

These principles have been put into practice at Hearthstone Alzheimer Care, a company that develops and manages assisted-living treatment residences for people in the middle and late stages of dementia. Hearthstone presently operates five assisted-living residences for those with Alzheimer's disease in the Boston and New York City areas. Each includes a 24-hour residential program, a respite program for families that need to have a family member cared for only occasionally for a week or two, and a day program for residents who are cared for by family members at night.

Each residence is presently a wing of a larger assisted-living complex, providing seniors with a continuum of living arrangements from relatively independent assisted living to assistance with problems of frailty and dementia care. This cooperative arrangement enables seniors to take advantage of an even fuller range of options. A resident can live full-time at Hearthstone, or a couple may decide to take advantage of the continuum by living in an assisted-living apartment, with the member of the couple who has dementia participating in the day program. And some couples live separately, with the person who has dementia living in the Hearthstone program and the spouse in an independent apartment. The particular arrangement is planned to maximize the quality of life of both members of the couple.

A typical Hearthstone day starts with each resident getting up when she or he wakes up, not on a regulated schedule. The morning includes a shower, grooming, dressing, and a breakfast served individually at the "Hearth" kitchen—the central design feature of each treatment residence. After breakfast the staff engages residents in activities such as cooking, laundry, bingo, seated aerobics, and gardening that help residents maintain a sense of self and develop a sense of the group as a whole. Lunchtime is another group activity, after which many residents rest in their rooms. The afternoon is full again, with several activities for small groups of about seven residents each. Residents move between activities if they lose interest or their attention wanders. After dinner, residents generally gather around the player piano to sing and dance before getting ready for bed. If a resident wakes in the middle of the night, aides engage him or her in conversation or play a game until the resident is tired again and goes back to bed.

Family members come to the residence often either to make informal visits during evenings and weekends or for organized occasions such as birthday parties or holiday celebrations. Support groups in which family members can share their experiences and joys and troubles are run by program directors once a month. Family members also are involved regularly with residents' medical needs, making decisions regarding medications and taking residents to doctors' appointments.

Each residence responds to the particular context created by the larger assisted-living context. One is located on three floors of a wing of a converted school; another on the seventh floor of a New York residential hotel; a third on the ground floor of a newly constructed building. Each, however, follows a basic program that reflects the design principles described earlier in this chapter:

- Common spaces
- Private spaces
- A garden
- Walking paths
- Safety
- Residentiality
- Supportiveness
- Understandability

A basic design concept that connects each design is the "dog bone" or "dumbbell" scheme. Rather than having social spaces in the center of a residence, or circular wandering paths, Hearthstone residences are designed to be straight walking paths with larger social spaces at both ends (Figure 12.1).

Social spaces generally include the Hearth kitchen, a living room, a

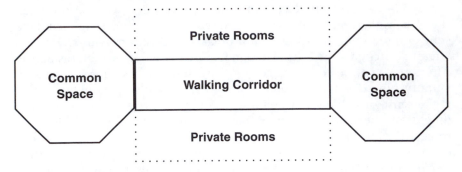

**FIGURE 12.1.** The Hearthstone barbell/dog-bone concept avoids dead-end corridors.

therapeutic laundry area, and a garden. Staff has a small office with private offices for the program director, the nurse, and the life-quality activity coordinator. Private suites include singles and rooms for two residents separated by a full wall or high piece of furniture. The walls along the walking path are highly decorated with photographs chosen by residents. Outside each private room is a "shadow box"—a framed-in glass box—that residents' families decorate with photographs and other mementos of residents' achievements and grandchildren.

## ☐ Evaluation of the Technique

Theory, informal observation, and common sense all lead to the conclusion that environment can reduce symptoms and improve the quality of life of people with Alzheimer's disease. The results of our study indicate ways in which elements of the physical environment affect health and quality-of-life factors.

1. In SCUs with unobtrusive and secure exits there are fewer paranoid delusions, less misidentification syndrome and paranoid delusions, and reduced social withdrawal.

   In SCUs with highly rated exit design, doors are painted the same color as the walls or as other residential doors in the SCU. Doors also are placed along the sides of hallways and therefore are less visible to residents walking down the hall than if they were located straight ahead of them at the ends of hallways. Doors straight ahead tend to invite residents to use them to leave. Windows in doorways also make the doors more apparent to residents. Windows allow residents to see what is outside the SCU, attracting them to elope towards that activity. If such windowed and otherwise obtrusive exits are locked, residents become frustrated and agitated.

Higher-rated exit doors have no signs other than an exit sign above the door, and they are fitted with little or no hardware—especially no panic hardware. Hardware offers a clear message to residents to use the exits and leave the building. Secure doors have regulation-compliant delayed-opening devices with coded push-button releases.

One extreme example of a particularly obtrusive nonsecure door was observed. The exit door from one SCU was painted bright green, was located at the end of a corridor, and had shiny silver panic hardware across the middle, and there was a black line drawn on the light tile floor in front of the door. Staff members reported being told that patients with Alzheimer's disease would not cross a black line and that this would prevent residents from leaving. However, residents frequently left the unit and had to be brought back by staff.

Providing exit doors that do not generate such frustration encourages residents and staff members to focus more of their attention on life within the SCU, interacting more with each other and participating more in shared activities within the SCU. With fewer distractions from eloping residents, the staff can focus more on interpersonal exchanges with residents. With fewer distractions, residents are more likely to recognize those around them. With less fear of the unknown, residents tend to be less anxious and paranoid and more likely to join other people in activities provided in the SCU.

2. In SCUs with increased bedroom privacy and more common-area "away places," there is less verbal agitation among residents, less physical agitation and aggression, and less misidentification syndrome and paranoid delusions.

Highly rated bedroom privacy means there is a higher percentage of private bedrooms than of shared ones—especially those with three or more beds. Multiple-person bedrooms rated higher in privacy are large enough to accommodate an easy chair or recliner for each occupant.

Common-space "away places" shield residents from public observation and full community participation but keep them in view. For example, away places might be small alcoves adjacent to living rooms or in hallways that allow residents to sit quietly alone. Outdoors, benches in remote corners of the garden offer residents the opportunity to remove themselves from group activities. Away places enable residents to withdraw from threatening social confrontations. Alert staff members can diffuse a tense situation by steering an individual away to a quiet place. Such environmental support helps residents act less aggressively toward others. Residents find themselves less frequently in situations in which they might be verbally and physically agitated. Inversely, without such privacy options, patients must interact with more people and more unfamiliar situations, increasing misidentification and paranoid delusions.

3. In SCUs with more adequate and variable common space there is less physical agitation among residents.

Some SCUs, minimally renovated from traditional nursing-home design, have one large common room that usually is located across from a nurse's station. Other SCUs have a range and variety of rooms for communal activities, for example a dining room, a therapeutic kitchen, one or two activity rooms, a sunroom, a quiet room, and a games room. Having too many common spaces confuses staff members. Equally stressful and confusing is the task of supervising a large group of residents together in one large room. Most understandable and manageable for both staff and residents are SCUs with a small number of rooms that may include only a dining room, living room, activity room, and staff office.

If there is variety of decor, colors, and surfaces among common rooms, residents find the environment more manageable and comprehensible. Variety includes some rooms carpeted and others tiled. Other forms of variety include some rooms with curtains and others with shades; varied furniture with easy chairs and sofas in some rooms; and card tables and simple chairs in others. Such quality differences help residents feel as if they are less confined and have places to go if they are bored in one of the common rooms.

Residents tend to release energy by walking from one space to another if there is variety, rather than becoming physically agitated. In such varied environments, residents rely less on staff and occupy themselves more with activities appropriate to the location. Residents thus feel less confused, less agitated, and more competent.

4. In SCUs with controlled and understandable sights and sounds, there is less misidentification of self and others but more social withdrawal.

SCUs with highly rated sensory environments are neither so quiet that you can hear a pin drop nor too noisy. The overhead paging and piped-in music systems are turned off because they confuse many residents. At the same time, naturally occurring sounds, smells, and sights of everyday life are encouraged: a group making bread, a resident playing the piano, decorations to celebrate holidays, a dinner bell to announce meals, and visitors chatting with residents.

A balance of understandable sensory experiences such as these reduces residents' confusion and helps residents recognize others as well as themselves. For some residents, however, even such stimuli, if not strictly controlled, are overwhelming. For those residents, even such understandable stimuli may make them withdraw socially from their surroundings.

5. In SCUs that are supportive of residents' autonomy through a safe and prosthetic environment there is less misidentification of self and others.

The most prosthetic environment for residents is one that holds no mystery, that easily can be understood and negotiated—for example one with a centrally located activity room visible from every hallway. An outdoor garden visible from every corridor and a common room used as a reference point also support residents' independence. Staff members working in SCUs that are safe—few sharp corners or hidden areas that patients might hurt themselves on or get lost in— tend to be less overprotective of residents, allowing them to walk around more freely. Staff members also are less restrictive if SCU design cues residents to appropriate behaviors, with explicit cues such as signs and implicit cues such as visible destinations.

Staff members appear to be explicitly aware only of direct physical support for autonomy. In group interviews, they mentioned only toilet seats high enough for residents to raise themselves on their own and hallway railings that residents use when walking.

It appears that the more environments support residents and make them safe, the more staff members allow residents to move about on their own. But the inverse may be even more true: The less safe for residents and the less easy to use the environment is, the less staff members who are responsible are willing to allow residents to walk around by themselves. Such environment-induced staff behavior—being overprotective and doing more "for" residents—creates excess disability among residents. The less residents can do on their own, the less they feel in control of themselves and their surroundings, and the less oriented they seem to be with respect to themselves and people around them.

6. In SCUs that are higher in quality on all eight environmental variables combined, there is less aggression and depression.

Higher-quality environments as defined by all eight criteria are less threatening, more calming, and more supportive of residents' independence. Such SCUs provide:

- Exits that are unobtrusive and safely lockable
- Clear walking paths
- Opportunities for privacy both in bedrooms and common areas
- Manageable and varied common areas
- Outdoor access to supportive gardens
- A residential and homey setting
- A sensory environment that is well controlled and understandable to residents
- A safe environment supportive to resident autonomy and independence

Fully supportive environments engage, sooth, and nourish residents. Residents who are thus engaged generally are less aggressive to others and tend to be less withdrawn and depressed.

# ☐ Conclusion

A strong theoretical argument can be made that environment has therapeutic effects for those with Alzheimer's disease. Without the full range of cognitive abilities to appraise what they see in their physical environment (Goleman, 1985), people with Alzheimer's disease react with aggression, agitation, paranoia, and other common symptoms that may lead to early institutionalization. Environmental design can be used to prevent events from occurring that patients with Alzheimer's disease might appraise as threatening, and thus to help patients cope with stress. The research presented indicates a strong "influence" of environment on health outcomes, if it does not establish positive treatment outcomes of specific environmental-design characteristics.

Pleas have been made for "the assembly of combined treatments that together may make a major difference" in the lives of people with Alzheimer's disease (Drachman & Leber, 1997). Environment is one of at least three modalities—pharmacological, behavioral, and environmental—for improving the quality of life and health outcomes of those with Alzheimer's disease. If these three approaches can reduce the symptoms of Alzheimer's disease and thus contribute individually, cumulatively, and interactively to the delay or prevention of nursing-home placement among people with Alzheimer's and related dementias, they all might be considered "treatments" for these diseases.

As the world's aged population increases, each society will be required to serve ever-increasing numbers of people with Alzheimer's disease and related dementias. The greater the challenge, the greater the need to link various treatments and maximize all their effects. Cooperation among therapists, caregivers, designers, researchers, and pharmaceutical companies will become the rule, not the exception.

# ☐ Note

[1] The expert panel included Margaret Calkins, AIA, University of Wisconsin, Milwaukee; Paul Chafetz, PhD, University of Texas, Southwest Medical Center; Uriel Cohen, AIA, University of Wisconsin, Milwaukee; Betty Rose Connell, Rehab R&D Center on Aging, Atlanta VA Medical Center; Irving Faunce, Exeter Hospital, New Hampshire; M. Powell Lawton, Philadelphia Geriatric Center; Nancy Mace, MA, California Pacific Medical Center, San Francisco; Jon Sanford, Rehab R&D Center on Aging, Atlanta VA Medical Center; Philip Sloane, MD, MPH, University of North Carolina at Chapel Hill; and Myra Schiff, PHD, Canadian Alzheimer's Association, Toronto.

# ☐ References

Bryk, A., & Raudenbush, S. (1992). *HLM: Applications and data analysis methods.* Newbury Park, CA: Sage Publications.

Bryk, A., Raudenbush, S., Seltzer, M., & Congdon, R. (1988). *An introduction to HLM: Computer program and user's guide.* Chicago: University of Chicago, Department of Education.

Calkins, M. P. (1988). *Design for dementia: Planning environments for the elderly and the confused.* Owings Mills, MD: National Health Publishing.

Cohen, U., & Weisman, G. (1991). *Holding on to home: Designing environments for people with dementia.* Baltimore, MD: Johns Hopkins University Press.

Cohen-Mansfield, J., Marx, M. S., & Rosenthal, A. S. (1989). A description of agitation in a nursing home. *Journal of Gerontology, 44,* 77–84.

Coons, D. H. (1991). The therapeutic milieu: Concepts and criteria. In D. H. Coons (Ed.), *Specialized dementia care units.* Baltimore, MD: Johns Hopkins University Press.

Drachman, D., & Leber, P. (1997). Treatment of Alzheimer's disease: Searching for a breakthrough, settling for less [Editorial]. *New England Journal of Medicine, 336,* 17.

Goleman, D. (1985). *Vital lies, simple truths: The psychology of self-deception* (pp. 53). New York: Simon and Schuster.

Helmes, E., Csapo, K. G., & Short, J. A. (1987). Standardization and validation of the Multidimensional Observation Scale for Elderly Subjects (MOSES). *Journal of Gerontology, 42,* 395–405.

Hiatt, L. (1992). *Nursing home renovation designed for reform.* Boston: Butterworth.

Hyde, J. (1989). The physical environment and the care of Alzheimer's patients: An experimental survey of Massachusetts Alzheimer's units. *American Journal of Alzheimer's Care and Related Disorders & Research, 4,* 36–43.

Lawton, M. P. (1995). Environment approaches to research and treatment of Alzheimer's disease. In E. Light & B. D. Lebowitz (Eds.), *Alzheimer's disease treatment and family stress: Direction for research.* Rockville, MD: U.S. Department of Health and Human Services.

Mathew, L. J., Sloane, P. D., Kirby, M., & Flood, R. (1988). What's different about a special care unit for dementia patients? A comparative study. *The American Journal of Alzheimer's Care and Related Disorders & Research, 3,* 16–23.

National Institute on Aging. (1993). *Manual of procedures: National Institute on Aging collaborative studies: special care units for Alzheimer's disease* (Vol. 1). Bethesda, MD: Author.

Office of Technology Assessment. (1992). *Special care units for people with Alzheimer's and other dementias: Consumer education, research, regulatory, and reimbursement issues.* Washington, DC: U.S. Government Printing Office.

Ohta, R. J, & Ohta, B. M. (1988). Special units for Alzheimer's disease patients: A critical look. *Gerontologist, 28,* 803–808.

Ory, M. (1994). Dementia special care: The development of a national research initiative. *Alzheimer's Disease and Associated Disorders: An International Journal, 8*(suppl. 1), 41–53.

Raia, P., & Koenig-Coste, J. (1996). Habilitation therapy: Realigning the planets. *Newsletter of the Eastern Massachusetts Alzheimer's Association, 14*(1), 12–14.

Reisberg, B., Borenstein, J., Salob, S. P., Ferris, S. H., Franssen, E., & Georgotas, A. (1987). Behavioral symptoms in Alzheimer's disease: Phenomenology and treatment. *Journal of Clinical Psychiatry, 48,* S9-15.

Sacks, O. W. (1987). *The man who mistook his wife for a hat and other clinical tales.* New York: HarperCollins.

Sloane, P. D., & Matthew, L. J. (1990). The therapeutic environment screening scale. *American Journal of Alzheimer's Care and Related Disorders & Research, 5,* 22–26.

Teresi J. (1994). Overview of methodological issues in the study of chronic care populations. *Alzheimer Disease and Associated Disorders, 8*(1).

Weisman, G. D., Cohen, U., Ray, K., & Day, K. (1991). Architectural planning and design for dementia care. In D. H. Coons (Ed.), *Specialized dementia care units*. Baltimore, MD: Johns Hopkins University Press.

Zeisel, J., Epp, G., & Demos, S. (1978). *Low-rise housing for older people: Behavioral criteria for design*. Washington, DC: Office of Policy Development and Research, US Department of Housing and Urban Development.

Zeisel, J., Hyde, J., & Levkoff, S. (1994). Best practices: An environmental-behavior (E-B) model for Alzheimer special care units. *American Journal of Alzheimer's Care and Related Disorders & Research, 9*(2), 4–21.

Zeisel, J., Silverstein, N., Hyde, J., Shi, L., Levkoff, S., & Lawton, P. (1999). *Environmental contributors to health outcomes in Alzheimer special care units*. Manuscript submitted for publication

Zeisel, J., Welch, P., Epp, G., & Demos, S. (1983). *Midrise elevator housing for older people: Behavioral criteria for design*. Washington, DC: Office of Policy Development and Research, US Department of Housing and Urban Development.

# INDEX